The Life and Death of
THE AFRIKA KORPS

The Life and Death of
THE AFRIKA KORPS

Ronald Lewin

Quadrangle/The New York Times Book Co.

Library of Congress Catalog Card Number: 76-50824
International Standard Book Number: 0-8129-0682-9

Contents

For
Major Ted Andrews

List of Illustrations

MAPS

Acknowledgments

The Author and Publishers are grateful to the following for permission to reproduce the maps in this book: Major General J.M. Strawson, CB, OBE, for nos 1, 5, 6 and 8; General Sir William Jackson, GBE, KCB, MC, for nos 2a, 2b, 2c and 3; Field Marshall Sir Michael Carver, GCB, CBE, DSO, MC, for no 4. The maps are drawn by Arthur Banks except for nos 2 and 3 which are by Carolyn Metcalf-Gibson.

Foreword

Some time in 1972 I received an unexpected letter from New Zealand. It came from a Major Ted Andrews, who had been reading with approval my *Rommel as Military Commander*. Rommel was no stranger to Major Andrews, who served with the famous New Zealand Division throughout the bad and the good days of the desert war. There was a natural pleasure in receiving a friendly signal from one who could judge out of hard experience.

But I was particularly interested to learn from Major Andrews that in the course of the campaign he had acquired a unique stock of photographs of the Afrika Korps. During the final advance westwards from El Alamein, at the point where Montgomery feared that Rommel would make a stand in the region of El Agheila, the New Zealand Division in one of its characteristic 'left hooks' attempted to cut off the retreat of the Axis troops. While they were carrying out this manoeuvre Andrews and his men over-ran a German position, in which he came across a substantial quantity of undeveloped film. When he later obtained prints from the negatives he realised just what he had found.

He sent me the bulk of the collection which is now, with his approval, lodged in the Imperial War Museum. What struck me immediately was its authenticity. There are, of course, many photographs of the Afrika Korps, but a considerable portion – perhaps particularly those of Rommel – has a slightly 'staged' air, like studio portraits. These new ones were natural – most interestingly so because they tended to be concerned with the humdrum rather than the grandiose: with the domestic life of the Afrika Korps rather than with martial glory and themes for Dr Goebbels' propaganda machine.

One saw the Afrika Korps behind the lines, *en pantoufles*: at sick-parade, at the canteen, using a makeshift shower, celebrating Christmas. And if there were shots of action they were *cinéma vérité*, the casual transient moment caught by a man who (though not identified) may have been an amateur rather than one of the Propaganda Ministry's professionals. I found myself becoming grateful to Major Andrews for a most valuable reminder.

For what the photographs vividly brought home was the fact that at the

9

time we tended to think of the Afrika Korps merely in terms of men in panzers, men behind the guns, men who laid minefields: belligerents. But here were images of a different way of life. In the 8th Army we created our own *modus vivendi* – very like that of a well-knit family, with our own language, our own private jokes, our own idiosyncrasies. But here was another family – living in the same neighbourhood, as it were, but with a style recognisably its own.

And this led me to observe that the Afrika Korps possessed not only the social characteristics of a family well adapted to its environment, as well as a passionate sense of self-identity, but also that inner unity, that cohesion of part with part, which makes such a smooth-functioning organism not only biologically but also militarily efficient. These were thoughts to carry further, and I am grateful to Major Andrews for having started me on my journey.

RONALD LEWIN

I

'Operation Sunflower'

'German troops fighting shoulder to shoulder with our allies
in the Mediterranean must be conscious of their lofty military
and political mission.'

Hitler, *Conduct of German Troops in Italian
Theatres of War*, 5 February 1941

The Afrika Korps was a child of chance. At no point before 1939 did Hitler
contemplate fighting a 'colonial' war – even a war to recover Germany's lost
colonies. It is true that the question of the colonies cropped up in negotiations
with Britain, but in so far as the *Führer* hoped to regain them for the *Reich* he
expected to do so as a result of bargaining or threats. Military planning was
always restricted to a larger, European purpose which – however one inter-
prets its methodology and its time-scale – consisted in separating Russia from
the West, then overwhelming the West, then subduing Russia.* Since the
thinking of the German High Command was canalised in these continental
directions, which were in any case traditional for the German armed forces,
the consequence was that by 1940 the *Wehrmacht* possessed not a single unit
specifically trained for an African campaign. No attention had been given to
research and development of appropriate equipment. No war games or even
more modest exercises had examined the tactical problems. The orientation,
the training and the armament of the force that finally disembarked at Tripoli
were entirely those of a formation designed for European conditions.

The British in North Africa, by contrast, were the heirs of many years'
experience. The techniques of moving modern formations and employing
modern weapons in this difficult theatre had been studied and practised in one
way or another since the First World War – which in itself had supplied useful
precedents, in Palestine for example; in the Duke of Westminster's operations

---

* A main reason for MENACE, the abortive amphibious operations against Dakar in September 1940, was
the fear, based on reports of German infiltration, that Hitler intended to move into this area. In fact there
were virtually no Germans in French West Africa at the time, and neither before nor after MENACE was
Hitler actively concerned with these territories.

against the Senussi: in T.E. Lawrence's armoured cars; in the work of the Light Car Patrols between 1915 and 1918, which in their T model Fords identified and named many desert features and resulted, in 1919, in 'Report on the Military Geography of the North Western Desert of Egypt', by Captain Claud Williams, MC, of the Pembroke Yeomanry. Later, the extensive use of the armoured car for peace-keeping in the many overseas areas of British interest built up during the '20s and '30s a valuable *expertise*. Moreover, the permanent British presence in Egypt meant that units and commanders regularly acquired the habit, at however rudimentary a level, of manoeuvring in desert conditions. Reports were often filed on the viability or hazards of particular routes, and the performance of tanks and vehicles in a world of rock and sand. In particular, the Abyssinian crisis gave Britain coincidentally an opportunity denied to Germany, for the establishment of a Mobile Force at Mersa Matruh in 1936 – an insurance against the Italians beyond the frontier – was in fact the first *operational* assembly of a mobile task force with modern weapons prepared to fight in desert conditions. Much was learned, and it is significant that the chief units in this *ad hoc* combination later became the basis of the 'Desert Rats', 7 Armoured Division.

In the characteristic British way, amateur initiative added to professional knowledge. The Long Range Desert Group, which was to hang like a leech on the flanks of the Afrika Korps, derived from the private explorations of the Libyan Desert by a small group of enthusiasts led by the future Brigadier Bagnold. 'Their expeditions, beginning in the late '20s with weekend trips from Cairo to Siwa or Sinai, had grown into large-scale explorations in the '30s, journeys of 5,000 and 6,000 miles during which we covered most of the desert between the Mediterranean and the northern Sudan.'* One of these enthusiasts was Vladimir Peniakoff, better known as Popski of the Private Army, who made many such expeditions, often alone and dangerously. 'By 1939,' his biographer wrote, he had 'moved far towards meeting the demands which were to be made of him by the war. He was no longer merely fascinated by navigation but practised in it; he had learnt to be patient and lonely; the technique of desert driving he now knew; with the Arabs he had at least a rudimentary acquaintance, and a sound grasp of their history.'† It was a limiting factor for the Germans that they were never able to draw on a similar accumulation of specialist knowledge, or to call on men whose peace-

---

* W.B. Kennedy Shaw, *Long Range Desert Group*, p. 14.

† John Willett, *Popski*, p. 90. In May 1933 Peniakoff made an expedition to the Siwa oasis in the company of Paolo Caccia-Dominioni (Count Sillavengo) who fought as a major in the 31st Engineers of the Italian army in the North African campaign. See his *Alamein 1933–1962*, the best picture of the campaign's realities from an Italian viewpoint.

time passion for the desert equipped them uniquely for services in war.*
Indeed, their chief exhibit was not German at all, but Hungarian – one Ladis-
laus Edouard de Almasy. During the '30s Almasy made frequent journeys in
the Libyan Desert, and in 1942 there was evidence that a *Sonderkommando
Almasy*, or special unit, was operating on behalf of the Germans in the wild
desolation of the Qattara Depression, south of the Alamein line.

Such a wide discrepancy between the British and German experience
suggests that the Afrika Korps should have been at an immense disadvantage.
By comparison with its opponent it was an innocent abroad – or so it seemed.
But the British squandered their inheritance while Rommel, against all prob-
ability, achieved over them the dominance of a desert fox over its prey. Yet
hero-worship of Rommel alone, which Auchinleck condemned and Churchill
encouraged, is militarily misleading, for if, as the saying goes, a regiment is as
good as its Colonel, it is often the case that a Colonel is only as successful as his
regiment permits him to be. Rommel's personal achievement is now beyond
dispute, but the instrument of his success has not been fully examined. What
was this impromptu expeditionary force which, without training or tradition,
adapted almost instinctively to the requirements of an unknown theatre of
war and developed a sense of identity so strong that it survived, after many
victories, an absolute defeat – so strong, indeed, that over 30 years after
Germany's collapse the veterans of the Afrika Korps are still a brotherhood?

Hitler's unintentional involvement in the North Africa campaign only
occurred after a series of tentative and almost casual moves. The first followed
the fall of France, when an alternative to the invasion of England was prudently
sought by the High Command in case Operation SEALION, which Hitler had
set in motion on 16 July, proved impracticable. Six days later the Commander-
in-Chief, von Brauchitsch, suggested a number of Mediterranean ventures
including armoured support for the Italians in North Africa. This idea was
approved in principle by Hitler, and as a result 3 Panzer Division was ordered
to make preparations while General von Thoma (later to be captured on the
field of Alamein), was sent across the Mediterranean to visit Marshal Graziani
and report. But if these events implied a growing enthusiasm, it was soon to
be deflated.

First there came a humiliating discovery: the Italians were indifferent if not
opposed to German assistance. When the Duce and the *Führer* held their
meeting at the Brenner Pass on 4 October, Hitler's offer of tanks and specialist

---

* Alan Moorehead, in *The End in Africa*, noted that, 'It appeared to me as I travelled among the prisoners,
especially the Germans, that they lacked the power of individual thought and action. They had been trained
as a team, for years the best fighting team in the world. They had never been trained to fight in small
groups or by themselves . . . they never tried out the odd exciting things we did – things like the Long
Range Desert Group.'

troops was received by a lukewarm Mussolini with the reply that he would not need any until he got to Mersa Matruh, though panzers and Stukas would come in handy for the final advance on Alexandria. (It is ironical to think that this aid was being rejected only two months before O'Connor pulverised a complete Italian Army between Sidi Barrani and Beda Fomm.) More cogent was the result of von Thoma's mission. On the one hand he emphasised the logistical problems of maintaining supply not only in the desert, but also across a Mediterranean dominated by the Royal Navy. On the other hand he stated that no less than four German armoured divisions would be necessary to ensure success.* Since Hitler had no intention of dissipating his precious panzers on this scale the whole project now lost impetus, though staff planning still continued in case a move were authorised. On the contrary: Mussolini's swaggering invasion of Greece on 28 October, concealed from Hitler until the last minute, produced not admiration but fury, and at a meeting with the High Command on 4 November the *Führer* announced that the Libyan operation was postponed.

According to the account which von Thoma gave to Sir Basil Liddell Hart after the war,† he discovered during his interview with Hitler on his return from Africa that the *Führer* was noticeably indifferent to the idea of ejecting the British from Egypt – a fact not so surprising when one recalls Hitler's ambivalence about the invasion of the British Isles. Like his Army chiefs, Brauchitsch and Halder, he never wished to make more than the minimal military commitment in Africa – nothing beyond a prop to sustain the tottering Italians. Thus it was not difficult for Hitler, piqued by the Greek affair, to put everything off and transfer 3 Panzer Division to the force earmarked for Operation FELIX, the projected attack on Gibraltar. The child of chance seemed a very long way from birth. Yet it was the Italians, in the end, who brought the Germans to the point of decision, for the disaster they suffered at O'Connor's hands had a strategic significance for both of the Axis partners – as Admiral Raeder and the German Navy were quick to point out. Suppose the British obtained a permanent grip on the Mediterranean? Reluctantly, on 11 January 1941, Hitler issued his Directive No. 22, which ordered the General Staff to have ready a *Sperrverband*, or special blocking detachment, for moving to Tripolitania, while *Fliegerkorps* X from Sicily operated generally against British ports and shipping throughout the Mediterranean. Directive No. 22 was the birth certificate of the Afrika Korps. As in some biological

---

* He also recommended that no Italian troops should be employed – a military ideal which was, of course, politically unattainable.
† B.H. Liddell Hart, *The Other Side of the Hill*, p. 163.

evolution, the British by their very success in the desert had thrown up their own antibody.

When the two dictators met a week later at Obersalzberg Hitler was still unenthusiastic: indeed, he told Mussolini that he saw little point in committing German troops to months of stagnation in Tripoli. However, the child was growing, for the operation had acquired a code-name, SUNFLOWER (*Sonnenblume*), and a special unit, christened 5 Light Division, was being prepared for despatch about mid-February. The pace now quickened. When the Italians lost Tobruk on 22 January, and General von Rintelen, the German Military Attaché in Rome, reported that Graziani believed all Tripolitania must be surrendered except the *enceinte* of the city itself, more drastic action seemed necessary. The Italians must fight and the Germans must support them if the minimal strategic requirements were to be maintained of an Italian presence in North Africa. In rapid sequence, therefore, the first elements of 5 Light were sent down to Naples on 31 January for onward movement; the *Sperrverband*, originally conceived of as an anti-tank formation, was thickened up immediately by the addition to 5 Light of 5 Panzer Regiment, and was soon to be followed by 15 Panzer Division; pressure on the Italians compelled them to agree that Tripolitania must be defended much further to the east;* Graziani was sacked and replaced by Gariboldi; and on 6 February Erwin Rommel, unexpectedly summoned from leave, was instructed at Hitler's HQ by the *Führer* himself that he was to proceed to Libya forthwith, as commander of the German troops which would shortly be arriving there and would be called the German Afrika Korps. (The title of *Deutsches Afrika Korps*, DAK, was formally promulgated on 19 February.)

Whatever may have been thought or written about Hitler's limitations as a War Lord, there can be no doubt that his personal approval of Rommel for this difficult command was brilliant – nor was it casual. He had observed Rommel's qualities at first hand during the Polish campaign. His careful reading of the General's *Infanterie grieft an*, published in 1937, had shown him, by its vivid accounts and analyses of Rommel's dramatic operations in the First World War, the calibre of his mind and the skill, urgency and daring of his approach to battle. The performance of Rommel's 7 Panzer Division, the 'Ghost Division', in France in 1940 had supplied a superb confirmation. From Hitler's point of view, at the time, there could have been few better choices for a semi-independent command in a new terrain, where the moral and physical weakness of their ally would demand from the German general exceptional initiative, stamina, originality, stubbornness and sheer battle skill.

---

* This sensible condition, insisted on by Hitler, was aimed at providing the Afrika Korps with adequate room for manoeuvre and less exposure to attack from the air.

Rommel's terms of reference gave him great freedom, though the qualifications implied a possibility of friction. The orders for SUNFLOWER issued by the German High Command on 10 February laid down that the Afrika Korps, except in unusual circumstances, would be employed as a whole under a German commander and not fragmented over the front. If that commander received an order prejudicial to his troops – i.e. one likely to lead to failure – it was his right and duty to appeal direct to his superiors in Germany. The only way the Afrika Korps could be subordinated to the Italian Commander-in-Chief was for tactical purposes.

If Hitler's Directive No. 22 was the birth certificate of the Afrika Korps, these orders from the German General Staff were its charter. As Rommel's personal ascendancy increased, and as it became clear that the Afrika Korps was the bone and muscle of the Axis Army in Libya, the charter was strained to its limit – and beyond. Yet there was nothing extraordinary in the terms laid down for the operation of one country's forces under the command of its ally. The instructions given to Lord Gort for handling the BEF under Gamelin's command in 1940 were similar, as, for example, were those given by their respective governments to the generals at the head of the Australian, South African, and New Zealand forces in the Mediterranean theatre. All this was straightforward, and the charter of the Afrika Korps was well suited for a cautious policy of bolstering the Italians, which was Hitler's purpose. In selecting Rommel he undoubtedly chose a man with the qualities for this tricky task. What he failed to foresee, however, was that he had started something self-perpetuating and the obverse of what he intended: that Rommel's initiative and thrust would create successes which cried out for exploitation, and that the very qualities of independence which fitted Rommel for dealing with the Italians might also be exercised in exploiting those successes against the will of his masters in Germany. Hitler intended the Afrika Korps to be a stone wall: Rommel made it an avalanche, moving under laws of its own.

The first elements of 5 Light Division reached Tripoli by sea on 14 February. By working all night under lights they unloaded their transport in time to draw tropical kit and parade under the palm trees at 11 next morning. After an inspection by Rommel they marched past – and continued marching towards the enemy. A day later they were in contact with the British. This little spearhead, consisting of Reconnaissance Battalion 3 and Anti-tank Regiment 39, was steadily followed over the next few weeks by the rest of the Division, which was more or less complete, under General Streich, when in April and May the second component of the Afrika Korps gradually arrived. This was 15 Panzer Division, which began life as an infantry division in 1936 and fought as such in the French campaign of 1940. It was only converted to armour in November of that year. Then, in August 1941, the 'Afrika Division z.b.V' (for special purposes) was put together from various independent units already in Africa, plus others flown in for the purpose. With the alteration of its name to 90 Light on 27 November, and the earlier conversion (in August) of 5 Light to 21 Panzer the classical period of the Afrika Korps may be said to have started, for it is with 15 and 21 Panzer and 90 Light that its most memorable achievements are associated.

The striking fact about this summary and anticipatory record is the extraordinary speed with which such an amalgam of oddments became a coherent force. 5 Light is patched up from bits of 3 Panzer and other sources, then acquires 5 Panzer Regiment, then is further strengthened and converted to 21 Panzer. 15 Panzer has an infantry tradition and experience, and little training as an armoured division before it arrives in Africa. 90 Light is an improvisation, thrown together only a couple of months before it is plunged into the great CRUSADER battle. Yet all three divisions, though they grew in efficiency as the months went by, seemed at home and self-assured from the start. There are relatively few instances of the Afrika Korps running into disaster because of raw troops or naïve commanders. This is in sharp contrast to the performance of the British. Right up to Montgomery's victory at Alamein we see Wavell, Auchinleck and Montgomery himself insistently requesting more time for training or arguing for the deferment of an offensive because the troops are not ready. And when offensives occur we see grave losses sustained – even whole armoured brigades shattered – because of behaviour which can only be described as militarily puerile. The historic fact is that, broadly speaking, German units coming new to the desert adapted to its special conditions more rapidly and more efficiently than British newcomers.

Yet it was not that the units which went into the Afrika Korps had received much indoctrination even during the short period after they had been warned for service overseas. A staff to examine military requirements in North Africa was indeed proposed as early as July 1940 by General Kirchheim, and in August the High Command approved its formation. Had it been able to function, its work must have been beneficial for the Afrika Korps. But the Italian *Comando Supremo* resisted – it will be recalled that at the Brenner Pass meeting in October Mussolini turned down Hitler's offer of immediate aid – and the group was disbanded. Though it was resuscitated later in 1940 and actually reached Tripoli at the end of February, Rommel again disbanded it and used its officers to fill gaps in his existing establishment. This whole episode suggests a short-sightedness on the German side, for the *Sonderstab Lybien*, or Special Staff Libya, was an exceptional example of the bringing together of Germans who actually knew something (however superficial) of Africa – primarily those who had served there in 1914–18. On the other hand it is a reminder that whereas the British in the Middle East tended to diversify into a wide spectrum of Private Armies – the Long Range Desert Group, the Special Air Service, Commandos, SOE – the German practice, stemming from the High Command and upheld by Rommel, was to employ their limited resources in Africa on strictly conventional lines. Putting it another way one might say that Rommel had no time for frills.

There was a popular British notion in 1941 that the Afrika Korps had been carefully trained and acclimatised as part of Hitler's grandiose plan for world conquest. Indeed, Rommel's swift and unexpected success seemed to imply a special aptitude on the part of his troops. But this was moonshine. It was not until much later that an area at Grafenwoehr in Bavaria was devoted to the occasional hot-weather training of reinforcements for Africa. All that was done in the early days by way of preparing the troops was to warn them about hygiene and provide lectures by travellers, and other 'experts', on geography and similar rewarding subjects. When they moved forward to the front from Tripoli after disembarkation, wearing their unfamiliar olive-green pith helmets, they were advancing to all intents and purposes into Terra Incognita.

Conceived and brought into the world in this haphazard fashion, the Afrika Korps nevertheless reached its military maturity with astonishing speed. But even more remarkable is the fact that a formation so miscellaneous in origin could have found and maintained so strong a sense of identity. There were only three major forces during the Second World War which made the subtle but transforming shift from being a mere agglomeration of units to having a feeling of unity – that binding unity which holds together a tribe or family, and converts a collection of human beings from a disconnected assortment into an organism. Two were British – 8th Army under Montgomery and 14th Army under Slim: the third was the Afrika Korps. No American or Russian, and no other British or German army developed the sense of individuality which distinguished these three,* and though the constituents of each were radically different their common factors are marked. What, then, are the prerequisites if an army is to become self-aware, so that all its members feel part of a whole and part of one another – so that anyone not of them is alien?

First, the Army's theatre of war must be sufficiently remote from the homeland or, as they used to put it in the desert, 'out in the blue'. Remoteness breeds togetherness. Yet this in itself is not enough, for the Americans in the Pacific were further from the States than the Afrika Korps from Germany. It seems that an essential requirement is a certain permanence of the same army in the same area: in this sense 8th and 14th Armies, and the Afrika Korps, had a stability which allowed them to take root in their terrain like colonists, and,

---

* Patton's Third Army made a certain approximation. Perhaps the best analogy is Bomber Command, united in its self-sacrificial task by the mysteriously pervasive personality of Sir Arthur Harris.

in gradually adapting to it, to develop their own distinctive attitudes, myths, behaviour, language, ways of making war – even their own idiosyncrasies about boiling water or making the best of rations. In each of the three instances it is also clear that the foil of a notable enemy was important. As an army grows in self-awareness it wants to do well, it wants to know it is doing well, and it wants the world to know: a good enemy supplies the necessary measuring-rod. And success there must be, somewhere on the road. 8th and 14th Armies marched from defeat into victory, and the Afrika Korps from triumph to tragedy, but all three knew the sweet sight of their enemies' backs. If an army is to be truly self-confident it must *know it can do it.*

Above all, a self-identifying army comes to think of itself as a unity and a superior caste because of the personality and the military skill of its commander. It is significant that the leaders of the armies in question were Rommel, Montgomery and Slim, for in any country in the Second World War there were none better than these at making their troops a corporate projection of themselves. Their methods were wholly dissimilar. The Slim known to his men as 'Uncle Bill' bound 14th Army to him by his humanity, his utter honesty, his friendly calm, his humour. Montgomery's certainty that he was master of his trade seeped through to his men in a thousand ways, but he was also known affectionately throughout his army as a person – rather odd, wearing hats covered with regimental badges and given to issuing Godly Messages of the Day, but unmistakeable, unforgettable and unbeatable. Rommel's appeal was more narrowly professional, and perhaps more German. Leading from the front, he typified to the Afrika Korps an ideal soldier, fearless, resourceful, tireless, swift to spot the point of danger or the opportunity to exploit, a hard but not an unjust taskmaster. No stories went round 8th Army of Montgomery dangerously leading a supply column through the battle (as Rommel did at Gazala), or himself rushing his anti-tank guns to a threatened gap (as Rommel did at Sidi Rezegh).* Montgomery never dropped from the skies in his light plane to upbraid or re-direct his forward troops. Since Rommel's energy took him everywhere and his perfectionism never accepted the second-rate, he truly unified the Afrika Korps: they were manifestly his and he was manifestly theirs, while his devotion and dedication became the air men breathed. They tried to go and do likewise.

The matter is put quite plainly in the recollections of Heinz Werner Schmidt,† who served with the Afrika Korps from the beginning, and as chief

---

* Characteristic feats like these acquired their own name throughout the Afrika Korps – *Rommelei, Rommelisms.*

† Heinz Werner Schmidt, *With Rommel in The Desert.* At this late date Rommel, of course, had finally returned to Europe.

ADC came to know Rommel and his methods intimately. During the last
weeks of the war in Africa he was commanding a special unit in Tunisia.

> The American tanks now began to concentrate their fire on our position on
> the rise. And a few minutes later the three German assault-guns broke cover
> and sped past us. As if to excuse his flight the officer in charge of them
> shouted to me as he passed: 'Tank attack! We must get back!'
>   No, I said to myself. This would never have happened in Rommel's old
> Afrika Korps. We are facing defeat in Africa.

Courage, efficiency, *élan*, self-respect and a sense of identity – here is a sum of
commendable military qualities which had and still has a distorting effect. The
admiration they induce is liable to obliterate something which nevertheless
must always be kept in mind – the fact that the Afrika Korps crossed the
Mediterranean to further 'the lofty military and political mission' of Adolf
Hitler's *Reich*. The scope of that mission may have been limited – in the
Führer's calculations, if not in Rommel's: all the same, the specific purpose of
the Korps was to buttress the southern flank of Nazism's New Order in
Europe. To avoid the risk of idealising this remarkable formation it is therefore
prudent to take out an insurance policy, by asking how its ethos compared
with the attitudes and behaviour of other German armies on the other fronts
of the war.

The immediate point that strikes the observer is that there was nothing
exceptional about the contents of the Korps. As has been seen, its composition
was gradual and almost haphazard, while the units from which it was con-
structed were no more than characteristic *Wehrmacht* battalions and regiments.
The Afrika Korps was simply a representative cross-section of the sound core
of the German Army, and as such it contained its natural quota of ideological
fanatics, its main bulk of men who contentedly followed Hitler's star without
much thought for the implications of his philosophy, and a residue who were
merely Germans fighting for Germany. That at least a sprinkling of fanatics
existed was familiar to anyone dealing with the arrogance of captives under
interrogation or in prisoner-of-war camps. But the notable truth about the
Afrika Korps, nevertheless, was that its men fought not like ideological bigots
but as good soldiers have fought at all times – hard, well, but without brutal
excess. All contemporary witness and all subsequent evidence indicate that in
the main the Korps survived until the end in Africa with its hands clean. There
was no Oradour, no Malmédy massacre to stain its image. When one recalls
the outrages committed by German troops on civilians and on their military
opponents in Russia, Yugoslavia, Greece and North West Europe this conclusion is at first surprising. But there were important contributory factors –

the terrain itself, Rommel, and above all the unpolluted control by OKH and the *Wehrmacht* of the African theatre.

It is a cliché that the desert was an ideal place for the making of war: as vast, as undefiled, as sanitary and almost as viable as the sea. The analogy drawn between its armoured conflicts and a naval battle was often wildly inexact, but there was this truth: in CRUSADER, at Gazala, at Alamein or Mareth the struggle occurred as it did at Jutland or Midway, in what might be described scientific-ally as a pure state. There were none of the infinite and, in a sense, irrelevant complications which arise when war is conducted amid an inhabited area – no maquis, no partisans,* no underground, no refugees: no significant occupa-tion problems: none of the demoralisation which cities in war zones create for both conquering and liberating armies. Black markets, brothels, informers – all the degrading aspects of warfare in and around civilised communities were (with minute exceptions) missing in that great wilderness which stretches from Tunisia to the Delta of the Nile. Both sides, 8th Army as much as the Afrika Korps, felt the psychological effect of operating in this aseptic vacuum. With-out indulging in the romanticism of T.E. Lawrence, it is still possible and necessary to assert that in some indefinable way the purity of the desert purified the desert war.†

In such an ambience the personality of the commander was crucial. From the records of Nuremberg and the subsequent War Crimes Tribunals, for example, it would be simple to extract the names of a number of generals who, had they been given command of the Afrika Korps, might have fashioned out of it something different and contemptible. In spite of the moral influence of the desert spaces a Nazi tough like Sepp Dietrich could easily have perverted or bullied these young and malleable men into fighting dirtily, lawlessly, un-pardonably. Rommel made this impossible. In battle he might reveal all the dourness and lack of compromise which stemmed from his Swabian origins, but his character was as upright as his body, and his moral principles as firmly rooted as his love for his wife or his country. With Swabian common-sense marched a Swabian respect for common decency. It was no coincidence that British officers and other ranks who came Rommel's way as prisoners tended to refer to him as a gentleman, because he was incapable of behaving like a cad. He might lose his temper, but never his honour. By the evidence of his personal behaviour, by his refusal to obey commands from above which he thought morally degrading or to order those beneath him to degrade them-selves, he created for the Afrika Korps an essentially wholesome climate of

---

* The Arabs, intermittently and surreptitiously agents for both sides, form an irrelevant shadow within the larger picture.

† There was nothing spurious about the title given to the German edition of Rommel's narrative of the African campaign – *Krieg Ohne Hass*, 'War Without Hate'.

opinion. Like the desert wind, the gusts of his authority might blow fiercely, but their tang was untainted.

There is a revealing paragraph in his *Papers,* referring to the period in mid-May 1941 when the attacks on Tobruk had come to a halt.

> At about this time officers and men of the *Trento* Division were responsible for several excesses against the Arab population, with the result that the Arabs killed a number of Italian soldiers and kept the Italians away from their villages by armed force. There are always people who will invariably demand reprisals in this sort of situation – for reasons, apart from anything else, of expediency. Such action is never expedient. The right thing to do is to ignore the incidents, unless the real culprits can be traced.

This is not the spirit which burned the women and children of Oradour-sur-Glane alive in their church and razed their homes, or caused the tragedy of Lidice. It is the voice of a man who, when Hitler issued his notorious order that captured commandos should be shot out of hand, tore up the instruction and ignored it. In November 1941 Geoffrey Keyes, the elder son of the hero of Zeebrugge, landed by submarine with a small commando group to raid what was mistakenly thought to be Rommel's headquarters. The object was to kill or capture Rommel himself on the eve of the CRUSADER offensive. Keyes was mortally wounded. After that night there were five graves in the little village cemetery of Beda Littoria. They stood in a row, each with its wooden cross. Four were German: on the fifth cross was inscribed

MAJOR GEOFFREY KEYES

VC, MC

gef. 17.11.41.

What sweetened the situation was the absence of SS or Gestapo from the theatre of the Afrika Korps. Nothing carried corruption behind the advancing Korps as did the infamous *Einsatzgruppen* or Special Extermination Squads in Russia, nor were Rommel and his troops exposed to the pressures from secret police and other agencies which bore so unremittingly on the armies of occupied Europe. The units in the Korps, and their officers, were *Wehrmacht*: there were no SS Divisions, with their warped standards and dubious allegiances. Only for a short while, at the time of Alamein, did the introduction of a *Luftwaffe* Parachute Brigade inject an alien element, and it is instructive to note how swiftly the Italians summed up Ramcke's hard-eyed zealots. The result of all these factors was a German formation in Africa which, while believing in itself, seemed also to believe in the traditional decencies of war.

There are well-recorded incidental instances of brutalities (and even worse) on the part of the Afrika Korps – just as similar acts can occasionally be registered against their opponents. But on neither side were they acts of *policy*, and none would have been condoned by Rommel any more than by Wavell, Auchinleck or Alexander. War brutalises individuals, just as it can ennoble them, and battle at all times has bestial by-products. But if the Afrika Korps be considered as a whole it is impossible to think of it without respect not only for its military, but also for its human virtues. The child of chance acquired good manners.

2

Restrictive practices

'Parameter: a quantity which is constant (as distinct from the ordinary variables) in a particular case considered . . .'
The Shorter Oxford English Dictionary

If the Afrika Korps be considered as a developing organism (the biological viewpoint from which this book is written), one observes that the environment within which it struggled to realise its potentialities was the sum of three elements – the policies of Hitler, Mussolini and their High Commands; the distance from Europe and the physical character of the desert; the military capabilities of the British. The history of the Korps is the record of its success and failure in adaptation to this complex environment. But it is essential, at the outset, to understand that within each of these three constituent elements there was, in truth, a constant factor inimical to growth. The history of the Afrika Korps is only properly intelligible if these constants are always present to the mind. They are the parameters of frustration within which (and in spite of which) Rommel achieved his victories and the Afrika Korps matured into a self-aware and supremely efficient organism.

Of the three impediments, distance had the most obvious effect on Rommel and his men – distance in terms of sea miles from Europe and, at least as important, of land miles from their administrative base to the front line in Africa. The consequences of this parameter were almost always hampering, vexatious, unpredictable: it was only rarely that the traffic over this distance brought the Afrika Korps a bonus of supplies or equipment to improve its living conditions or provide a quantitative superiority over the enemy. Too often things went the other way.

The British, who had to fight their convoys through the Mediterranean or drag them round the Cape, knew from bitter experience that any army operating in the desert must take with it all it needs: there are no cities to sack, no cultivated lands to plunder. Logistically the desert's value is zero. The same limitation applied to the Afrika Korps, whose Tripolitanian base was even shorter of indigenous resources than the British base in Egypt. Thus virtually everything the Korps needed for life or battle had to be shipped across the Mediterranean. (Air transport was attempted fitfully, but never attained anything like a regular programme.*)

The problem can be expressed numerically. There was little difficulty about ports at the Italian end – Bari, Brindisi, Naples, Taranto. (There were, however, perennial difficulties over Italian inefficiency, lethargy or indifference, and the lack of fuel oil for the Italian Navy was another constant impediment.) More significant was the fact that in Africa itself, as a result of the Italian débâcle during the winter of '40/'41, Tripoli remained as the *one* viable port for Axis traffic. At best, Tripoli could handle five cargo ships or four troop transports at the same time.† Not only did this mean that there was a bottleneck at the very entry to Rommel's base: it meant, too, that large convoys of merchant ships were pointless if there was no hope of a quick turn-round. (Assuming they got to Tripoli, they would have to wait their turn, sitting ducks for the RAF.) Moreover, on those occasions when the Italian Navy nerved itself to fight a convoy through, the amount of precious fuel oil consumed by the escort could be disproportionate to the small scale of the convoy itself. Van Creveld points to a classic case in December 1941, when four battleships and three light cruisers, with 20 destroyers, conducted four vessels to North Africa – 100,000 tons of warships to escort 20,000 tons of merchantmen. The arithmetic was absurd, except for such crisis situations as, for example, the British attempts to relieve a beleaguered and starving Malta.

During the shuttlecock movements of the campaign the first advance of the Afrika Korps, in 1941, brought it to Benghazi: returning in 1942, it re-captured Benghazi and at last acquired Tobruk. But to Rommel's infuriated disappointment, often registered in his signals back to Germany, neither of these harbours enabled his quartermasters to expand significantly the bottleneck which so constantly blocked his supplies. During the first occupation of Benghazi only 700–800 tons a day reached the quays, as compared with the port's notional capacity of 2,700 tons a day – partly because of lack of coastal shipping, partly because Benghazi is only 300 miles from the Egyptian frontier and was therefore much exposed to the night bombers of the RAF. During the second occupation, though there was some improvement in the delivery figures they

---

* The effort made in July and August 1942, when 500 aircraft were used to transport men and supplies, was not characteristic. 24,600 men for the army and 11,600 for the *Luftwaffe* were flown in, as well as stores and equipment. Nevertheless, on the eve of Alam Halfa at the end of August the Afrika Korps was short of 6,000 tons of fuel.

† See M. van Creveld, 'Rommel's Supply Problem, 1941–42', in the *Journal of the Royal United Services Institute*, September 1974, an illuminating survey to which this chapter owes much.

still remained low: the grave lack of fuel for Italian ships in the summer of 1942 meant that convoy tonnage fell (so that in May 32,000 tons were landed instead of 150,000), and it was more economical to off-load at Tripoli than to make the voyage to Benghazi. Tobruk made little difference.

In any case, the use of the more easterly harbours increased the danger of interruption by submarines and light task forces of the Royal Navy – and this was only one aspect of the uncertainties Rommel and his Korps constantly endured because of the need to haul their sustenance over the disputed sea lanes from distant Italy. It has been calculated that 'only 15 per cent of the supplies, 8.5 per cent of the personnel, and 8.4 per cent of the ships sent from Italy to Libya in 1940–43 were lost at sea'.* Such an average, however, is dangerously misleading. Certainly the Afrika Korps was not always in desperate straits: what is relevant is that from time to time the Navy hit hard, accurately and destructively; that such inroads on Rommel's supply lines often occurred at critical points in the campaign; and that constant misgivings about the logistic flow introduced into his planning a huge element of contingency, which might well have broken the nerve of some less buoyant commander.

The disconcerting effect of this unreliable logistic channel is easily demonstrated. For the months of January to May 1941, the vital and dangerous phase when the Korps was landing and seizing the initiative in Africa, the British Official History† gives the following figures of merchant shipping losses: Italian, 102 ships of 233,448 tons; German and German-controlled, 15 ships of 53,119 tons. (The Italian figure includes some losses outside the Mediterranean: over 50,000 tons, for example, captured or scuttled in the ports of Somaliland.) And it is an old story that at the time of Alam Halfa and Alamein in 1942, when Rommel was desperately hard-pressed for fuel, the selective sinking of his supply ships came near to grounding his army.

The fact is that even in its earliest days the Axis Army in Africa, which with the Italians comprised seven divisions and would later be larger, required – but by no means always received – some 70,000 tons of supplies each month. Every sinking in the sea lanes made it more important for the stocks which did reach Africa to be landed and sent forward as expeditiously as possible. Too often there were delays – unloaded ships or accumulations on the docks. No wonder that in May 1941 Hitler, under pressure from Rommel, asked permission from Admiral Darlan for the use of Bizerta – through which it was hoped to transmit 20,000 tons a month. But though a Franco-German agreement was signed in Paris at the end of May, granting transit rights through Bizerta, neither party was happy about the plan, which was never imple-

---

* M. van Creveld, *op. cit.*, note iii.
† S.W. Roskill, *The War at Sea,* Vol. I, p. 439.

mented. The Afrika Korps thus had to depend, for most of its existence, on whatever reached and was forwarded from Tripoli, plus the intermittent and minor benefit of landings at Benghazi and Tobruk.

In the last paragraph the key words are 'sent forward as expeditiously as possible', for if the interdiction of the sea lanes, though constantly on the cards, was actually intermittent, the transit of supplies from the ports to the front was a matter of almost daily concern. The ideal of all armies in the field is an efficient line of communication. In the particular case of the Afrika Korps there were two constants which hindered Rommel's *bêtes noires*, the quarter-masters.

The first was a matter of geography. Both British and Germans suffered from the fact that only one tolerable road skirts the northern rim of Africa. But whereas the British, at least as far west as the bulge of Cyrenaica, had the option of various inland routes across the desert and along the escarpments, the eastward haul of supplies from Tripoli had a more restricted scope, particularly abreast of the Gulf of Sirte. An unfriendly terrain made detours on a generous scale impracticable, and to a large degree lorry convoys were compelled to use the Via Balbia. This was another form of bottleneck. Moreover, whereas the British had the convenience of a railway running some considerable distance forward from their base, the Afrika Korps, with no railway between Tripoli and Cyrenaica, could only enjoy this alternative means of transport once they had advanced far to the east and captured a section of their enemy's track.

Shortage of routes was compounded by a shortage of transport vehicles and by Rommel's dynamic temperament. The Afrika Korps never had enough lorries. Windfalls, like 2,000 vehicles and 1,400 tons of fuel captured at Tobruk in 1942, only temporarily disguised the basic truth, which was that the logistic situation of the DAK must inevitably deteriorate in direct proportion to the distance it travelled to the east. However Rommel might rage at the quartermaster, this was an inescapable parameter. It was all very well for him to write in his *Papers*: 'in fact, the battle is fought and decided by the quartermasters before the shooting begins'. In practice, by exploiting every victory to the uttermost and driving the Afrika Korps to the furthest attainable limit, he ignored the advice of his administrative staff and increased the difficulties of supply. From Tripoli, even from Benghazi to Alamein was simply too far for his inadequate transport pool, and the moment of truth came in the climacteric battles of July–November 1942. When Auchinleck stopped Rommel in July the German infantry, on Rommel's own admission, were being carried for the most part in captured vehicles. When the main battle of Alamein started, 'Rommel's troops were down to three *Verbrauchssätze* of fuel – one of which was at Benghazi – and eight to ten *Ausstattungen* of ammunition' – and the railway from Tobruk was under water.* The fire and skill of its leader inspired the Afrika Korps to memorable feats, but they were achieved in spite of his indifference to logistic reality.

The second constant factor, which it might be said checked the full flowering of *Sonnenblume*, was the attitude of the High Commands in Germany and Italy. Every commander at war in an overseas theatre needs a secure home base: he should possess, and know he possesses, the confidence and support of both the political head of state and his military chiefs. Otherwise it is a case of 'sweet bells jangled': however well he may seem to do there will always be critics near to the political seat of power, ready to carp and undermine and depreciate. Even if the political head is well disposed, his goodwill may be eroded. Both Wavell and Auchinleck discovered what it means to lose the confidence of the home command.† Dismissal is usually the ultimate consequence, but while the commander is still in the field an atmosphere of distrust at home can affect him and his army in a number of ways, all deleterious. His plans are peremptorily altered, unpalatable new plans descend from on high, essential supplies and equipment are rationed or denied, wounding signals are dispatched, inquisitions and witch-hunting flourish.

Rommel, and because of Rommel the Afrika Korps, were constantly at risk in these respects. Though Hitler himself had given Rommel his opportunities, in Poland, France, and now in Africa, the *Führer*'s favour was unpredictable – as easily withdrawn as it was suddenly granted. Until the plot of 20 July 1944, he did indeed continue to employ and promote Rommel, even after acts of insubordination and military defeats which would have destroyed a less fortunate man. But though Goebbels built up a propaganda image of Rommel as a model Nazi, the truth was that he rode light to politics and ideologies: accepting the Nazi system in so far as it worked well for Germany (and ultimately rebelling against it because of its failure), he was not bound to Hitler by anything other than his military skill and, so long as the *Führer* trusted it, his loyalty. The relationship was thus pragmatic. Rommel always knew he was expendable.

In this sense the Afrika Korps was constantly at risk since Hitler's policies for North Africa were variable, dogmatic and sometimes disastrous. When its first units disembark he has no desire for an offensive advance: when it has reached Alamein and come to a dead end, unless it admits defeat and retires, Hitler shouts 'Stand fast'. Between these two extremes his policies constantly wavered (his change of heart over Malta in the summer of 1942 is a good

---

* M. van Creveld, *op. cit.* A *Verbrauchssatz* is the amount of fuel required to move a panzer division 100 km across. country. An *Ausstattung* is the amount of ammunition required for one day's heavy firing.
† In each case, the Chiefs of Staff did not resist when Churchill demanded their removal.

example). Thus the Afrika Korps was always in danger of being compelled to do the wrong thing or prevented from doing what the situation on the spot, and not Hitler's map in his command post, demanded. And every time its leader chased a shattered enemy in defiance of his *Führer*'s orders he was gambling – and knew that he was gambling – with his career, if not his life. Here was a parameter of instability.

Nor had Rommel a true friend at court to plead his cause – and the cause of the Afrika Korps. So far as Brauchitsch and Halder at OKH were concerned, the Korps and its commander were problem children, an irrelevant nuisance to be kept within bounds. At OKW Keitel and Jodl were mere weathercocks revolving at Hitler's will: moreover, like the men at OKH they felt no sense of solidarity with Rommel. He was not of the *Brüderschaft*, a Samurai of the General Staff. Hitler had heaved him up the Army List. He was a nobody from Würtemburg, not an élite Prussian. From the viewpoint of his military superiors he was not *echt*, the genuine article. And Rommel knew this. In his *Papers* he hurled bitter taunts at the desk-soldiers in their supreme headquarters who ignorantly thwart the fighting general, taunts ages old, but Rommel meant Brauchitsch, Halder and their peers. His sense of insecurity was revealed when OKH sent out a group of officers under General Gause in June 1941 to provide Rommel with an adequate operational headquarters (and, so OKH hoped, to keep him under control). The future Major-General von Mellenthin was in the team. As Rommel's chief intelligence officer, after *Panzergruppe Afrika* was formed,* he came to respect and admire his chief. But on his arrival he was acutely conscious of frost in the air.

> I shall never forget his reserved and frigid manner when he received us at Gambut. We were all very much officers of the General Staff, and yet we were all obviously new to African conditions. As a fighting soldier Rommel looked at us with a sceptical eye; moreover he had never been on the General Staff himself and was clearly uneasy that we might attempt to supervise and even supersede him.†

As will be seen, Rommel trumped this ace thrown on the table by OKH, but the main point stands. He was as suspect to the high officers of the General Staff at the Army and Armed Forces Commands in Germany as they were to him.

If Rommel was a doubtful quantity, his Afrika Korps – particularly to Brauchitsch and Halder – was an even more dubious proposition. It is easy to

---

* See p. 70.
† von Mellenthin, *Panzer Battles 1939–1945*, p. 42.

understand why: to see how, personal antipathies apart, these essentially professional soldiers felt a profound distaste for what they considered to be an adventure on a distant, irrelevant shore. From the autumn of 1940 onwards their main obsession was first the preparation and then, after July 1941, the execution of operation BARBAROSSA, the invasion of Russia. The magnitude of its initial requirements in men and *matériel*, and the subsequent varying fortunes of the German armies, the scale of the battles and the vast logistic problems created by the Russian *Lebensraum* made the aggressive expeditionary force in Africa seem, in this perspective, a wasteful distraction to the cool staff minds of OKH. Admiral Raeder keenly appreciated, from the naval point of view, the critical importance of the Mediterranean, but it is fair to say that at no time were the heads of the German Army excited about either the strategical or the political significance of an absolute victory over the British in North Africa. And DAK had hardly begun to deploy and fight before the German High Command was grappling with what, from the point of view of planning and launching BARBAROSSA, was a huge and complicating diversion – the assault on the Balkans, Yugoslavia, Greece, Crete. To get the measure of the way that their military superiors thought about Rommel and the Afrika Korps it is worth studying what the Westerners – Haig or Wully Robertson – had to say about Gallipoli.

Such, then, was the second parameter of frustration – a constant atmosphere of hostile indifference at the heart of the Supreme Command.* Hitler's unpredictable waves of enthusiasm could stimulate energetic support for DAK from time to time, yet even he was fettered by the increasingly adverse conditions of the Russian campaign where armour, infantry and aircraft were swallowed as in some vast slough. Thus, though the record shows that Rommel was spasmodically furnished with a fair stock of good equipment, fine troops and able staff officers, the overall effect of scepticism and disregard at OKH was to deny him the quantitative superiority he needed to ensure a final decision, while his aggressive forward plans were too often negated or emasculated by directives from Germany. Broadly speaking, the Afrika Korps achieved results in spite of the High Command – by Rommel's insubordinate generalship, by quality rather than by quantity of weapons and men, by exploiting brilliantly the persistent inadequacy of the enemy. All this would end in later 1942, when the British were re-invigorated by Montgomery, fresh divisions, and an abundance of American equipment; Alamein and the Allied landings in NW Africa rang the death-knell for DAK. But by then Stalingrad,

---

* This is well reflected in Halder's diary. During the weeks before DAK began to move across the Mediterranean there are many entries about staff planning for BARBAROSSA, but on 16 January 1941 he noted; 'The war in Africa need not bother us very much.'

the symbol of BARBAROSSA's failure, meant that not even Hitler could stretch a helping hand to the Korps which had done so much with so little.

The logistic stringencies imposed by the first two parameters had, however, at least one fruitful result. Unlike its opponent, DAK was rarely wasteful. This was mainly a by-product of its superior military skill: ends were perceptively assessed and the means to them professionally calculated. There was no waste because there was nothing to waste – attacks would go in with minimal forces supported by minimal gun-fire. But what is striking, in a review of the whole campaign, is how often the British would squander a complete armoured brigade in some useless assault on a fixed position, as though consideration of good housekeeping exercised no restraining influence on bad tactical judgement. 22 Armoured Brigade at Bir el Gubi in the opening phase of CRUSADER, or 23 Armoured Brigade losing most of its tanks in a Balaclava charge during the second Ruweisat battle in July 1942, are instances of an amateur extravagance hardly to be paralleled in the record of the Afrika Korps. The heavy artillery bombardment which preceded the botched 'Aberdeen' attack during the Gazala battle fell on empty miles of desert and a few DAK outposts – all those shells transported round the Cape, north to Egypt, and over weary miles to the front at who knows what cost. How rarely does one read of the artillery of the Afrika Korps (grouped as it was sometimes under Rommel himself, or the able General Böttcher), firing into the empty blue? Where every shell and every tank had to count, the need for economy combined with professional skill to produce the desired result without excessive waste. Yet the British possessed a paradigm of how this could be achieved; O'Connor did it on the way to Beda Fomm.

The Italian alliance brought small alleviation for the Afrika Korps. In the field of high policy Hitler's vagaries and the restrictive indifference of his military henchmen were matched by the Duce's volatility and the caution of his generals. It is difficult to find any policy decision taken by Mussolini in respect of the Axis campaign in Africa which was founded on exact military judgement. For him the Afrika Korps was a convenient tool to enhance his prestige – or to be prevented from diminishing it. As the fighting sways to and fro along the Mediterranean shore we find the Duce against an advance if he fears that his colonies or his divisions may be endangered by defeat, and his glory tarnished; eager for an advance if glory beckons – as when he thought Rommel might enter Cairo; and obstinately against retreat, even when all military logic demands it, if that means surrendering yet another strip of his Empire. Rommel could never rely on rational guidance from Rome. The Duce's decisions were subjective – like Hitler's order to stand fast at Alamein.

Mellenthin's comment on Mussolini's African army is about right, damning as it does with faint praise. 'Senior commanders and staff officers were fairly

well trained, and proved reasonably capable.' Some sensible battle commanders were thrown up – Messe,* for example. But within the parameter of
policy Cavallero, the Duce's Chief of Staff, and Gariboldi, who replaced the
discredited Graziani as C-in-C North Africa, were as restrictive in their attitude
as the high-ranking doubters in Germany. The story of DAK's advance to
Alamein and successful retreat to Tunisia is of a continuous struggle on
Rommel's part to avoid Italian demands which would have prevented the
former and ruined the latter. He usually treated his Italian counterparts with
an appropriate courtesy, but in his battle decisions the disregard for their
views, and even their orders, was so open as to imply contempt. Such an
implication was not wholly correct. Several of Rommel's staff officers certainly
despised the Italians without qualification. Rommel, however, respected a
number of the senior commanders, and went out of his way to commend
courageous acts by regimental soldiers. On strategy and tactics, however, he
found Italian thinking unacceptable, and continued a law unto himself.
Courtesy did not imply kow-towing.

Before we define the third parameter we must exclude 'the ordinary variables'. The leadership, equipment, and battle performance of the British were
not a constant throughout the campaign. The painful amateurishness of the
first retreat before the DAK (and the second), of BATTLEAXE and of Gazala
matured into the considerable professionalism of Alamein, Medenine, the left
hook at Mareth. Equipment advanced from the obsolescent Crusaders to
Grants at Gazala and Shermans at Alamein. Field guns, once scattered in
batteries, were ultimately massed to fire by the score in unison. Like the Afrika
Korps, in fact, the embryo of the Western Desert Force grew organically into
the adult 8th Army. In other words, if one looks back over the whole campaign
one sees that while at any given moment – particularly in the early days of the
DAK – Rommel could count on a predictable performance by his opponents,
the quality of that performance was progressively and, in the end, decisively
improved. In itself, therefore, the battle skill of the British forms only an
imperfect parameter.

But behind the variable was a constant, unknown to Rommel, but of
immense importance as a positive factor throughout the campaign. The contribution of ULTRA to the British survival and ultimate victory in North Africa
has not yet been fully documented and analysed, but enough is already known
to make it clear that it played a critical and perhaps crucial part. Here was a true
parameter of frustration, whose existence was never suspected by the Germans
throughout the whole of the war.

When hostilities commenced the British had already acquired an Enigma

---

* But Messe had already served on the Russian front.

machine, that sophisticated electronic device on which the Germans encoded the top-secret signals transmitted by radio between their High Command and the chief operational headquarters or, for example, between the U-boat command and vessels on station. Interception and de-coding of these signals was developed by the British into an efficient and elaborate system which, in effect, provided Churchill, his Chiefs of Staff and his commanders in the field with ears at the German keyhole, a surveillance of which the Germans never became aware because of their total – and not unreasonable – confidence that the marvellously diversified scrambling of their signals could never be unravelled by the enemy.*

The Germans were wrong – and their ill-judged complacency had a direct significance for the Afrika Korps. A Special Liaison Unit of the ULTRA organisation, shrouded in security, was established at Headquarters, Middle East soon after DAK arrived, and from then until the close of the campaign Rommel's opponents were receiving transcripts, sometimes almost immediate, of the vital – as well as routine – signals that passed between himself and OKH, OKW and Hitler. Interception and de-coding by ULTRA of the radio traffic relating to his supply convoys across the Mediterranean were also of immense value in enabling the small British naval and air forces to strike with accuracy against Axis shipping instead of dissipating their effort in vain searches.

It will be seen, as the story of the Afrika Korps unfolds, that there were numerous occasions when the information supplied by ULTRA – unimpeachable information – about the logistic situation of the DAK or of Rommel's battle plans was of central importance for the British commanders in Africa. So this third parameter was certainly one of frustration and certainly a constant, since its effects applied throughout the whole period of the DAK's service and, unknown to Rommel, steadily worked against him and his troops.

Usually, but not always. There were many reasons why the powerful weapon of ULTRA was not, as some have assumed, an absolute means of achieving swift and inevitable victories. All kinds of contingencies qualified its power. Commanders could misinterpret the significance of the information with which they were fed. For technical reasons de-coding might be delayed, and information could arrive too late. Too often, as the record from the spring of 1941 to the summer of 1942 reveals, a situation favourable to the British could be thrown away by simple ineptitude in the conduct of the battle. And there was another limitation. The ULTRA source was so precious, in terms of the broader aspects of the British war effort, that the information it furnished was restricted, at any Army headquarters, to the Commander-in-Chief himself and

---

* See *The Ultra Secret*, by Group Captain F.W. Winterbotham, the first published account of this outstanding triumph of British Intelligence.

not more than a handful of his most senior and trusted staff officers. They could not convey this information 'pure' to their subordinates, the commanders in the field, but had to disguise it by attaching it to some more generally known source. To compromise ULTRA would have been disastrous. But this need for security could sometimes have a hampering effect.

Nevertheless, the parameter existed – from the beginning. As one thinks of the armoured strength of the DAK's panzers thrusting against their adversary the image comes to mind of a gladiator in the arena of some Roman circus, vainly seeking to destroy his opponent the *retiarius*, who foils and finally entraps him with his net before finishing him off with the three-pronged spear. Group Captain Winterbotham explains how the net of ULTRA began to close around the DAK even as it disembarked for its African adventure.

> Hitler . . . had already sent the Xth German *Fliegerkorps*, under the command of Kesselring, down to Sicily in December 1940 in order to help the Italians harass our shipping in the Mediterranean, and now a signal to the *Luftwaffe* headquarters informed them, and us, that General Rommel would be taking command of the German Army units to be sent over to North Africa. . . . By mid-February an Ultra signal to Berlin told us that Rommel had arrived in Tripoli. . . . In reply to Churchill's note to me as to how soon we could expect German forces in Cyrenaica, I was able to send over to him the OKW signals giving Rommel the approximate dates of the arrival in Tripoli of the units which were to constitute his Deutsches Afrika Korps, coming direct from Germany. *

That Wavell under-estimated the capacity of the Afrika Korps to lunge forward violently soon after its arrival demonstrates how a commander's misuse of his secret information was one of the contingencies to which ULTRA was always exposed. But it does not invalidate the general truth, that the Afrika Korps began to be entangled in the net of ULTRA from its very inception. Indeed, had Wavell listened to his Director of Military Intelligence, Brigadier Shearer, the DAK might have received a more hostile welcome.

> Early in March I submitted a paper to my C-in-C in which I predicted that, after a few weeks' training in desert warfare (and unless our own forces in Libya were substantially reinforced) the German Armoured Corps (for such we now knew it to be) could successfully re-take Cyrenaica. . . . He told me quite unequivocally that he thought I was being unduly pessimistic. 'Your evidence,' he said, 'is far from conclusive.'†

---

* Winterbotham, op. cit., p. 65.
† Brigadier John Shearer, unpublished memoir.

The Afrika Korps, for its part, was not without ears attuned to the secrets of the British. One of Rommel's most valuable, though unwitting, informers was the American military attaché in Cairo, Colonel Fellers, who acquired an immense amount of information about plans, equipment states, unit capability etc.,* and transmitted it in regular signals to Washington. Unfortunately in the autumn of 1941 a safe in the American embassy in Rome was burgled through the connivance of an Italian employee, and the 'Black Code' was photographed. 'The military intelligence service has come into the possession of the American secret code,' Ciano noted in his diary on 30 September. The 'Black Code' was the one used by Fellers for the encipherment of his signals to Washington. In consequence Axis listening stations were able to intercept this traffic and pass it to cryptanalysts for de-coding and re-transmitting, in a suitable German code, to Rommel. This agreeable state of affairs continued until the summer of 1942, when British and American suspicions led to the recall of Colonel Fellers and the introduction of a new, safe code for the communications of the next American attaché in Cairo.†

At the operational level of tactics and manoeuvre the Afrika Korps was exceptionally well served – again until the summer of 1942. Rommel's Wireless Intercept Section, directed by Lieutenant Seebohm, whom von Mellenthin considered 'brilliant', achieved a remarkably high standard of field intelligence, placing enemy units by the identification of call-signs and direction-finding, reading signals transmitted in the lower-grade operational codes, and so on. In addition, the British themselves for long provided an inexhaustible flow of information by their lax wireless discipline. Far too often critical conversations were conducted in clear, or officer speaking to officer would attempt to protect his message by the use of privately concocted codes of a schoolboy simplicity. The Afrika Korps, by contrast, maintained a professional security in its communications. It is noteworthy that when the Germans broke triumphantly into Greece, and saw victory within reach, their units lapsed into excessive communication in clear, and Brigadier Shearer was struck by the comparison with the DAK.

But Seebohm died. During the struggle at Tel el Eisa on 10 July 1942, when von Mellenthin had to lead Rommel's headquarters, staff and all, in an attempt to help the Italian Sabratha Division hold off a savage assault by the Australians, the Lieutenant was killed and many of his *Fernmeldeaufklärung* detachment also lost their lives or were taken prisoner. The Afrika Korps never obtained an equivalent replacement for this highly skilled unit. At the same time the

---

* Not only in Cairo. Alan Moorehead, for example, came across Fellers up at the front in the early days of CRUSADER. See *A Year of Battle*.
† See David Kahn, *The Codebreakers*, p. 472 foll., for a detailed account of the Fellers affair.

8th Army made great strides in improving its own signal security.

If a balance be struck, however, it becomes clear that in the wide field of Intelligence the Afrika Korps was out-matched by its opponents. In the tactical area Seebohm's *Fernmeldeaufklärung* was outstanding, but the British too had valuable sources – the reports of the Long Range Desert Group; agents; their own operational intercepts. On the highest level the de-coding of Colonel Fellers' signals, immensely fruitful though it may have been, occurred only between the autumn of 1941 and the summer of 1942. But the service from the ULTRA organisation, in spite of temporary interruptions and delays, was in effect a weapon which, unknown to Rommel, had a high place in the British Order of Battle from the beginning to the end of the campaign. It constitutes, without doubt, the third parameter.

Other armies, of course, had their own constants. The Germans in Russia faced the inescapable snow and ice and mud, the vast distances, the logistic strains, the inexhaustible manpower of the enemy, the consequences of Hitler's personal intervention. Slim's 14th Army fought in a hostile environment of jungle and decimating disease, of vile communications, of recurrent monsoons, of shortages more severe, at times, than those which weakened the DAK. The Afrika Korps was not a special case. Still, as one studies the brilliant series of military achievements which followed its arrival at Tripoli in February 1941, it is important to recall throughout that they occurred against a background of apathy and volatile judgement in Berlin and Rome, of uncertain and inadequate supplies and reinforcement, and of the secret surveillance of ULTRA. And, when that is said, it must also be remembered that the corporate spirit which gave the DAK its vitality was never dissipated, in spite of all these adverse factors. Indeed, it was unquenched by final defeat, so that on the eve of that last day in Tunisia, at just before midnight on 12 May 1943, a signal was transmitted to Germany which encapsulates the theme of this book.

Ammunition shot off. Arms and equipment destroyed. In accordance with orders received Afrika Korps has fought itself to the condition where it can fight no more. The German Afrika Korps must rise again. Heil Safari!

3

The Tortoise and the Hare

'Speed is the one thing that matters here.'
Rommel to his wife, 5 March 1941

In war as in peace, first impressions count. When Montgomery arrived in Egypt he created an immediate effect by the speed with which he assimilated and analysed the tactical situation at Alamein, while the troops in the line were no less rapidly stimulated by the rumours that reached them of this new little man who issued orders like 'No more retreat' and 'All vehicles to the rear'. But Rommel was no less expeditious in imposing the style and the pattern of command he proposed to employ, and in seeing that these were fully understood throughout his Korps. To catch the flavour of the opening days in Africa one must remember, first, that Rommel was just as shadowy a figure to most of his men as was Montgomery when he reached Cairo: each had a reputation, but neither was familiar. Secondly, one has to recall that until the beginning of March, when suspicion began to dawn that the British were weaker than had been assumed, the prospect facing Rommel and 5 Light was of an imminent attack. It was calculated that O'Connor's offensive would be extended further west. Rommel in his *Papers* described the atmosphere on 11 February, as he paused in Sicily on his way to Tripoli.

The latest news from Africa was very grave. Wavell had taken Benghazi, destroyed the last Italian armoured division south of the town and was about to advance into Tripolitania. It was not impossible that the next few days would see the arrival of the leading British troops in the outer environs of Tripoli. As the first German division would not be complete in Africa until the middle of April, its help would come too late if the enemy continued his offensive. Something had to be done at once to bring the British offensive to a halt.*

'Speed is the one thing that matters here.' Even before he left Sicily Rommel arranged with General Geisler, commanding *Fliegerkorps* X, to bomb Benghazi;† no simple matter, for it entailed obtaining permission from Hitler's HQ to over-ride their ally's embargo on the bombing, since so much of the real estate in Benghazi was Italian! And when Gariboldi, at their first meeting next day in Tripoli, was unenthusiastic about Rommel's idea for a forward defence of Tripolitania, arguing that he was inevitably ignorant of the terrain, Rommel's answer was, 'It won't take me long to get to know the country. I'll have a look at it from the air this afternoon and report back to the High Command this evening.' An 'action this day' tempo was maintained, to the discomfiture of the Italians and the edification of the German troops, who saw for themselves that this brisk and bustling Württemberger was a man to be reckoned with. As Rommel flew up and down the desert between Tripoli and the front his Reconnaissance Battalion 3 and Anti-tank Battalion 31 were thrust rapidly eastwards along the Gulf of Sirte, and by 19 February they were in position at Nofilia: meanwhile 50 dive-bombers and 20 fighters of *Fliegerkorps* X were arriving from Sicily under General Fröhlich, now entitled *Fliegerführer Afrika*, to give them support. At the same time the Italian *Ariete* Division (armoured but short of tanks) and *Pavia* and *Bologna* (infantry, but short of artillery) were brought up behind the Germans. By the first week in March a mined defensive line was being established amid the salt marshes just short of El Agheila, where the coast of the gulf bends northward in its run up to Benghazi. Here at Mugtaa, 500 miles east of Tripoli, Rommel began to feel comfortable, for he now discovered that the British threat was far less than he had feared.

An episode at this moment tells one a great deal about how Rommel's own drive and initiative became habitual throughout the Afrika Korps. By assuming and expecting that others would act up to his standards, he caused them to do so. Heinz Werner Schmidt had been a young infantry platoon commander in the Polish campaign. He then found himself in Eritrea, in charge of a group of German Merchant Navy volunteers cut off by Anglo-Italian hostilities. Escaping on the last plane from Eritrea, after the Italian defeat, he reached Tripoli and was taken on to Rommel's staff as having some 'African' experi-

---

* There is an intriguing might-have-been. If the transfer of troops to Greece had not prevented O'Connor from advancing to Tripoli, as he yearned to do, would Rommel and his Korps have arrived in Africa?

† '. . . a series of concentrated attacks on the port which forced the British to abandon it as a supply base. This German success was to have dire consequences for the British later.' General Sir William Jackson, *The North African Campaign 1940–1943*, p. 93.

ence.* Almost immediately, on 12 March, he was summoned to Rommel's office and ordered by the Chief Staff Officer (Operations) to undertake a special assignment. South of the German defences at Mugtaa lies the oasis of Marada. Schmidt was instructed to take a mixed column, occupy Marada, and explore the routes for a possible attack on Jalo, another oasis lying 150 miles to the east across the desert. Armed with one of the only three operational maps in German hands, he set off next day with four armoured cars, a wireless truck, six Volkswagen, two anti-aircraft trucks and two with anti-tank guns, three other officers and a detail of riflemen. In his head rang his orders: 'If Marada is occupied, you will take it. And if Marada is attacked, you will defend it at all costs.' Schmidt carried out his mission – and incidentally, having been promoted to Rommel's chief ADC, later returned to the firing line at his own request and survived the war.

The point is that this was a sizeable assignment and a considerable command for a soldier of Schmidt's experience and seniority, yet he was given the task as a matter of course. A year later, as the Afrika Korps was once again slicing at speed through the British south of Benghazi, and there was an acute shortage of fuel, another officer confessed to Rommel that he was unable to get petrol. Rommel told him to go and get it from the British. His tone was no doubt a sergeant major's, but the principle was right. The Afrika Korps would always be a starveling, short of supplies, short of men, short of equipment. It could survive only by being rich in initiative, resourcefulness, ruthlessness, daring. This was the lesson Rommel constantly taught by precept and example: making others believe that the impossible was attainable by themselves, he showed them by his own behaviour how to get there. It was not a method that elicited affection: the Africa Korps never felt for Rommel as 14th Army felt for Slim. He could be surly, unpredictable, abrasive: his antennae did not reach far into the human condition. Yet he carried the Afrika Korps in the palm of his hand. Men would get up and face death at his bidding – because they knew he would be beside or in front of them.

There was a simple but fundamental reason why the adolescent Afrika Korps did not break under Rommel's rough handling but rather survived and increased in stature. This was the German system of military training, with its two main principles – first, the doctrine of always making ground, of maintaining a forward momentum; and secondly, an insistence on the interchangeability and mutual interdependence of units of all arms. The *Wehrmacht* was conceived as a team designed to advance. During the years since Hitler came to power, indeed (the youth and early manhood of most of the Afrika Korps),

---

* An indication of the extent to which the infant Afrika Korps (as compared with the British) lacked officers with first-hand knowledge of Africa.

it had been designed for *aggressive* advance. These ideas were deeply implanted, going back to before 1918, and certainly to 1921 when General von Seeckt, who raised the German Army like a phoenix from the ashes of defeat, announced that he sought an army of leaders, *ein Führerheer*. In his *Basic Ideas for the Reconstruction of our Armed Forces*, written in 1921, von Seeckt declared that, 'the whole future of warfare appears to me to be in the employment of mobile armies, relatively small but of high quality, and rendered distinctly more effective by the addition of aircraft. . . .' This was a blueprint for the Afrika Korps.

But it was forward motion as a *team* that mattered. The German soldier was taught to take it for granted that armour, artillery, aircraft, infantry, engineers exist to co-operate, and that co-operation must be expected in all kinds of combinations of arms. Writing about the Afrika Korps in 1941 the British *Official History* makes the point lucidly.

> The German aptitude for organisation is proverbial. Having foreseen – as did the British – that changing tactical situations would often call for rapid changes in the grouping of units, the Germans made allowance for this in their organisation. But they went much further, and by insisting upon a clear and well-understood doctrine, thoroughly instilled by training on uniform lines, they made it possible for units and even sub-units to settle down quickly in new groupings and under new Commanders with the minimum of confusion.

This is why it was possible to despatch young Lieutenant Schmidt on his mission to Marada with a mixed group hastily put together, just as it is why, throughout the desert campaigns, the Afrika Korps may be seen dissolving effortlessly into fragments and as effortlessly reforming. If Rommel had not been able to count on men indoctrinated in these attitudes, his idiosyncratic conduct of his battles would either have had to be different or else it would have been disastrous.*

After O'Connor's offensive, on the other hand (that is to say, after the first appearance of the Afrika Korps), the British were exposed to disaster after disaster precisely because of the lack of a similar doctrine. There were other main factors, to be analysed later, such as inadequacy of command and inadequacy of equipment. But once the veteran force that carried O'Connor to Beda Fomm – in particular, 7 Armoured Division – was dissipated, it would be

* See his 'Africa in retrospect' in *The Rommel Papers*, p. 523. 'From the outset it was our endeavour to turn our army into an instrument for the most rapid improvisation and to accustom it to high speed of manoeuvre. Officers who had too little initiative to get their troops forward or too much reverence for preconceived ideas were ruthlessly removed from their posts and, failing all else, sent back to Europe.'

long before the British in the desert attained an equivalent measure of effective flexibility. The reasons were manifold. At bottom lay the fact that there was no basic common doctrine in the British Army comparable with the German, as described above by the *Official History*. Co-operation between arms was not instinctive and automatic. Then there was a hangover from the '30s, whose influence prevailed for far too long – the impression, derived from the more extreme of the pioneer protagonists of armour, that tanks and infantry must necessarily function in independence. The late conversion of horsed cavalry to armour meant that far too many cavalier ideas had still to be eradicated – ideas of gallant 'going it alone', ideas of social superiority, antediluvian ideas. And at some point one has to diagnose a defect of the British regimental system. Its merits are beyond question and need no exposition. But these very merits – pride of unit, sense of difference, powerful but limited traditions – all militated in some indefinable way against 'settling down quickly in new groupings and under new commanders with the minimum of confusion'.

The coherence of the various elements in the Afrika Korps, and their ability to work as a team in whatever combinations might be necessary, was a considerable factor in the early days. Their rapid tactical readjustments came as a surprise and a shock to the British, who were often thrown off balance and thus provided further opportunities for exploitation. For them, unfortunately, improvement only came slowly – perhaps not sufficiently until Montgomery's arrival – for in some ways the exhaustion and tensions of defeat increased instead of curing the tendency to separatism. Often unjustly, the cynicism and suspicion of the infantry for the armour intensified. By the summer of 1942 such feelings were widespread. The future Major-General Sir Howard Kippenberger was then commanding 5 Brigade in 2 New Zealand Division. In his memoirs* he describes how his Brigade, having carried out a successful attack on the Ruweisat Ridge, was left unsupported in the open and counter-attacked by panzers. His men were being massacred. He drove for help.

After ages, perhaps 20 minutes, we reached a mass of tanks. In every turret someone was standing gazing through glasses at the smoke rising from Ruweisat Ridge four miles and more away. I found and spoke to a regimental commander, who referred me to his Brigadier. The Brigadier received me coolly. I did my best not to appear agitated, said that I was Commander of 5 New Zealand Infantry Brigade, that we were on Ruweisat Ridge and were being attacked in the rear by tanks when I left an hour before. Would he move up and help? He said he would send a reconnaissance tank. I said there was no time. Would he move his whole brigade?

* Major-General Sir Howard Kippenberger, *Infantry Brigadier*, p. 169.

While he was patiently explaining some difficulty, General Lumsden drove up. I gave him the same information. Without answering he walked round to the back of his car, unfastened a shovel and with it killed a scorpion with several blows. Then he climbed up beside the Brigadier, who was sitting on the turret of his tank. . . . The General asked where we were and the Brigadier pointed out the place on the map. 'But I told you to be there at first light?' General Lumsden then said . . .

Kippenberger's Brigade in this operation lost four battalion commanders out of six, and 1,400 other ranks. He commented: 'The fundamental fault was the failure to co-ordinate infantry and armour. *This is impossible without a common doctrine, a sound system of intercommunication, and training together.*'* It is fair to say that at no stage in its history could such an incident have occurred in the Afrika Korps, and even for lesser aberrations heads soon rolled.

The first success in that history was about to be registered, for now, in March 1941, the Korps was on the eve of its opening offensive, a true *blitz* during which it would overrun Cyrenaica, capture three generals, and so savage an armoured division that it would be instantly deleted from the British Order of Battle. Hitler's miscalculation, in thinking that the man who had crashed through France at the head of the Ghost Division could be tied down to command of a *Sperrverband* or blocking detachment, was already being revealed, for by mid-March Rommel persuaded Gariboldi that with more German reinforcements they might capture not only Cyrenaica but even NW Egypt and – why not? – the Suez Canal. With Gariboldi's agreement, and convinced that the British were no longer formidable, he set off for Berlin on 18 March to put his case to the High Command.

But Suez was no magnet for an OKH† and OKW preoccupied with plans for the Balkans and Russia (which they prudently withheld from Rommel). On 21 March he was instructed in writing that his job was simply to defend Tripolitania and only tentatively prepare to recover Cyrenaica. He would get no more reinforcements after 15 Panzer arrived in mid-May. There was no hurry: he could report his plans within a month. With this restrictive brief in his pocket Rommel returned to Africa – and immediately disobeyed it. 'I have to hold the troops back to prevent them bolting forward', he wrote to his wife on the 26th: Reconnaissance Battalion 3 had in fact just pushed the British out of El Agheila. It was in such a spirit that, at the end of the month, the Afrika

---

* Author's italics.

† *Oberkommando der Heeres*, the German Army's High Command, headed by von Brauchitsch with Halder as his Chief of the General Staff. *Oberkommando der Wehrmacht*, the central Command of the Armed Forces, with Keitel at the head and Jodl as his chief staff officer. OKW was, in effect, the *Führer*'s personal channel of command.

Korps embarked on an offensive which would carry it to the frontiers of Egypt.

With that sixth sense which sometimes converts war from a science into an art Rommel had realised that the British in Cyrenaica were no more than paper tigers* – a situation created by Wavell out of a mixture of misunderstanding and necessity. At his heavily burdened Middle East Headquarters he was aware, as has been seen, of Germans landing at Tripoli, but made the rational deduction that their supply problems would prevent any attack for some little time. Thus he was less worried when the imminent threat to Greece compelled him to strip his desert defences. All that remained, therefore, to face Rommel west of Tobruk was 2 Armoured Division, fresh from England, at a true strength of one weak armoured brigade, equipped with worn-out tanks and short of transport, special units, and, above all, desert experience. (As, of course, was the Afrika Korps.) To the north, around Benghazi, lay part of 9 Australian Division, also weakened in personnel and equipment by the urgent calls of Greece: its third brigade lay further back, in Tobruk.

This was not a force to hinder Rommel. After an initial probe and the capture of Mersa Brega on 1 April the Afrika Korps exploded over Cyrenaica like a bomb-burst. Only a graphic display on a map can sufficiently illustrate the dynamic effect of the many columns which Rommel composed from the nearest troops and commanders and then hurled in every direction, confusing the enemy and seizing at a whirlwind pace the main focal points, Msus, Benghazi, Mechili, Derna, Tmimi. So we see Graf von Schwerin's group (signal and anti-tank units, and Italians from *Ariete*) cutting inland to Mechili; Colonel Olbrich takes his 5 Panzer Regiment, with a machine-gun battalion, field artillery, and tanks from *Ariete*, up to Msus and then to Mechili; General Kirchheim, who is only in Africa for a visit, is given *Brescia* Division and sent round the coast via Benghazi–Derna–Tobruk: General Streich, commanding 5 Light, is also making for Tobruk across the hinterland with tanks, machine-guns and anti-tank guns, but on the way Colonel Ponath breaks northward with 8 Machine-gun Battalion to drive for Mechili and Derna. The *brio* of these and other *ad hoc* groups was such that, though the Australians got away to Tobruk, by 8 April the unfortunate 2 Armoured Division had been eliminated and its commander, General Gambier-Parry, had been taken prisoner as Mechili was finally over-run.† Already, moreover, during the night of the 6th/7th, Colonel Ponath's group making for Derna had captured a greater prize. General O'Connor, sent up by Wavell to bring his experience to bear on

---

* He was, nevertheless, afraid that unless he broke rapidly through the Mersa Brega bottleneck and penetrated into Cyrenaica, the British would so improve and strengthen their defences that he would be halted along the arid shores of the Gulf of Sirte. He was a man in a hurry.

† It was here that Rommel acquired the armoured command vehicle, or ACV, which he forthwith made his own, and which was known to him and his men as 'the Mammoth'.

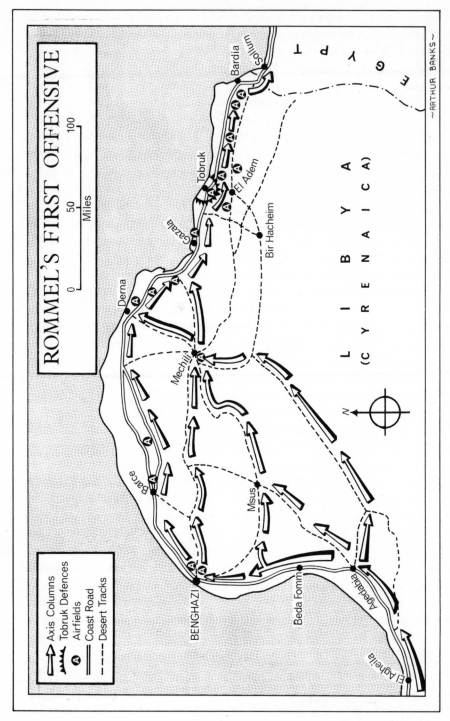

ROMMEL'S FIRST OFFENSIVE

MAP 1   Rommel's first offensive, April 1941

the battle, was driving through the night for Tmimi along with General Philip Neame, VC, who at Cyrenaica Command controlled the British operations. Mischance turned them northwards to Derna, and into Rommel's arms. His victory was absolute. By the 10th he was talking in terms of Suez again, and by the 11th Tobruk was under siege.

First impressions indeed count. Coming as a direct successor to the German *Blitzkrieg* in France, this runaway conquest in Africa seemed to confirm the superiority of the *Wehrmacht*'s men and methods. As the garrison of Tobruk was shortly to demonstrate, this did not mean that British and Dominion troops were immediately demoralised, but there was an undoubted psychological effect, and this April week saw the beginning of the Rommel legend. From the victor's point of view 5 Light was, of course, only the spearhead of the Afrika Korps, but the swift and total success increased an already high morale while Rommel's handling of the battle, brief though it had been, taught many hard lessons and laid down many precedents.

For the Germans were not gods, but human beings, and in assessing their performance accurately one must take into account their advantages and their errors. In every department 2 Armoured Division was unfit for action. Worn tracks and failing engines made its tanks no match for the efficient enemy – one battalion, 6 RTR, was only equipped with the death-trap Italian M13s – and it is to be noted that by the afternoon of 2 April General Gambier-Parry was reporting that he only had as runners 22 cruiser and 25 light tanks, and now expected breakdowns at the rate of one every ten miles. The tank was the queen of the desert, and here was the first evidence of what was inevitably to occur in so many subsequent actions: no armour, no hope. Once this frail façade was pierced there was nothing behind. Moreover, the Germans had better weapons. Their larger, well-gunned, eight-wheeled armoured cars were soon at an advantage over the British. Of 5 Panzer Regiment's 150 tanks about half were light early marks, but the rest were the medium Mk. III and Mk. IV.* The process of replacing the 37 mm anti-tank gun by the excellent 50 mm was under way, and 5 Light had a ration of the latter. There were even a few 88 mm, though perhaps these were not always well commanded, to judge from Rommel's description of how he found one in the middle of the battle, disabled by a British tank but still able to fire – except that its officer had sent to fetch help a gunner with the firing-pin in his pocket!

The fumbling moves of the British had been further complicated by an inadequate system of supply. Fuel, in particular, was short, owing to a lack of

---

* Until the arrival of the Sherman tank in the autumn of 1942, the British had nothing to compare, for tactical purposes, with the high explosive shell of the Mk. IV fired in a 360 degree traverse. The British addiction to armour-piercing shot for their tank guns was a severe limitation. (A few 'close support' Crusaders armed with a 3-inch howitzer were no equivalent to the Mk. IV.)

transport and the premature burning of dumps. But the Germans also had their difficulties, since the lorries allocated by the High Command to the establishment of 5 Light were insufficient for the long hauls of an African campaign. Moreover, the great lesson they had to learn – and were brusquely taught by Rommel – was that the kind of warfare in which they were now engaged required foresight, self-help, improvisation if logistic shortages were not to restrict freedom of manoeuvre. The advance had hardly got beyond Agedabia before 5 Light was reporting that it required four days to replenish its petrol! Rommel very properly ordered the division to off-load all its vehicles and rush them back down the coast road to the dump at Marble Arch, 'whence they were to bring up sufficient petrol, rations and ammunitions for the advance through Cyrenaica within 24 hours'. This followed a brush with the commander of the division, General Streich, who, Rommel noted, 'had some misgivings on account of the state of his vehicles, but I could not allow this to affect the issue. *One cannot permit unique opportunities to slip by for the sake of trifles.*' There is the authentic voice of the man who created the Afrika Korps in his own image. And again, when the operation was over and Tobruk the next target, it was urgent to get 5 Light on the move so that the fortress could be assaulted while the enemy was still off balance. Rommel therefore flew in a sandstorm from Derna down to Mechili, to check that all was well. He found the whole of 5 Light still there.* 'They had imagined they could allow themselves a couple of days for maintenance work on their vehicles. This was far from being my idea and I ordered the division to move on through Tmimi that night.' This was bullying to be kind, for in the great mobile battles that lay ahead the Afrika Korps would discover that such comforts as leisurely maintenance and regular supplies were non-existent. However, in Cyrenaica the Korps had passed its first test with distinction. As to error and weakness, there was little that experience and a few dismissals could not rectify.

The learning process would continue, and indeed shortly enter a new phase around the perimeter of Tobruk. But that very fact is a reminder that in one respect the commander of the Korps was himself unteachable. 'The pursuit,' says the *Official History*, 'had been a great personal triumph for General Rommel, of whom it could be truly said that he led one advance after another, and was everywhere at once, except at his own headquarters.' It was mainly to the good that in this battle he had acted like an infuriated gadfly, rushing hither and thither by plane, car, tank – whatever lay to hand – with orders, abuse, inspiration. His troops were willing pupils, but they were still in the

---

* Sometimes he did not even need to land in his Fieseler Storch. When he found himself flying over a company which seemed to have halted for no good reason, he simply dropped a message. 'Unless you get going at once I shall come down. Rommel.' This was the sort of *Rommelei* which, recounted and embroidered throughout the Korps, gave it a sense of unity under its leader's all-seeing eye.

kindergarten so far as the desert was concerned, and they needed a school-master. Yet though in this first operation Rommel had amply demonstrated his claim that 'a commander's drive and energy often count for more than his intellectual powers', he had also disclosed the inherent weakness in his personal application of that principle. There are times in most battles when a com-mander ought to apply his intellectual powers, and at such times he needs to be where the data on which to form a judgement are most freshly and fully avail-able, i.e., at his headquarters. By disregarding this truth, by disappearing 'into the blue', by getting out of touch with the nerve-centre of his command Rommel threw unnecessary and agonising burdens on his staff officers while he himself mis-read the battle picture. Even in this first action, successful though it was – and successful largely because of his dynamic leadership – there was a prophetic instance of how inaccessibility could lead him into dubious decisions.

Back at Agedabia his *Führungsstaffel* or tactical headquarters, composed of his operations and intelligence officers, formed the opinion that increasing evidence of a British retreat was rendering out-of-date Rommel's order of 5 April for 5 Light to concentrate on Mechili. It looked as though the better and bolder course was to strike straight for Tobruk before the fugitives could arrive and strengthen its defences. But there was no Rommel to consult: he was somewhere up forward, doing what with whom nobody knew. The staff therefore decided to act on their own responsibility. Putting a surprised Lieutenant Schmidt in Rommel's private light plane, they ordered him to fly to the front, contact the scattered group-commanders and instruct them to concentrate on Tobruk; but Schmidt, delayed and diverted by sand-storms, failed to arrive before Rommel had fully committed his troops to Mechili. Since by this time 2 Armoured Division was so enfeebled that it could have been left to be mopped up later, it is an interesting question whether the *Führungsstaffel* was right. If Tobruk had been attacked at the earliest possible moment it is conceivable that it might have been carried by surprise and shock – which would have radically altered the whole strategic picture in North Africa. But setting speculation aside, the episode is sufficient to indicate the dangers as well as the benefits for the Afrika Korps of Rommel's tendency to total immersion in the front line. It also illustrates the good fortune for the Korps in being under-pinned by an efficient central staff whose loyalty to Rommel stopped short of subservience. The German tradition of a General Staff capable and responsible enough to act independently of the titular com-mander in the field would more than once restore reason when Rommel's intuitive procedures had seduced him towards the irrational.

But Churchill got hold of the wrong half of the metaphor when on 26 March, his instinct for trouble already alert, he signalled to Wavell:

We are naturally concerned at rapid German advances to Agheila. It is their habit to push on when not resisted. I presume you are only waiting for the tortoise to stick his head out far enough before chopping it off. It seems extremely important to give them an early taste of our quality.

In fact the tortoise might well stand for the British and the hare for the Afrika Korps. 'It was principally our speed that we had to thank for this victory.' So Rommel in his *Papers*; whereas Major General Strawson, in *The Battle for North Africa*, rightly observes of the British commanders that, 'they suffered then, as so often later in the desert, from a command system which was not just slow in making up its mind what to do, but even slower in giving orders when its mind was made up. There was in this battle no clear tactical aim, and if there had been there were few means of carrying it out.' Of course the British, like the tortoise in the fable, would win the race in the end, but throughout its opening stages they had the appearance of sluggards doomed to defeat.

And now, since Tobruk had not been taken on the run, it remained to be taken – for if the advance was to continue into Egypt, not to speak of Suez, it must constitute a permanent threat to the flank of the Afrika Korps. Its harbour, moreover, limited though its capacity might be, would immensely strengthen the exiguous German lines of communication.* By the early hours of 10 April, therefore, Rommel had hustled forward an advance force under General von Prittwitz, the commander of 15 Panzer who had arrived ahead of his division and characteristically been thrust immediately into the line, re-placing the wounded Kirchheim. An attack was launched but, Rommel noted, 'we had at that time no real idea of the nature or position of the Tobruk defences'. By midday the attempt was over, and von Prittwitz dead, killed by a direct hit from an anti-tank gun.

In the final reflections on his campaigns which Rommel composed in 1944, while he was recovering from his injuries in Normandy, he recalled that in Africa, 'from my officers I demanded the utmost self-denial and a continual personal example, and as a result the army had a magnificent *esprit de corps*'. But the premature death of von Prittwitz is a reminder of the heavy cost in leaders that this principle of front-line leadership imposed on the Afrika Korps. Of its corps commanders Crüwell was shot down in his light plane at Gazala in May 1942, and taken prisoner; Nehring was wounded the following August at Alam Halfa; Stumme died in action of a heart attack and von Thoma was captured at Alamein; Fehn was wounded in January 1943 and his successor, von Liebenstein, in February. In 15 Panzer, apart from von Prittwitz, von Esebeck was wounded at Tobruk in July 1941, Neumann-Silkow was killed at

---

* So it was hoped, but, as indicated in Chapter Two, Tobruk never provided a great alleviation.

his command truck by a shell-burst during the CRUSADER battle in December, and von Vaerst was wounded the following May. In 21 Panzer von Ravenstein was captured by the New Zealanders in November 1941, during CRUSADER; von Bismarck was wounded the following July and killed in the minefield at Alam Halfa in August; von Randow was killed near Tripoli at the end of the year. 90 Light lost Sümmermann from a fighter attack on 10 December 1941, while Kleemann was wounded on a mine the following September. This was a heavy butcher's bill – nor was von Prittwitz the only price to be paid at Tobruk.

The truth was that after Wavell had flown up to Tobruk, as he did on the 8th, and ordered the port to be held by an aggressive and mobile defence, the task of taking it was beyond the present powers of the Afrika Korps. 15 Panzer was hardly complete until mid-May, and apart from investing the 30 miles of the Tobruk perimeter there was a forward group to be maintained under Colonel von Herff in the frontier area of Fort Capuzzo, Sollum and the Halfaya Pass. Even with the Italian divisions under his command Rommel was hard pressed both to contain the extensive outworks of Tobruk and, with his relatively few Germans, to assemble a sufficiently powerful force for a break-in. Moreover, though 2 Armoured Division had proved a passive victim the four Australian brigades in Tobruk, under Morshead (perhaps the best Australian field commander of the war), were ingenious, ferocious and successful.* The war of movement had turned into a siege, and whereas the élan of the young Afrika Korps was perfectly suited to the former, for the latter techniques were necessary which had still to be acquired. Rommel's verdict on 5 Light in the spring of 1941 was that 'the division's command had not mastered the art of concentrating its strength at one point, forcing a break-through, rolling up and securing the flanks on either side, and then penetrating like lightning, before the enemy had time to react, deep into his rear'.

All this became evident when 5 Light made a more calculated assault, starting on the night of the 13th. A small bridgehead was secured and 5 Panzer Regiment passed through, only to run head-on into the guns of 1 RHA, firing over open sights, and tanks in hull-down positions. Halted and enfiladed, the panzers withdrew with a loss of 16 out of 38. 'I was furious,' Rommel wrote, 'particularly at the way that the tanks had left the infantry in the lurch, and ordered them forward again immediately to open up the breach in the enemy line and get the infantry out.' In fact the Australians had the infantry well in

---

* At the beginning of this first siege of Tobruk, General Lavarack and the HQ of his Cyrenaica Command stayed in the fortress to organise the artillery support system, the counter-attack plan and rehearsals, and the logistic backing. 'It did not leave by sea until Morshead was satisfied that all was well and that the command system had settled down into a properly co-ordinated machine capable of handling the defence.' General Sir William Jackson, *op. cit.*, p. 237.

hand, particularly Machine-gun Battalion 8 which lost three-quarters of its strength and its excellent Colonel Ponath, who had just been decorated with a Knight's Cross for his work in Cyrenaica. This attack was made on the southern sector of the perimeter. A further one, on the 16th, went in from the west, since Rommel was worried about possible interference with his supply lines. But though he personally directed the assault he had been compelled to use the armour of *Ariete*, 90 per cent of which failed mechanically before action was engaged, and an infantry regiment of *Trento*. Though the Italians were stiffened by officers from the Afrika Korps, they lacked heart, and one Australian counter-attack caused a surrender of no less than 26 officers and 777 men. Rommel's adjutant, Major Schraepler, did not mince words when he wrote to Frau Rommel on the 22nd: 'We have too few German forces and can do nothing with the Italians. They either do not come forward at all, or if they do, run at the first shot. If an Englishman so much as comes in sight, their hands go up. You will understand, Madam, how difficult this makes the command for your husband.' This was more perceptive than Rommel's own observation to his wife a few days later: 'the battle for Egypt and the Canal is now on in earnest'. He ought rather to have confessed that he was baulked, as a last desperate attack at the end of the month demonstrated.

Once a force is committed to maintaining a siege with only a vast barren hinterland behind it, it is as much exposed to the rigours of static warfare as are the besieged, and this, from the beginning of May, was the fate of the Afrika Korps. For the infantry of 15 Panzer, who were being flown by Junkers 52 into the airfield at Derna and then brought up to the line, it was a particularly deflating experience. Instead of palms and romance they were presented with shallow holes scraped out of the rocky ground – for the upland environs of Tobruk allowed of little digging. In these homes they had to lie all day under the sun, short of water, maddened by the swarming flies, and regularly shelled.* Rations, as always in the Afrika Korps unless British stocks had been captured, were meagre, dull and unvaried, as the war correspondent Hans von Esebeck told Desmond Young when he was writing his book on Rommel.

One of the reasons we had so much sickness, especially jaundice, was that our rations were too heavy for the desert. Our black bread in a carton was handy, but how we used to long to capture one of your field bakeries and eat fresh, white bread! And your jam! For the first four months we got no fresh fruit or vegetables at all. We lived all the time on Italian tinned meat.

---

* Though British ammunition was not abundant in Tobruk the 'bush artillery', created by the garrison from captured Italian weapons, could draw on huge stocks of shell, and was employed with an effective enthusiasm.

This unspeakable substance came in tins marked AM, and was therefore known to the Germans as 'Asinus Mussolini' (Musso's donkey), or 'Alter Mann' (potted old man). A little cheese and olive oil filtered through the Italians, but fresh bread was long a problem, for even when field bakeries arrived it was realised that their ovens were wood-fired. Potatoes, a staple of the German diet, were excluded because it was believed they would deteriorate in transit. For water supply the technical arrangements were adequate, though far from generous. There was little, in fact, to distinguish between the conditions of besieger and besieged.*

> The ever-present sand which blew up into periodic sand-storms; the flies, mosquitoes and insects; the lack of fresh vegetables and food or any variety of diet; the warm, distasteful, brackish water which only served to aggravate the thirst instead of quenching it; the difficulty of keeping clean or of cleaning our clothes; the lack of any of the small comforts of civilisation; the weeks and months without even a sight of a woman – these were the main trials and tribulations.

That vignette of Tobruk during the latter days of April was drawn by a British officer† who saw it from the inside, but it might just as easily have been composed by a member of the Afrika Korps. To the wretched Italians who filled in the gaps round the perimeter it applies with even greater force, since they were already men without hope. For the Germans and the Tobruk garrison there was always a shot of adrenalin amid the boredom – the Stuka knocked down, the successful patrol, the stratagem that worked – for these were means to an end in which each, for different reasons, passionately believed: victory. The majority of Italians already saw surrender as the best option – and why not? With obsolete artillery, paper-thin tanks, incompetent officers, a government that bred more cynicism than faith, they were coming to see themselves as cannon fodder, despised by their allies, ill served by their own command, a laughing-stock among their enemies. The Italians were necessary to the Germans – if only to provide more men on the ground. The Germans, by contrast, were vital to their allies, life-blood, for without the Afrika Korps the Italian Empire in North Africa must have collapsed in 1941. But on each side the marriage was one of convenience, without joy. An atmosphere charged with doubt and suspicion was certainly not stimulating

---

* Unlike the Italians, who had a double standard – one for officers, one for men – Rommel insisted that he and his staff had the same rations as the troops. Contempt for the Italian double standard and respect for their leader's austerity helped in establishing a sense of solidarity between Korps and commander.
† Cyril Joly, *Take These Men*, p. 127.

for the men who endured that sun-baked summer in their fox-holes round
Tobruk.

Unfortunately for Rommel and his Korps doubt and suspicion were precisely the feelings which now prevailed in the offices of the OKH. The
German High Command was not interested in the sound military principle of
reinforcing success in North Africa, because it was mainly apathetic about
success and certainly unwilling to reinforce it. There was an ambivalence. The
Goebbels propaganda machine naturally made the most of a dramatic story,
and to Rommel's fury presented his military achievements as a by-product of
his ideological zeal. 'Nonsense,' he commented on an article about himself in
Das Reich. In so far as this domestic reaction got through to the Afrika Korps
it was obviously a boost to morale.* But at the centre of power things were
very different. As early as 23 April Halder, who was consistently critical, noted
in his diary: 'Rommel has not sent in a single clear report, and I have a feeling
that things are in a mess. . . . All day long he rushes about between his widely
scattered units and stages reconnaissance raids in which he fritters away his
strength . . . the piecemeal thrusts of weak armoured forces have been costly.
. . . It is essential to have the situation cleared up without delay.'

The method chosen by OKH was the classic one – send out a safe man to
investigate and report. Just as the British High Command, when General
Monro was dispatched to examine the stalemate at the Dardanelles, secretly
hoped and expected that he would recommend evacuation, so now Brauchitsch
and Halder looked for 'appropriate' observations from the assessor of their
choice. This was a Deputy Chief of the General Staff, von Paulus: it is one of
history's ironies that the commander who surrendered at Stalingrad should
have been selected to advise on the siege of Tobruk. He came, he saw, he
watched Rommel fail to conquer, and on 12 May he submitted his predictable
report. The Afrika Korps was short of everything, and unless stocks were
built up to adequate levels no more troops should be sent out and no more
advances should be attempted. His statistics were compelling – 30,000 tons
required monthly for ordinary maintenance plus 20,000 monthly tons for
stock-piling, of which something like a half must be hauled the 1,000 miles
overland from Tripoli to Tobruk by a transport system chronically short of
vehicles and insufficiently staffed. Halder had chosen von Paulus because he
was 'perhaps the only man with enough influence to head off this soldier gone

---

* Morale clearly improved as the weeks went by and the DAK mastered the techniques of static siege
warfare, but the initial impact of this novel mode of war – perhaps particularly on those who had swept
through France in 1940 – was depressing. A German soldier's diary captured in mid-April noted: 'They
already have a lot of dead and wounded in the 3rd Company. It is very distressing. In their camp faces
are very pale and all eyes . . . downcast. Their nerves are taut to breaking point.' Inevitably, the early days
caused much homesickness. Schmidt observed that the first detachments of 15 Panzer 'hated the Africa
they saw'.

stark mad'. He exercised a creditable sanity. The military facts were inescapable. * None could argue over the logistics, and after observing the total failure of Rommel's attack on the western sector of the perimeter between 30 April and 4 May von Paulus was wholly justified, by any commonsense standards, in ordering the Afrika Korps to sit tight, to prepare a fall-back line at Gazala, and not to renew the assault 'unless the enemy left Tobruk of his own accord'. Nevertheless Lieutenant Schmidt, who was given the job of bear-leading von Paulus round the front line, commented that 'in truth, we noticed no important changes during the weeks that followed von Paulus's inspection. We did not fall back to Gazala, and we still ate "Old Man".'

It is usually profitless for the historian to concern himself with the might-have-been, but there is some interest in speculating about the possible future of the Afrika Korps if at this particular moment Rommel's confidence had collapsed. Suppose 'this soldier gone stark mad' had accepted, like OKH, the cold logic of von Paulus's analysis: suppose that he had been *sensible*. The whole emphasis of the 12 May report was on a defensive, static, unadventurous strategy. Its first priority was protection of the sea routes from Italy to Libya and an improved air defence of Tripoli and Benghazi. The sequence of reinforcement proposed was ammunition, petrol, rations, vehicles, and only then more troops. Retirement rather than advance was the keynote for dealing with the situation, which Halder called 'unpleasant'. Schmidt, indeed, records von Paulus as saying that 'the troops around Tobruk are fighting in conditions that are inhuman and intolerable. I am going to recommend to Berlin that we withdraw to a strong position at Gazala, where our supply lines will be shorter. The troops will live under better conditions, and we should be ensured greater reserves. . . . As I see it, every man here is on duty without a break.' There was a great deal to be said for this realistic evaluation, based, as it certainly was, on the larger General Staff picture which von Paulus had in mind – an expanding canvas filled by penetration into the Balkans and the imminence of Operation BARBAROSSA which would temporarily, and perhaps irreversibly, commit the main weight of Germany's armed forces to the Russian adventure. A man who controlled his instincts with his intellect more effectively than Rommel might well have capitulated to the pressure of these arguments – but such a man would never have driven in a whirlwind campaign what amounted to a small expedition from Tripoli to the frontiers of Egypt.

And Rommel had no intention of capitulating. On the contrary: instead of cramming the Afrika Korps into trenches he kept it on its toes. A rumour

---

* Von Paulus erred in one respect. He told Rommel that the unplanned advance of the Afrika Korps into Cyrenaica had caused the British to withdraw their troops from Greece, thus preventing the Germans from cutting them off. Any stick was good enough to beat Rommel with. In fact the British evacuated in the face of a massive German superiority.

spread among the troops that fighting would die away as the summer heat intensified – a theory particularly accepted by the panzer units. But far from stagnating at Tobruk, or withdrawing and thus affecting the morale of his men, Rommel adopted a policy of gradually extracting his mobile elements from the Tobruk perimeter and grouping them further forward to face a British attack out of Egypt, which in mid-May he anticipated almost hourly. Wireless intercepts had given him a clear warning that something was in the wind – a reminder that the Afrika Korps developed to a high degree the capacity to obtain hard intelligence from the reception of local British signals, aided by the prevalent lack of wireless discipline in the Desert Army. The expected attack, known to the British as Operation BREVITY, was launched in the early hours of 15 May: it was indeed brief, and a total failure. One armoured and one infantry brigade thrust up and along the escarpment above Sollum, into the Capuzzo–Sidi Azeiz areas, and after some initial success against Colonel Herff's frail outpost group they were decisively repelled when Rommel rushed up a battalion of tanks from 8 Panzer Regiment. For greater losses than the Germans' the British had only acquired control of Halfaya Pass. This was indeed invaluable, for here and at Sollum were the only two points where it was possible to ascend from the coastal strip and its low-lying eastern hinterland on to the great plateau of Cyrenaica. But even this key position was surrendered on 26 May when Herff, reinforced now by 160 tanks, pushed the British back on to the plain. Rommel in his *Papers* says that his enemy 'fled in panic to the east'. Since the unit in question was 3 Coldstream Guards this seems implausible, but undoubtedly the retirement cost 173 casualties, 12 field and anti-tank guns, and five tanks.

For the Afrika Korps the significance of this local success was far greater than could have been visualised at the time. There was an immediate dividend, for the battle had been stiff and genuine, not a relative walk-over like the first action in April: the self-confidence of the Korps was therefore enlarged. Moreover, the test of action was enabling Rommel to cut out dead wood. General Streich, a brave considerate man who lacked the necessary fibre, had dissatisfied Rommel at Tobruk by his weak handling of the armour. He now went 'on his camel', as the Afrika Korps put it – stellenbosched, *limogé*: all armies have a word for this painful experience. Together with Olbrich, the Colonel of 5 Panzer Regiment, he was shipped back to Germany. A tank battalion commander was also court-martialled for feebleness in the face of the British 'Matildas': at this stage of the war in Africa, as in France in 1940, it came as a shock to discover that the armour of these infantry tanks was impenetrable, certainly from the front, by any German gun less than an 88 mm.

But there were larger issues. Rommel and his Korps could not know that on 20 April Churchill, alerted by confirmation from Wavell of the arrival at

Tripoli of 15 Panzer Division, had instantly rushed through the Mediterranean the *Tiger* convoy, or that on 10 May *Tiger* would deliver at Alexandria 234 tanks and 43 Hurricane fighters. Still less was it known that ULTRA had caught from the air and de-coded the pessimistic recommendations from von Paulus to Berlin. These were immediately communicated to Churchill, who was not unnaturally stimulated by this 'hard' evidence that the Afrika Korps was stuck in an *impasse*. To repair British prestige in the Mediterranean, to get into action his Tiger cubs (as he called the new armoured reinforcement), and to hit Rommel quickly while his strength seemed low the Prime Minister pressed Wavell urgently and insistently, against his Commander-in-Chief's better judgement, to launch a major offensive in the desert. It will be seen that when this occurred, in mid-June, the ground which the Afrika Korps had gained during BREVITY was of critical importance.

Moreover, the launching of operation BATTLEAXE on 15 June was an instance of Rommel's actually benefitting from the close surveillance of his army's condition which the ULTRA intercepts provided. The flow of information into London from ULTRA about German plans and strength, before and during the invasion of Crete in the latter part of May, had greatly impressed Churchill once again with the value of this unique source. From the von Paulus dispatch he felt he had gained a deep insight into Rommel's difficulties, and Wavell, in consequence, was kept under constant pressure to attack an enemy who, in the Prime Minister's eyes, seemed ready for the *coup de grâce*. Why was he lingering? Wavell's knowledge that his operation was premature was brushed aside.

Yet premature it was, for some reasons which Wavell understood and Churchill ignored, and for others of which neither Prime Minister nor Commander-in-Chief was aware. Though they had achieved an easy superiority over the Italian armour in 1940, the British were now about to pay the bill for falling behind the Germans during the '30s in developing an effective long-term system for the production of tanks. Surprised and stripped at Dunkirk, they had been compelled to overwork their existing equipment and concentrate, for their new output, on still inadequate designs. The signal from Wavell to the CIGS of 30 May 1941 is a shocking reflection on the state of British armour one year after the German invasion of France. It is safe to say that no such complaint ever went back from Rommel to Berlin about the condition of a fresh consignment of panzers. Wavell's report stated:

A.P. Wavell to CIGS   *30 May 1941*

State of Tiger cubs on arrival Egypt.

    Light tanks Mark VI. Eight out of 21 require complete overhaul.

    Cruiser Mark IVA 15, average mileage 700 or half their life.

Cruiser Mark VI 67, in good order.

Infantry tanks, first 69 ready on 28 May required average 48 man-hours each in shops. Examples of heavier repairs are: two gear boxes, cracked and faulty, required exchange, broken sprockets, rackham clutches slipping, unserviceable tracks, one left-hand engine seized, top rollers seized, two engines over-heating and lacking power require top overhaul.

Had cubs only required to be fitted with desert equipment and camouflage painted, all would have been ready for operations by 31 May.

The other factor, which was to be of critical importance in BATTLEAXE and would remain so until the autumn of 1942, was that the miscellany of tanks with which the British were compelled to operate in the desert meant that differences in speed and armour made it difficult – and perhaps impossible – to employ the armoured regiments effectively *en masse*. In BATTLEAXE the pace and performance of the Matilda infantry tanks held them tactically apart from the swifter cruisers. But in the Afrika Korps all marks of panzer, bred from one family, were able to function together in relative harmony.

What neither Wavell nor Churchill knew was that between BREVITY and BATTLEAXE the Afrika Korps had developed to a decisive point what was to prove a continuing advantage on the battlefield throughout the desert campaign. This was the employment of the 88 mm AA gun in an anti-tank role, first from fixed positions and later as a mobile element within the rapidly moving armoured engagements. By early June Rommel had emplaced his 88s, and the new and powerful 50 mm anti-tank guns, in some half-dozen dug-in strongpoints which ran in a curve from the Halfaya Pass southerly to the Hafid Ridge, six miles south-west of Capuzzo, 'so that with their barrels horizontal', as Rommel put it, 'there was practically nothing to be seen above ground'. Their presence was a shattering surprise for the British.* Indeed, the Afrika Korps gained a further benefit, for much of the subsequent respect for their panzers was due to the fact that British commanders, seeing their tanks so unexpectedly demolished, failed to appreciate that the instrument was the 88 and not the guns of the German armour. Thus a legend unnecessarily pro-liferated about the superiority of the Mk. III and Mk. IV. Nevertheless, the domination of the 88 mm continued at least until April 1943, when in the battle of Wadi Akarit a mere handful of these guns stemmed what should have been a catastrophic breakthrough by the 8th Army.

The device which Rommel and his Afrika Korps evolved was essentially

---

* There were only 13 88s in all – five at Halfaya and four on the Hafid Ridge, the other four working with 15 Panzer. Yet this small technological increment was crucial.

simple. It consisted in standing a theory on its head. The general assumption of the '30s was that the prime purpose of tanks was to destroy tanks and then, having 'punched a hole', to penetrate and over-run the rear areas of the enemy. Gradually but steadily the Afrika Korps reversed this principle, establishing the anti-tank gun line as the killer on to which the enemy armour was drawn. The panzers were thus freed to deal in relative safety with the British infantry, field artillery and supply echelons. 'This significantly showed,' wrote Liddell Hart, 'that the Germans knew how to exploit the offensive potentialities of the long-disputed theory of armoured warfare but had also grasped the idea of the defensive counter to it. Rommel was the first Panzer leader to demonstrate the modern version of the "sword and shield" combination, and prove the value of the "defensive-offensive" method in mobile mechanised warfare.' But it also showed (particularly when it was later refined into the practice of keeping anti-tank guns mobile to operate offensively amid the manoeuvring panzers), that the Afrika Korps had comprehended more clearly then the British the military necessity of functioning as a unified team.

Yet this lethal use of the 88 mm should not have come as a shock. Pre-war intelligence reports had indicated that during exercises in Germany the gun was being employed in this novel fashion, while practical experience in France in 1940 had revealed its capability in action. For some reason the British commanders, with certain exceptions, were blinded by their own reluctance to use the 3.7 AA gun in a similar role. This was not due to partisan obstruction, for the C-in-C AA Command, General Pile, who was well grounded in the principles of modern mobile warfare, frequently propounded to his colleagues the merit of the 3.7 as an anti-tank weapon. Nevertheless, though it was used in a field artillery role during the latter stages of the war* this excellent British equivalent of the 88 was never pushed beyond the stage of half-hearted experiment as an anti-tank gun. Some have argued that as heavy anti-aircraft artillery was in short supply in North Africa the defence of ports, bases and communications deserved priority. But the same conditions applied with equal or even greater force to Rommel, and there can be little doubt that the cost/effectiveness of such 88s as were diverted to anti-tank purposes was exemplary.

Wavell was not alone in his difficulties with the authorities at home, for towards the end of May Rommel received what he called 'a major rocket' from OKH, and a sharp exchange of correspondence followed. There had been some misunderstanding over procedure, and he sent his Chief of Staff back to Germany to clear it up, writing at the same time to his wife, on 2 June, that 'it's easy enough to bellyache when you aren't sweating it out here'. Never-

---

* The Afrika Korps used the 88 in a field role, firing air-bursts, during the first siege of Tobruk.

theless, in all the circumstances he and the Afrika Korps were well prepared (apart from the perennial shortage of fuel) to face the battle which Rommel had anticipated and Wavell now launched with deep misgivings, having signalled to London: 'I think it right to inform you that the measure of success which will attend this operation is in my opinion doubtful.'

4

A midsummer night's dream

'Ecology: The branch of biology which deals with the
mutual relations between organisms and their environment.'
The Shorter Oxford English Dictionary

During the next six months the Afrika Korps came of age. The DAK that
fought, at the end of the year, in the great winter battles on the approaches to
Tobruk was technically mature and inspired by a self-confidence now based
on performance; the whole efficient body functioned through the harmonious
integration of its parts. In effect, here was an organism completely adapted to
its environment. Its development between BREVITY and CRUSADER is an
example of military ecology.

   The striking achievements of DAK in mobile warfare during 1941 have
tended to conceal the fact that from the first investment of Tobruk until its
relief in December there was always a substantial German presence on its
perimeter. Rommel did all he could to extricate his armour and motorised
infantry so that he could acquire the flexibility to be gained from an uncommitted panzer formation, but he dared not leave containment of Tobruk to the
Italians alone. Their record throughout the siege was too often one of panic,
inefficiency and apathy, qualified, in the old Italian way, by the incidental
courage or competence of individuals or small groups. The truth was that the
vigour of the offensive/defensive tactics of the Tobruk garrison was a constant
threat, preventing Rommel from building up his strength in the forward area
as rapidly as he would have wished. Auchinleck recognised this in his *Despatch*:

   Our freedom from embarrassment in the frontier area for four and a half
   months is to be ascribed largely to the defenders of Tobruk. Behaving not
   as a hardly pressed garrison but as a spirited force ready at any moment to
   launch an attack, they contained an enemy force twice their strength. By
   keeping the enemy continually in a high state of tension, they held back four

Italian divisions and three German battalions from the frontier area from
April until November.

But not even Auchinleck brings out the full effect of Tobruk as an influence
on the Afrika Korps. Apart from the fact that armour and artillery were
sucked into the siege, as well as infantry, the port and its unconquered garrison
came so to dominate Rommel's (and Hitler's) thinking that his planning during
the autumn of 1941 was devoted to breaking the defences of Tobruk with his
mobile divisions rather than hurling them onward into Egypt.

This was the debit. On the credit side was the invaluable knowledge about
techniques of static warfare gained during these four and a half months of
investment – techniques which, from Alamein onwards, the Afrika Korps
desperately needed and found itself able to apply with a high degree of
sophistication. All the units serving outside Tobruk (including the 'Afrika'
Division z.b.V., whose first troops arrived in the theatre during June, and
whose presence at Tobruk was confirmed by the Australians on 11 September)
were in a school which gave them the opportunity of learning an unfamiliar
discipline. This, the grammar of trench warfare, was a commonplace for their
fathers on the Western Front, but it had not received a high priority in the
Wehrmacht's training for the European *Blitzkrieg*. And the German ethos pre-
ferred operations by day, but the bare open country around the 30 miles of
Tobruk's perimeter put a premium on night tactics. It was necessary, therefore,
for the DAK to master the best methods of minelaying and minelifting, offensive and defensive patrolling, raiding and repelling raids – all in the darkness.

The inexperience of the DAK in what Rommel used to call 'position warfare' is well reflected in a report by Major Ballerstedt, commander of 115
Lorried Infantry Regiment (from 15 Panzer).* Written on 7 June, it praised
the defensive skill of the Australian and added: 'Our men, usually easy-going
and unsuspecting, fall easily into his traps, *especially as a result of their experiences
in the closing stages of the Western Campaign* [i.e. France 1940].' Ballerstedt commented on the Australians' skill with their weapons, particularly as snipers;
on their gift for observation and drawing the correct conclusions from what
they saw: and on their ability to create surprise.

Yet, as the Australian *Official History*† observes, 'if the Germans had anything to learn . . . they learnt it quickly'. Indeed, the *History* continues by
quoting from another report, written a few weeks later by Lieut-Colonel Ogle
of the 2/15th Australian infantry battalion, which weighs up the enemy in

---

* 115 Regiment was detached from its parent Division for many weeks as part of the investing force.
† *Tobruk and El Alamein*, by Barton Maughan, who served as a subaltern in an Australian infantry battalion
at Tobruk.

words curiously similar to Ballerstedt's. It first praised the accuracy of the Germans' mortar fire,* and the precision of their sniping. ('The only periscope in possession of the unit was hit as soon as it was raised above the post. In another case one man was shot through the temple when he raised his head above the parapet.' It sounds like Ypres or the Somme.) Then Colonel Ogle continued:

> Our own troops have learned the following lessons from the German.
> a. Camouflage – of positions and of muzzle blast, for they have found it extremely difficult to locate his guns.
> b. Dummy Positions – so many sangars have been constructed that we cannot in confidence assume that he is occupying one of them.
> c. Day Discipline – Practically no movement at all is seen. To the observer, the whole of the enemy territory appears unoccupied.

And there is another matter. If the thesis propounded in the first chapter has any validity – that if an army is to achieve a sense of identity, one requirement is that it should be opposed by a good enemy – then it should be observed that 9 Australian Division in Tobruk was the first good enemy the Germans had fought at length since their invasion of Poland. There and in France the strength of the steamroller had been too great. No battle was prolonged, and the few good troops the *Wehrmacht* encountered were normally overwhelmed. The destruction in the spring of 1941 of the British 2 Armoured Division was achieved at the gallop. But for months the Tobruk detachments of the DAK were facing, in 9 Australian Division, what by general consent must be considered as one of the finest formations in all the Commonwealth's forces. These alert volunteers, keen of mind and eye, combined with their athlete's physique the cavalier, unorthodox temperament of a frontiersman. There could be no greater contrast than between these independent, self-sufficient, iconoclastic Antipodeans and the inbred sense of order, discipline, and hierarchical values which conditioned the DAK just as it did all troops in the German Army.

9 Australian Division was also at school in Tobruk. But it had fewer presuppositions to shed, not having been trained in the National Socialist *Weltanschauung* of the *Blitzkrieg*, and unlike the DAK it contained many soldiers already accustomed at home to the space, the silence and the solitude of the Outback, to sun and sand and thirst, to fending for themselves in rough conditions of copper-mine or sheep-run. The way of life at Tobruk was

---

* Both German and Italian mortars had a better range than the British 3-inch weapon with which the Australians were equipped.

therefore accepted by the Australians with a natural relish, whereas the men of the DAK perhaps only endured it as a duty. They learned their lessons with scholarly care, but hardly with abandon.

In particular, the Australians perfected the arts of night fighting. Morshead's doctrine from the beginning was one of spirited aggression. His division must dominate the No Man's Land of the perimeter. There is no more graphic account in any of the Official Histories, British or Commonwealth, than the many pages which Barton Maughan devotes, in *Tobruk and El Alamein*, to the continuous series of patrols and raids executed by the Australians at night amid the German and Italian positions. Here was indeed a good enemy: Rommel's men learned by example, and by the sheer fact of having to counter, week in week out, so formidable an opponent.*

But while a portion of the Afrika Korps was being educated in the siege of Tobruk, on the threshold of Egypt its main body demonstrated by superior technique that in a war of manoeuvre the British in mid-1941 (as compared with O'Connor's veterans) had reverted to the *Kindergarten*.

The offensive which Wavell pessimistically launched in June under the code-name BATTLEAXE had been anticipated by Rommel. Herff's vigorous push at the end of May, which recovered Halfaya, gave the Afrika Korps control of all the higher ground from the sea south to Sidi Omar. This was actively developed as a defensive line, through which the British must pass if, as Rommel assumed, they sought to relieve Tobruk. As has been seen, the emplacement of 88 mm AA guns in anti-tank roles both strengthened the line and guaranteed surprise, but careful attention was devoted to each individual post – 'in accordance with the lessons learnt at Tobruk'. Anyone who, during the war, had the opportunity of inspecting a German position knows with what beaver-like energy and with what exact science trenches and weapon-points were sited and camouflaged. But what Rommel could not achieve by an order was a stock of supplies. The chronic shortage of transport meant that most localities only had enough for a few days, and had the DAK not finished off the battle with clinical precision victory might in fact have been replaced by disaster.

The defences at Halfaya, German and Italian, were under the command of one of the most remarkable characters in the Afrika Korps. This was Haupt-mann Bach, an officer from the reserve who in peacetime had been the pastor of the Evangelical Church of Mannheim. Gentle, considerate, the antithesis of the officer-corps tradition, he was known and admired throughout the

---

* Churchill wildly miscalculated the *timbre* of the Australians in Tobruk when he minuted to the CIGS on 22 April: 'There is no objection to them making themselves comfortable, but they must be very careful not to let themselves be ringed in by a smaller force, and consequently lose their offensive power upon the enemy's communications.'

DAK, for his gift of command was exceptional. Rommel thought the world of him. The only officer allowed a walking-stick, because of his limp and his years, he could hardly fail to be noticed as he removed his habitual cigar to issue a quietly conversational but decisive order. Bach, who would shortly win renown at Halfaya, is also a reminder that the desert allowed personality to flower from time to time even among the type-cast *Wehrmacht* soldiers in the Afrika Korps, as it so often did among their enemy. Lieut-Colonel Freiherr von Wechmar,* for example, whose Reconnaissance Unit 3 had the dash and efficiency of 11 Hussars, could well have been taken, with his beard and fleece-lined coat, for an officer from the Long Range Desert Group – the same environment, perhaps, generating a similar species.

The *Fernmeldeaufklärung* was in high gear. By 6 June Rommel and his staff had appreciated that Wavell was about to attack. 15 Panzer, under Major-General Neumann-Silkow, was moved forward and made responsible for the frontier defences, while 5 Light, under von Ravenstein, lay back in mobile reserve about El Adem/Acroma, capable of assisting in the main battle or dealing with an attempt to thrust from Tobruk against the German rear. The respective tank states were approximately equal. 5 Light mustered 96, and 15 Panzer about 100,† while the British under Beresford-Peirse had raised 90 cruisers and some 100 Matildas.

But here was the rub. Not for the last time British tactics were vitiated by the discrepancy in speed between Crusader and Matilda which prevented the effective use of all the armour *en masse*. And Wavell's doubts about BATTLEAXE, bravely confessed to Churchill and the Chiefs of Staff in spite of his own knowledge from ULTRA of von Paulus's comments on the DAK's condition, were eminently justified. To make desert-worthy the 'cubs' from the *Tiger* convoy took precious weeks, as has been seen, and their crews were denied the time to familiarise themselves properly with the new equipment. BATTLEAXE was launched 'off balance', as Montgomery would have said, by a force neither sufficiently trained nor properly integrated. Everything was done in a rush.‡

The Afrika Korps, by contrast, was comfortably balanced. Through the intercept service it was able to decide on 14 June that the assault would start next day. All units were alerted, including the Italians' *Ariete* armoured division back at Gazala, while 5 Light made preparatory forward moves of guns and

---

* He had already earned the Knight's Cross in the spring advance and received it from Rommel's hands. Of the DAK's two Reconnaissance Units, 3 and 33, Caccia-Dominioni observed that 'their experienced crews seemed to treat the desert as if it were a somewhat threadbare version of the Black Forest'.

† Compared with the thickest armour on the Crusader (40 mm) or the Matilda (78 mm) the Panzer Mk. III was only 30 mm thick overall. By BATTLEAXE a Model H of the Mk. III had been evolved by welding extra face-hardened plates on to the front and rear, giving a further 32 mm. Some of this model were possibly employed in the battle, but the number is uncertain. The front of the Mk. IV was also 30 mm thick.

‡ General Sir Reginald Savory, who then commanded 11 Indian Brigade, once recalled for the author how infantry reinforcements reached him on the very eve of the attack.

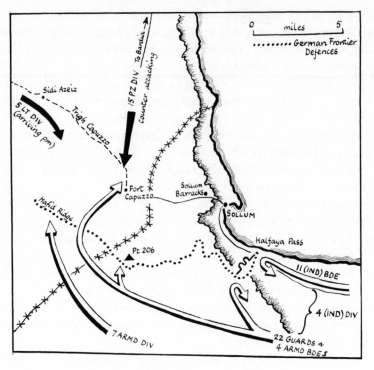

MAP 2a   Operation Battleaxe, Day 1

tanks. Outside Tobruk the whole of the investing artillery was instructed to
open a bombardment as the moon rose.

In the early morning of the 15th Beresford-Peirse moved three columns
forward. On his right, between the centre and the sea, 4 Indian Division under
Messervy sent 11 Indian Brigade against Halfaya, and 22 Guards Brigade with
4 Armoured Brigade (some of whose Matildas also supported the attack on
Halfaya) against the strongpoints in the Fort Capuzzo area. Wide on the left,
making through the frontier wire for the Hafid ridge, moved 7 Armoured
Division with the divisional Support Group. The result, by the evening, was
inconclusive. Neumann-Silkow was worried, Beresford-Peirse was unshaken,
but Rommel was optimistic, even though he over-estimated his enemy,
referring to 'some 300 British tanks which pressed stubbornly northwards'
and 'the tremendous strength of the British'.*

---

* Both the Afrika Korps and the British were constantly prone to such over-estimates, the sum of many
factors characteristic of the desert war – the all-prevailing dust, the tempo of tank battles, the difficulty of
obtaining accurate air photographs, the optimistic reports of tanks destroyed which caused alarm when,
next day, the opponent appeared as strong as ever.

In fact the careful training and superior armament of the Afrika Korps had already paid important dividends. Previously the Matilda, with its 78 mm of frontal armour, had dominated the battlefield, but the DAK now possessed an answer. In the attack on Halfaya Pass during the 15th 11 out of 12 supporting Matildas were destroyed by the upper defences and 4 out of 6 by the lower. Though the impression was that panzers were responsible (an impression of superior fire-power which was now to be almost indelibly stamped on the minds of British tank crews), the damage was mainly done by the 88 mms, though the excellent 50 mm *Pak* may have contributed.* At Capuzzo the attack went better: gun positions were over-run and 500 prisoners taken, a counter-attack by 15 Panzer was repelled, and by nightfall the area was in the hands of the Guards Brigade. But at the Hafid Ridge successive attacks by 7 Armoured Brigade failed. The third attack, in the early evening, was subtly misled into an ambush by an inviting 'Leaguer' composed of dummy vehicles, a mistake which caused the loss of 11 of the Tiger-cub Crusaders and the damage of six more. Later that evening the foremost tanks of 5 Light arrived on the scene, and held the ground.

A comparison of respective strengths next morning reveals the difference between a mature and naïve philosophy of armoured warfare. After butting stubbornly against fixed defences the British were already reduced to 48 cruisers in 7 Armoured Division and 40 Matildas in 4 Armoured Brigade. Their crews were exhausted by action. But the Afrika Korps, allowing the enemy to roll on to its powerful anti-tank armoury, had remained fresh and virtually un-committed. During the whole day only a handful of panzers had been lost. Within 24 hours the DAK had gained an irreversible advantage.

Though the next day brought some delusive British successes, the inevitable merely moved closer. 4 Indian Division beat off 15 Panzer from Capuzzo and swung across to the coast of Sollum, but beleaguered Halfaya stood like a rock, for the inimitable Bach inspired the defence like some fighting Bishop of medieval times. On the inland wing 7 Armoured Division and 5 Light swayed along the frontier wire from Hafid to Sidi Omar, spitting at one another until dark – when a count revealed that 27 more of 7 Armoured's 48 cruisers were dead. 'In these actions, the partially trained British units showed the tendency, to which they were to become prone, of attacking too soon without properly co-ordinated artillery support.'†

Rommel and his Korps now displayed their calibre. There were difficulties

---

* 15 Panzer had 18 of the 50 mm anti-tank guns in BATTLEAXE and 5 Light had 36. The numbers are approximate. Each division also had a supply of the older 37 mm but this was inferior to the British 2-pounder whereas the 50 mm had a better performance.

† General Jackson, *op. cit.*, p. 129.

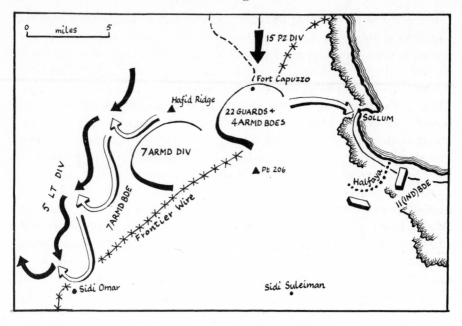

MAP 2b   Operation Battleaxe, Day 2

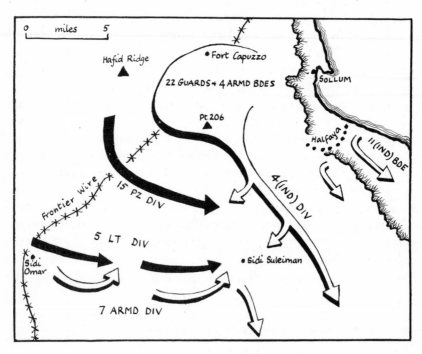

MAP 2C   Operation Battleaxe, Day 3

over fuel, the enemy had air superiority, a number of tanks had been lost on the 16th, the British inroads between Capuzzo and the coast were sinister. Nevertheless, 'to impose my plans on the enemy from the outset', as Rommel put it, he ordered both his divisions to get on the move before dawn on the 17th. 5 Light was to strike eastwards from the wire towards Sidi Suleiman while 15 Panzer curved round the left flank of the Indian Division. Then, linking up, they were to drive in concert for Halfaya, thus establishing themselves in the British rear. Though 4 Indian managed to fend off Neumann-Silkow, 5 Light reached Sidi Suleiman by 8 a.m. and the cat was among the pigeons. 'This operation,' wrote Rommel, 'had obviously taken the British completely by surprise. In wireless messages which we intercepted they described their position as very serious. The Commander of 7 Armoured Division sent a request to the Commander-in-Chief of the desert force to come to his headquarters. It sounded suspiciously as though the British commander was no longer himself capable of handling the situation.'

The DAK's intercepts had captured the truth. Wavell was already at Beresford-Peirse's headquarters, but before they could join the worried Creagh, in command of 7 Armoured, Messervy on his own authority had ordered the Indian Division to start a general withdrawal at 11 a.m. Wavell was a realist. He instructed Beresford-Peirse to break off the action and pull his men eastwards beyond the frontier. It was all over. Flying back to Cairo, Wavell sent off that same afternoon a doom-laden signal to London. 'I regret to report the failure of BATTLEAXE. . . .'

The Afrika Korps had not only won a clean-cut victory: it had overthrown the opposing Commander-in-Chief. Three generals outside Benghazi – and now Wavell! When Churchill received the news of the disaster to his 'cubs' he was down in Kent, at Chartwell, alone. 'Here I got the reports of what had happened. I wandered about the valley disconsolately for some hours.' Retribution followed. BATTLEAXE gave the Prime Minister conclusive evidence that his long-felt suspicions of Wavell were justified, and on 21 June he signalled to him that in the public interest he was to be replaced by Auchinleck. 'Rommel,' he bitterly observed, 'has torn the new-won laurels from Wavell's brow and thrown them in the sand.'

But to the Afrika Korps its swift success brought an immense accession of pride and self-confidence. For the first time it had functioned as a true panzer corps in a mobile battle against an enemy of roughly equal strength. 'I've been three days on the road going round the battlefield,' Rommel wrote to his wife Lucy on the 23rd. 'The joy of the "Africa" troops over the latest victory is tremendous.' And Schmidt observed: 'Everywhere that Rommel went now

---

* Caccia-Dominioni, *op. cit.*, pp. 68–70.

the troops beamed at him. He was already in the process of becoming a hero. He made short complimentary speeches to many groups of men. . . .' In particular he visited Halfaya, to thank the unyielding Bach and shake by the hand Major Pardi of the Italian artillery, whose personal courage and competence made him Bach's partner. 'These two had brought the collaboration between Italian artillery and German infantry to such a pitch of perfection that even in the heat of battle observers had been reminded of the timing and precision normally associated with acrobats and tight-rope walkers.'* Alas, Bach would be taken prisoner in the winter battle,* and Pardi, hit on his gun position while working with 21 Panzer on 9 July 1942, would die in hospital at El Daba, his groin, thigh and jaw all smashed by a shell-burst. 'As soon as he heard the news, Rommel dropped everything, leaped on to his little Storch and flew to visit him. Pardi must be saved at all costs. . . .' If the Italians had produced more officers like Pardi, and the Germans more men with Rommel's generous humanity? A might-have-been.

British studies of BATTLEAXE have tended to concentrate too much on the failure of Wavell and his troops and too little on analysing the DAK's success. The contrast is indeed marked. Apart from the usual courage of the regimental soldier there is nothing to place on the credit side for the British. But the Afrika Korps had demonstrated that it was already far advanced in sophistication – the skilful use of 88s, the baited ambush, the 4.30 a.m. night move by the panzer divisions, the quality of the *Fernmeldeaufklärung*'s service which constantly gave the DAK the initiative. And Bach's defence of Halfaya cannot be too highly praised, for it broke 4 Indian Division in half. The 'shift of weight' whereby Rommel switched 15 Panzer to link up with 5 Light was a centuries-old stratagem, but no less difficult to put into effect in 1941 and still demanding much self-assurance in the commander. Moreover, though 15 Panzer was finally prevented from operating side by side with 5 Light, Rommel's intention indicated at this early stage of the campaign that the armour of the Afrika Korps would fight, whenever possible, as a whole.

The learning process had not been dilatory, for already the DAK was a dangerously efficient fighting organism, self-confident and self-aware. Its doctrines were sound, its technical skill professional, its faith in its leader complete. From now until the end in Tunisia, it would be fair to say, only very rarely can one diagnose, on the occasions of its defeats, reasons for which the Afrika Korps was itself directly responsible. This is a high standard for any army at any time.

---

* Bach's personality penetrated to the British. Stuart Hood, an 8th Army staff officer now with the partisans in Italy, found himself in 1945 talking with a German deserter who had been on Rommel's staff. One of the first questions he asked was about 'Major Bach, the Protestant parson who had held out at Halfaya'. See Stuart Hood, *Pebbles from My Skull*, p. 110.

However, knowledge acquired by experience can still be consolidated and refined. This, a more adult stage of the DAK's learning process, continued steadily after BATTLEAXE. The War Diary of 15 Panzer, for example, contained an entry under the heading 'Experience gained in the defensive battle of 15–17 June 1941':

> In order to achieve surprise, all anti-tank weapons will hold their fire until it seems likely to be successful. Even if the *Flak* 88-mm has successfully opened fire, *Pak* 37- and 50-mms will remain silent in order to escape the attention of enemy tanks. They will wait until the heaviest English tanks are only a few hundred metres away before opening fire with the *Pzgr 40*.*

It would be long before the British fully applied the concept of a controlled and co-ordinated anti-tank defence implicit in this paragraph. Over and over again we read the tragic accounts of 25-pdr. field batteries firing in the open 'to the last man and the last round' as they self-sacrificially strive to hold off the panzers from their naked infantry. We read of the little 2-pdr. anti-tank guns 'portées' on trucks, which dashed boldly into the battle, as Michael Carver put it, like inefficient unarmoured tanks. But the truly co-ordinated anti-tank defence – so often to be organised by the Afrika Korps, and with such speed – was a rare feature on the British fronts until, at Medenine in March 1943, the 8th Army showed that it had learnt all the lessons and applied them with an absolute mastery.

And now, unexpectedly, the Afrika Korps felt the repressive hand of OKH. On 11 June Gariboldi had been surprised by the arrival at Tripoli of a Lieut-General Gause, accompanied by a large staff, whose function apparently was to provide a liaison team at the Italian *Comando Supremo* for OKH and to forward there the interests of the Afrika Korps, particularly in the field of supply. There is little doubt that the intention was, in the *Official History*'s words, 'to tighten the grip of OKH on affairs in Libya'. From their different viewpoints Gariboldi and Rommel strongly disapproved of this intrusion, and the latter made it very clear to OKH (as in similar circumstances Montgomery would have done) that Gause could not have two loyalties but must be directly subordinated to himself. For Rommel to have had a nominal responsibility to Gariboldi and *Comando Supremo* was hampering enough, as he sought to drive the Afrika Korps eastwards. Gause, with a private line to OKH, would be an intolerable addition.

---

* This *Panzergrenate*, the best anti-tank shot, had been specially designed to cope with the Matilda's armour, but it was in short supply. Ballistically unsound, it worked best at close ranges. *Pak* = anti-tank; *Flak* = anti-aircraft.

The deadlock was resolved in a way OKH had certainly not intended. On 12 July Gariboldi was replaced by a stronger character, General Bastico. Fearing that Mussolini aimed at reducing German influence in Africa,* von Brauchitsch accepted an arrangement which in fact gave Rommel greater power and strengthened the Afrika Korps' position. On 31 July a *Panzergruppe Afrika* was instituted, with Rommel in command, Gause as his Chief of Staff, and the team which had arrived with Gause as the headquarters staff of the Group. This was to contain two elements. First the Afrika Korps, composed of two complete panzer divisions, one German infantry division, and the Italian *Savona* infantry division. Secondly there was 21 Italian Corps, formed of the *Trento, Pavia, Brescia* and *Bologna* divisions. Rommel and his *Panzergruppe* were tactfully subordinated to Bastico, who was also in direct control of the Italians' mobile corps, 20, formed under General Gambara from the *Ariete* armoured and *Trieste* motorised divisions. But it would have been a more realistic recognition of what, for OKH, was an unpalatable fact, if the original title given to this new formation had been retained – *Panzergruppe Rommel* – for instead of reining Rommel in, as OKH had first intended, he had now been given his head.

The Afrika Korps profited in every sense. Its feeling that it was an élite formation, already keen, was if anything sharpened by serving under the same commander as the Italians, for the men in the DAK well knew that they were Rommel's chosen people.

> Between Rommel and his troops there was that mutual understanding which cannot be explained and analysed, but which is the gift of the gods. The Afrika Korps followed Rommel wherever he led, however hard he drove them. . . . The men knew that Rommel was the last man Rommel spared; they saw him in their midst and they felt, 'This is our leader'.†

The *Panzergruppe*'s commander himself,‡ and therefore the DAK, also benefited substantially from the quality of the officers who formed the new headquarters staff. Rommel's forebodings were soon dispelled. Before he arrived in Africa Gause had commented to Halder about Rommel's 'morbid ambitions': now they were in harness, and could take each other's measure, they achieved a warm working relationship so that by 28 August Rommel could write to his wife: 'I'm getting on famously with my new Chief of Staff.'

The new Head of Operations, Colonel Siegfried Westphal, was a soldier of

---

* But see below, p. 71, for other reasons.
† Von Mellenthin, *op. cit.*, p. 46.
‡ Who had just been promoted to Panzer General.

extreme distinction, later to become a Lieut-General, and Chief of Staff first to Kesselring in Italy and, in 1944, to von Rundstedt as Commander-in-Chief West. In the coming winter battle he would exercise a critically important initiative. And the new Intelligence staff officer, Major von Mellenthin, who had already proved himself in Poland, France and the Balkans, was also destined for high appointments later on in Russia and North-west Europe. Gause, Westphal and von Mellenthin composed, in fact, an outstanding team until the partnership was broken during the Gazala battle in June 1942, when in the fighting at Sidi Muftah both Gause and Westphal were wounded. Von Mellenthin then took over from Westphal, while Gause was replaced by Fritz Bayerlein, another figure of all-round capacity.* For the moment, in the reorganisation which followed the creation of the *Panzergruppe*, Bayerlein acted as Chief of Staff to the Afrika Korps, its new commander in place of Rommel being General Crüwell, a hard, practical, resolute officer. It must indeed be noted that however Rommel may have been stinted of equipment or supplies, he was extraordinarily well served with able staffs and battle-worthy corps and divisional commanders. There was very little dead wood at the top – particularly in the Afrika Korps.

In all these developments, however, another and a more powerful influence had been at work, and an analysis of the interplay of pressures illustrates exactly how the Afrika Korps could be affected by the dualism of authority in Germany. For while OKH was manoeuvring to restrict Rommel's responsibilities and put a brake on further advances by the DAK, Hitler and his servile† OKW were evolving entirely different policies.

On 11 June, assuming an early success in Russia, the *Führer* issued Draft Directive 32 in which 'Plan Orient' envisaged a converging assault on the British position in the Middle East from Libya, from Bulgaria via Turkey, and through conquered Caucasia. Implementing Hitler's dream, on 28 June Halder instructed Rommel to produce a draft scheme for invading Egypt after taking Tobruk. It was thus that OKH's desire to put chains on Rommel were defeated, for in this atmosphere of *Ran an den Feind, voll einsetzen‡* it was impossible for von Brauchitsch to block the formation of the *Panzergruppe* and the appointment of Rommel as, in effect, the Axis Land Forces Commander in Africa. Though policies in Germany fluctuated in the next few months (Rommel kept track of them by several visits to Italy and Germany), and though events in Russia temporarily shelved the grandiose 'Plan Orient',

---

* Bayerlein had arrived from the Russian front, where he had practised his trade under the pastmaster of panzer warfare, General Guderian.

† The tactful way of putting this, in the German of the time, was *führertren*.

‡ Admiral Scheer's signal to the German battle-cruisers at Jutland: 'Charge the enemy; make straight for him.'

nevertheless the central point remained firm. Tobruk must be taken – by September, it was assumed in Germany, but Rommel was strong enough now to insist that he would need all the forces committed to Africa, so that an assault could not be guaranteed until they were fully available, complete with equipment and the necessary stocks. October seemed the more likely month.

The idea that Rommel's preoccupation with Tobruk during the latter months of 1941 derived wholly from a personal obsession, which he cultivated in spite of his masters' disapproval, is thus a demonstrable fallacy. It was given a wide circulation in Desmond Young's early and impressionistic *Rommel* (1951). But whatever OKH might think, Hitler himself had shifted towards a forward policy of German domination in the Mediterranean campaign. Why else, for example, did he order the withdrawal of *Fliegerkorps* II from Russia in October, to be employed under Field Marshal Kesselring along with *Fliegerkorps* X for the establishment of naval and air superiority between Italy and Africa? Kesselring himself was made an overlord of the skies and seas, as Commander-in-Chief South, controlling the two *Fliegerkorps* and both Italian and German naval forces. Based in Italy, he was subordinate only to Mussolini: to Bastico and Rommel he was a supporter rather than a superior. His orders to paralyse Malta and co-operate with the *Panzergruppe* were evidence enough that the old concept of the Afrika Korps as merely a 'blocking group', to which OKH still tended to cling, was temporarily dead. The capture of Tobruk was thus in the forefront of German policy, and as late as 14 November, after Rommel had visited Rome for discussions with Cavallero, the latter confirmed the Italian attitude by writing to Bastico and telling him to launch the assault 'as soon as he could with the strongest possible forces'.

The truth is that for the time being Hitler's aims and Rommel's converged. The cliché about the garrison of Tobruk is precise: it was a thorn in the side of the Axis Army, whose presence irritated and disturbed the Panzer General, so that now that he was, as it were, officially back in business Rommel devoted himself to capturing the port with a single-minded intensity. Remembering the abortive attempts in the spring, he decided this time to penetrate the south-east corner of the perimeter. His detailed tactical ideas are graphically illustrated by the sketched plan for the attack, drawn by him as usual in bold and multi-coloured strokes, which is reproduced at the front of *The Rommel Papers*. There were two central considerations. He was fully aware that the British under their new commander Auchinleck must inevitably strike in due course for the relief of Tobruk,* and though he remained convinced that he could

---

* Bayerlein recalled that 'in the middle of October, our Army intelligence circular notified all formations that with large quantities of enemy war material and strong contingents of troops steadily pouring into Egypt, there was a grave danger that the British would soon launch a major offensive'.

move first, prudence required a capability to hold the British off. This meant strengthening the frontier defences, and retaining a mobile armoured reserve ready to make a quick riposte. But since Tobruk was the priority, his assault force must also be strong – and mobile, for as the draft plan indicates he intended to crack a hole in the perimeter and then pour his armour relentlessly through the breach. It was the Afrika Korps which would have to carry the main burden.

During the late summer and autumn, therefore, the DAK trained with a practical relevance which was not to be equalled by the British until Montgomery laid down his curriculum before Alamein. The harbour and hinterland of Tobruk were steadily pounded – an average of 500 *Luftwaffe* sorties per month between July and November, while the artillery bombardment, switched in August to the eastern sector of the perimeter, usually produced between 500 and 1,000 shells a day. As new units for the 'Africa z.v.V.' division flew in – one, 361 Afrika Regiment, containing many Germans from the French Foreign Legion – 115 Motorised Regiment* of 15 Panzer was at last able to withdraw from the siege, during which it had held the south-west sector since its arrival. At the seaside east of Tobruk the regiment now rested and recuperated, before practising its old mobile role; but Schmidt observed a classic phenomenon:

> The physical reaction among the men was immediate and patent. About 70 per cent of the unit went down at once with diseases such as dysentery and jaundice. The fighting strength of the unit, which had always been about normal in the Tobruk line, was at once reduced so gravely that companies were only of platoon effectiveness.

This pathology of reaction was a marked feature in most armies (in Burma, for example, and doubtless in Russia). Once the mental tension of the front line was relaxed the body asserted itself. In this respect DAK was at a disadvantage – less prepared by experience and less equipped than the British for the treatment of desert ailments, it also lacked the medical resources of the highly developed Egyptian base.

Nevertheless, around the perimeter preparations continued. Air photographs were now available – in April and May the Afrika Korps had scarcely possessed a single map of the Tobruk layout: it was rumoured that the Italians had intentionally withheld their accurate knowledge of the defences. This

---

* At this stage the motorised infantry of the Panzer divisions were called *Schützen Regimenten*. The more familiar title of *Panzer Grenadier* was not introduced until July 1942. The 'Afrika' Division (later 90 Light) was not yet motorised and relied on *ad hoc* transport.

time detailed photographs of the area to be attacked were issued right down to companies. And this time, too, there was a siege train. To the south east of Tobruk, in the El Duda/Belhamed area, General Böttcher's Artillery Command 104 built up a bombardment group of nine 210 mm howitzers, 38 150 mm and 12 105 mm. The British had nothing like this. Such medium guns as they possessed were scattered by regiment or battery. And the inherent flexibility of the Afrika Korps' dispositions would be revealed during the winter battle when, turning through 180 degrees, Böttcher's artillery pointed south and made its massive contribution to the conflict around Sidi Rezegh. Flexibility and economy in fuel consumption was in any case improved by the construction of a by-pass road. As the *Via Balbia* ran through Tobruk itself, the Axis transport was compelled to use a rough route skirting the perimeter until Rommel persuaded the unwilling Italians, with a labour force of 3,000, to construct a proper by-pass encircling Tobruk via Acroma, El Adem and El Duda. (The DAK troops rebelled at this corvée and demanded to be returned to the front line.)

But Rommel never forgot the war of movement – which might, indeed, become a high priority if the British struck first. In the coastal region between Tobruk and the frontier both panzer divisions*therefore carried out intensive exercises to perfect the co-ordination of armour, anti-tank and conventional artillery in mobile operations. Neumann-Silkow of 15 Panzer was rated as one of the most efficient panzer leaders. Von Ravenstein of 21 Panzer was an unusual mixture. An elegant intellectual, the former head of a news agency, he had won the coveted *Pour le Mérite* in 1918. In 1939 he commanded a panzer regiment in Poland, and had seen further action in the Balkans before BATTLE-AXE introduced him to the problems of the desert. Both these able men now took their divisions to school again.

In a sense these days were the consummation of the DAK's learning process, since from this time onward its deadly battle drill became habitual. The essence of the method consisted of a reversal of British doctrine, symbolised in the emotive notion that desert fighting was akin to naval warfare in which the tank represented the battleship, the capital ship. To 'destroy the enemy armour' in Jutland-like clashes between the capital ships of the desert – this was the British ideal. But already Rommel and his generals were coming to see that tank *v.* tank was a futile formula. Far better to decimate the enemy's armour with your anti-tank guns by tactical boldness and calculated stratagem: then, and only then, the panzers could wreak their will on exposed field artillery, defenceless infantry, headquarters and the 'soft' echelons of supply.

The hidden 88s and the ambush baited with dummies in BATTLEAXE had

---

* 5 Light was up-graded to 21 Panzer on 1 August.

disclosed the value of luring an innocent enemy to destruction. In the latest exercise, however, a more elaborate device was perfected which, in fact, had already been tried out in the day-long running fire-fight between 7 Armoured and 5 Light from Hafid down to Sidi Omar. This was the technique of keeping anti-tank guns, both 88s and 50 mms, manoeuvring on wheels amid the panzers so that, when they clashed with an enemy force, the guns could immediately drop into action and very significantly amplify the killing-power of the armour.* Suddenly taking post in the forefront of the panzers, they introduced not only surprise but also the effect of firing with good sights from stable platforms, and of normally propelling armour-piercing shot at a higher velocity and greater penetrative value than the guns of the Mk. III – the work-horse of the DAK – and the rarer Mk. IV could attain.

Other variants became possible. If a panzer body was unexpectedly attacked by British armour while moving in the open, its mobile anti-tank guns could rapidly switch to flank or rear and 'see off' the assailants before they got to close quarters – a weakness of British equipment, particularly the American-built 'Honey' which reached the desert in the autumn of 1941, being that they needed to close in to make a kill. In the battles to come all these techniques would be employed by the Afrika Korps with results the more lethal because after BATTLEAXE, as has been pointed out, British tank crews tended to believe that the 'brewing up' of their Matildas and Crusaders was the work of opposing panzers rather than of the accompanying anti-tank guns. Field Marshal Sir Michael Carver, a first-hand witness of what happened, puts the point forcefully when assessing what he calls the bitter lessons of BATTLEAXE and the later CRUSADER. 'It is clear beyond all doubt that throughout this period the true enemy of the British tanks was the German anti-tank gun.' The German *Pak* guns, he affirms, 'were boldly and aggressively handled as offensive weapons in the forefront of the battle alongside or even in front of the tanks'.†

He could well have made a further point. The two main processes, either of luring the enemy's armour to within a few hundred yards of a defensive line before opening fire, or, in mobile operations, of blending panzer and *Pak*, made great demands on mutual confidence between the different elements of the Afrika Korps – the panzer regiments, 8 and 5 :‡ the *Schützen Regimenter*: and the *Panzerjäger* or anti-tank battalions. The suspicion which existed between infantry and armour among the British had a divisive effect, whereas the very battle doctrine of the DAK, based on co-operation and interdepend-

---

* After BATTLEAXE a new trailer was introduced for the 88 mm, towed by an 8-ton half-track. This immensely facilitated its employment in mobile operations.

† Michael Carver, *Tobruk*, pp. 258–60.

‡ Regiment 8 contained the armour of 15 Panzer; Regiment 5 that of 21 Panzer. A German panzer regiment was the rough equivalent of a British armoured brigade.

ence, was yet another factor generating a sense of solidarity.

The pivot of Rommel's developing plans was a stiffening of his fixed defences along the Egyptian frontier. BATTLEAXE had demonstrated their value. By improving them the *Panzergruppe* would prevent the enemy from making a rapid advance down the coast, thus benefitting from the *Via Balbia* and picking up not only Bardia (where von Ravenstein's headquarters lay), but also the Gambut area further west, where Rommel had established his Group Command and where the main Axis dumps, workshops and other base installations had been painfully built up. Moreover, a blocking position at Halfaya and Capuzzo would compel the British armour to swing wide and south into the open regions of the Trigh el Abd, thus consuming more fuel and exposing a vulnerable flank. *Savona* and some units of the 'Afrika' Division (for which seven battalions had arrived by November) were stationed along this defensive line. Bach, now a Major, remained at Halfaya. It is significant, too, that from the slightly increased stock of 88 mms no less than 23 were positioned on the frontier, while only 12, together with the full tally of 96 50 mms, were kept mobile with the two panzer divisions. Rommel's concern for the frontier was emphasised by frequent personal visits, during which he supervised the defences with meticulous care. Schmidt draws a convincing picture of him addressing Bach's company commanders at Halfaya, giving precise instructions about the layout of each defensive locality, and elevating the spirit of the defenders.

All these busy preparations added up to a coherent and sensible plan which was, however, violated by two grave flaws. By his dynamic energy, eye for detail and tireless exercise of will-power Rommel brought the Afrika Korps, by November, to an athletic peak. But the supplies and reinforcements which were a pre-condition of its success – as he had laid down in the summer – failed to arrive, while Rommel himself committed as foolish an error as a commander can make. He formed a picture of his enemy's intentions, and by convincing himself that Auchinleck was still not about to attack he might well have lost the coming battle before it began – if his enemy's generalship had been adequate.

The graph of damage to the sea convoys which sustained the Axis in Africa was always variable, as was indicated in Chapter Two. Unfortunately for DAK the summer and autumn of 1941 was a phase when British naval and air strikes were dominant. Between July and October 20 per cent of the cargoes from Italy were sunk, and the average monthly landings of 72,000 tons was insufficient for the daily maintenance of the *Panzergruppe* as well as stockpiling for a major battle. Yet even these figures fell in the key months of November and December. 30,000 tons in the former and 39,000 in the latter month was unacceptably low. And all these figures, of course, reflect not only sinkings but also the turning back of convoys to Italy or Greece for fear of interception. The deprivation of fuel alone, on the eve of a mobile battle, was sinister: but the significance of the sinkings* (and perhaps of the influence of the Russian campaign) can be illustrated in another way.

Between the aftermath of BATTLEAXE and the opening of CRUSADER the total of effective tanks in 15 and 21 Panzer Divisions rose, roughly, from 180 to 250. Yet this increase was hardly due at all to the arrival of new equipment. The rise in figures is to be accounted for almost entirely by the repair of damaged tanks –a reflection of the superiority of the skill of the Afrika Korps, as compared with the British, in recovering their wounded panzers from the battlefield and the efficiency of the workshops which they established at forward points like Gambut. Alan Moorehead arrived as a war correspondent at Gambut in December:

> The tank workshops eclipsed anything we had in the forward areas. Bedded in concrete and under canvas were big lathes and a heavy smithy. Cases of tank precision instruments worth many thousands of pounds lay about. One was full of periscopes. Several huge boxes contained new fifty-milli-metre guns which apparently could be fitted to damaged tanks in this place. There were sheets of armour, new tracks and tyres, a mass of woodwork and steel parts. It almost seemed that they could have built a tank here in the desert by the sea.†

There is no doubt that as the date for his cherished attack on Tobruk approached Rommel sealed his mind against any suggestion that it might be anticipated by a British offensive. On 26 October he issued his orders: preparations to be completed by 15 November, D Day the 20th – to take advantage of the moon. Cavallero has recorded in his memoirs‡ that during his November visit to Rome Rommel declared that a large-scale British attack was 'extremely un-likely': 'an action with small forces on the part of the enemy' was more prob-able. The Italian official history, *Seconda Offensive Britannica*, says that Italian fears of an offensive were attributed by the Germans to 'an excessive Latin nervousness', and even quotes von Mellenthin as stating, as late as 11 Novem-ber, that there was nothing to worry about.

Rommel's euphoria is often ascribed to a curious sally which occurred in mid-September and was appropriately named *Midsummer Night's Dream*.

---

* The official historian of the Italian Navy says that in November 1941 62 per cent of all stores embarked in Italy were lost. (M.A. Bragadin, *Che ha fatto la Marina?*, p. 259.)

† Alan Moorehead, *A Year of Battle*, p. 76.

‡ *Comando Supremo*, p. 150.

Either to identify and sack supply dumps which the British were thought to be setting up in the forward zone, or to improve his intelligence picture, or, as is more probable, to exercise his troops realistically in the combination of all arms in the mobile battle, he suddenly shot off with von Ravenstein and 21 Panzer into the wilderness south of Sidi Omar. As the column swept eastwards his ADC, Captain Schmidt, thought he looked like a U-boat commander on his bridge as 'with an even more than usual boisterousness' he cried: 'We're off to Egypt.'

But the 'rude mechanicals' of 21 Panzer were not only in a delusive mid-summer dream: it was a bad dream. No dumps were discovered. The tanks ran out of fuel and were carpet-bombed by the RAF whose close formations the DAK later nicknamed 'Party Rallies'. A captured South African office truck contained papers which suggested that the enemy was more concerned with retreat than advance – as misleading an implication as that produced by the non-existent dumps, since elsewhere the British were stock-piling steadily. A raid which might surely have been more economically and effectively conducted by Reconnaissance Unit 3 or 33 was called off by a panzer General even more convinced that he was right.

Though the dispositions of the *Panzergruppe* were, in fact, entirely adequate to cope with the British advance, Rommel has nevertheless been often rightly criticised for his assumption that nothing serious impended. But apart from the great skill with which Auchinleck's army concealed its widespread preparations, there was another counter on the chessboard of deception which must have added great weight to Rommel's presuppositions. This was the Gauleiter of Mannheim.

Brigadier Shearer's unpublished memoirs describe how, in June, it was observed during an Italian bombing raid on Haifa that a parachutist, on landing, had set about digging holes in the ground. He was apprehended and brought to Cairo: from the ground a small but powerful transmitter was unearthed. The man's credentials seemed impeccable – a Jew seeking to join relations (who, of German origin, actually existed in Jerusalem). But the transmitter raised doubts, and without being informed of its discovery the man was lodged in the Combined Services Detailed Interrogation Centre outside Cairo. Here it was observed that even senior officers among the prisoners treated him with respect. Finally, an injudicious attempt to pass a message to the Red Cross in Switzerland revealed his identity – The Gauleiter of Mannheim.

Then, by chance, a staff officer experimenting with the transmitter obtained an answer from Bari. Exchanges followed, and the Gauleiter was soon established as having succeeded, in his role as a Jew, in obtaining a waiter's job in a senior officers' mess in Cairo where secret matters were discussed. As

Director of Military Intelligence Shearer now got the permission of the Commanders-in-Chief, Middle East, to use this ventriloquist's dummy. By feeding to Bari various true and verifiable bits of information Shearer had already created such credibility that Rommel, he learned, had ordered all Bari bulletins to be brought directly to him.

As in one of those deployments of a 'bent' agent so brilliantly described by Sir John Masterman in *The Double Cross System*, the moment now came to exploit this unique advantage. Auchinleck was, in all truth, sufficiently disturbed by the possibility of a German breakthrough in the Caucasus. What more reasonable than that his preparations in the desert should be a carefully calculated cover for the transfer of British reinforcements from the Middle East to Russia. Such ideas were sedulously conveyed to Bari, sometimes meeting with the response of a direct query from Rommel himself. And an intentionally arranged visit by Auchinleck to Jerusalem enabled the hot news to be fed to Italy that the C-in-C was actually there to discuss a move of the 9th Army northwards from Palestine.

No doubt this was but one of many factors increasing Rommel's assurance, and certainly the miasma of delusion spread far in this atmosphere of a midsummer night's dream. What more misguided, for example, or more tragic than the raid by Lieut-Colonel Geoffrey Keyes and his commandos on a house at Beda Littoria during the night of 17/18 November, which was intended to dispose of Rommel? That night Rommel was in Athens on the way back from Rome, and in any case it was some time since he had made his base the *cantoniera* or roadhouse at Gambut, on the other side of Tobruk, leaving the establishment at Beda Littoria to his quartermaster staff. It was an odd coincidence that only two nights earlier an equally abortive raid had been carried out by 15 men of the Brandenburg Regiment (which, like the Commandos or SAS, functioned not so much as a complete unit as in small detachments highly trained in demolition and destruction). These, landed on the coast near El Daba by U-boat, were intended to cut the railway which, by intensive effort on the part of two New Zealand railway construction companies, had by now been pushed forward beyond Matruh to the foot of the escarpment at Misheifa. All the Brandenburgers were taken prisoner, and the line stayed unscathed.

But the despised Italians had been justifiably nervous. On 18 November, two days before Rommel's own deadline, the recently re-christened 8th Army moved westwards through the frontier wire in a mood of extreme elation. The bear, as Churchill was fond of saying, blew first. Apart from Alamein, no battle would test the Afrika Korps so long or so severely as the coming conflict, CRUSADER.

5

The Sunday of the Dead

'The fact is that the Commander in the field will always be subject to great and often undue pressure from his Government. Wellington suffered from it: Haig suffered from it: Wavell suffered from it. Nothing will stop it. . . .' What might have been a summary of Hitler's relations with his generals at the front, whether Rommel in Africa or the men in Russia, was actually a prescient piece of advice sent privately by Churchill's Chief Staff Officer, the sage 'Pug' Ismay, to his friend Auchinleck when the latter took over from Wavell responsibility for the Middle East. From July to November 1941 Auchinleck was exposed to constant and often peremptory demands by Churchill that he should open a major offensive against the *Panzergruppe*, in spite of his professional judgement that an attack would be premature until his troops were properly trained and his reserves of men and equipment fully replenished. Like Wavell, Auchinleck finally succumbed, and the result was CRUSADER.

His obstinacy was beneficial – except in the mind of his Prime Minister, who maintained that 'once Rommel was beaten and his small, audacious army destroyed and Tripoli was ours it was not thought impossible for four divisions of our best troops, about 80,000 men, to land and conquer Sicily'. In mid-1941 such a concept was as unrealistic as Hitler's 'Plan Orient'. Nevertheless, when he came to write *The Second World War* Churchill still maintained that 'General Auchinleck's four and a half months' delay in engaging the enemy was alike a mistake and a misfortune'. In view of what is known about Rommel's 'small, audacious army', the unreliability of British armour, the indifferent standards of tactical command and the absence of a coherent doctrine for mobile war, it is doubtful whether any serious military student would now support Churchill's dogma. ULTRA told him much, of course, about the realities of Rommel's situation, but however impoverished that might seem to him, however reasonable it might appear to assume that one hard blow would dispose of the Afrika Korps, he never grasped – perhaps he never understood it about any theatre – that in the circumstances of the desert war mere quantity was not enough to overcome quality.

Certainly Auchinleck's obduracy had produced for him a quantitative advantage by the start of CRUSADER. 600 cruiser tanks (half Crusaders, half the American Stuart*), 170 infantry tanks, 600 field guns and no fewer than 34,000 vehicles were only part of the stocks that poured into the Middle East. By November, too, a sufficient muster roll enabled Auchinleck to divide his 8th Army (which in September replaced the existing Western Desert Force) into two Corps. 13 Corps, comprising the New Zealand and 4 Indian Divisions, with 1 Army Tank Brigade's infantry tanks in support, had the task of enveloping and overwhelming the Axis defences on the frontier. 30 Corps was the true striking force – 7 Armoured Division, 4 Armoured Brigade, 1 South African Division and 22 Guards Motor Brigade. 2 South African Division lay in reserve. By the end of October most of the Australians had been removed from Tobruk, after acidulous exchanges between the British and Australian Governments, but a force capable of breaking out had been built up there from 70 (British) Division, the Polish 1 Carpathian Brigade and a mixture of armour in 32 Army Tank Brigade.

Auchinleck was thus not stinted. To match the 139 Mk. III and 39 Mk. IV available in the DAK (its 70 Mk. II light tanks and the 146 Italian M 13/40 hardly counted†) he had at the front 62 of the older cruisers, 210 Crusaders and 173 Stuarts (apart from 132 infantry tanks with 13 Corps and the mixed brigade in Tobruk). And the Afrika Korps had no reserves, while in base workshops or in convoy at sea several hundred more tanks were in the pipeline to 8th Army.

Yet quality was critical. The Crusaders, and still more the older A13 cruisers, were mechanically unreliable: the Stuart's weaknesses have been noted. The uncapped ammunition fired by the British 2-pdr. gun tended to disintegrate on the face-hardened armour with which a number of the panzers had been strengthened before CRUSADER. And even perfect weapons are stultified in the hands of inept commanders. It was here, in spite of his numerical strength and preparations for the offensive more elaborate and meticulous than ever before, that Auchinleck was least secure.

For the command of 8th Army he chose Alan Cunningham, the brother of Admiral A.B. Cunningham, the naval C-in-C in the Mediterranean. Cunningham had acquitted himself well in East Africa, but he was wholly inexperienced

---

* Light tanks which the British at first tended to use in a medium role. Fast and reliable, they were crippled by their short range of action, and crews felt that they had to close well within the scope of the panzers' guns before they could use their own 33 mm to effect. The Stuart was christened and universally known as the Honey. The affection it aroused was not always justified by its fighting capability.

† In strictly qualitative terms this is true. Nevertheless, as will be seen, the *Ariete* armoured division was a valuable ally to the Afrika Korps in CRUSADER.

in armoured warfare, his health was uncertain, and there was a vein of pessimism or debility in his temperament. 30 Corps, which was intended to 'seek and destroy the enemy armour', should have been commanded by Lieut-General Vyvyan Pope, who arrived in Cairo in October, only to die almost immediately when his aircraft crashed on take-off at Heliopolis. It was a case of scratching round at the last minute for a successor, and the most convenient man available was Willoughby Norrie, who had reached the Middle East ahead of his 1 Armoured Division which was still in transit from England. For the British Pope's death was an unqualified tragedy. He had served in armour since the early '20s, consorted with pioneers like Hobart, commanded the Mobile Force at Mersa Matruh in 1936, acted as armoured adviser at Gort's HQ in France in 1940, and thereafter held the key post of Director of Armoured Fighting Vehicles at the War Office. Above all, his robust temperament and informed mind were supported by a fundamental creed – armour must always be used *en masse* and never dissipated. Norrie's outstanding record of gallantry in the First World War was no more an equipment for command in an armoured conflict than was that of Philip Neame, VC. Courage was the small change of the desert war. More ominous was the fact that Norrie's service in the '30s had largely been with the cavalry. He lacked, and would reveal that he lacked, the built-in capacities needed for decisive command in an armoured conflict. Against men like Cunningham and Norrie a battle-line containing hardened practitioners of the armoured art like Rommel, Crüwell, von Ravenstein, Westphal and Bayerlein was like a confrontation between the Order of Teutonic Knights and its innocent victims.

Nevertheless, during CRUSADER commanders in both armies would make critical errors. It was well for Rommel that he had trained the Afrika Korps to so high a pitch, for there were occasions when only the skill and tenacity of his troops enabled him to stage a brilliant recovery from the edge of disaster. On the British side, there can be no question that ultimate victory flowed from the quality of the regimental soldiers rather than from the tactical abilities of their generals. And when a battle has to be settled by front-line troops it means that, the commanders having used up their stock of ideas, victory will fall to the men who hold out longest. So it was in CRUSADER. Neither the *Panzergruppe* nor 8th Army had a monopoly of courage and stoicism, but a steady injection of supplies and armour refreshed and renewed the British, whereas the strength of the Afrika Korps simply drained away. On 7 December, when Rommel finally decided to withdraw, he had only 40 tanks left in DAK and some two battalions in 90 Light. Moreover, he had been warned that no significant reinforcements or resupply could be expected within a month. CRUSADER presents itself, therefore, as a battle which both sides deserved to lose; in which, however, the British were able to benefit from their logistic superiority because the intervention of Auchinleck, a commander whose will was as strong as Rommel's, prevented them from collapsing before the Afrika Korps had 'fought itself to the condition where it could fight no more'. But the honours, in truth, were about equally divided.

Opportunities for a decisive action were thrown away by both armies during the first 48 hours of CRUSADER. In his brilliant book on the desert campaigns, *Approach to Battle*, General Sir Francis Tuker coined the phrase, 'If the approach is good, the battle will be easy.' Rommel's mental approach, in mid-November, was adrift, and for the Afrika Korps many difficulties ensued. On 14 November, visiting Rome, he defended his plan for an assault on Tobruk (now fixed for 21 November) against the objections of an Italian High Command which, with the clearer vision of an enlightened self-interest, more accurately appreciated 8th Army's intentions. Rommel's blinkered outlook is forcibly recorded in Cavallero's diary:

> I asked Rommel whether it might not be possible for the enemy to make a large-scale enveloping attack. Rommel regarded the possibility as extremely unlikely as the enemy would be afraid of having his line of retreat cut by the Italo-German divisions. He anticipated nothing more than an action with small forces, supported by the enemy air force. *

The fact that Rommel only flew back across the Mediterranean as 8th Army was beginning to move is a sufficient indication of his self-assurance – an assurance which, it could be argued, had been fortified by the many deceptive arrangements of the British,† were it not that the *Panzergruppe*'s general had flatly rejected Intelligence pointers – air photographs, unit identifications – which should have alerted a man who had not already 'made a picture'.

The obsession with Tobruk did not mean that the *Panzergruppe* was ill-disposed to meet an attack from the east. After final readjustments the three main headquarters lay – Rommel's Group HQ at Gambut, Crüwell's DAK HQ at Bardia, and Navarini's HQ for the Italian XXI Infantry Corps at El Adem. South-west of El Adem was the HQ of Gambara's mobile XX Corps with *Ariete* at Bir el Gubi and *Trieste* in reserve at Bir Hacheim. 15 Panzer was on the coast between Bardia and Tobruk, while 21 Panzer was poised on the Trigh Capuzzo at Gasr el Arid, south of Gambut and west of Capuzzo. Reconnaissance Units 3 and 33 had been combined under Baron von Wechmar, as Group Wechmar, and placed under 21 Panzer's command with the function

---

* *Comando Supremo*, p. 150.
† 'Never in a large operation had tactical surprise been more completely achieved since Gustavus Adolphus crossed the frozen Baltic,' observes the Australian Official History, adding 'never had it been achieved to less purpose'.

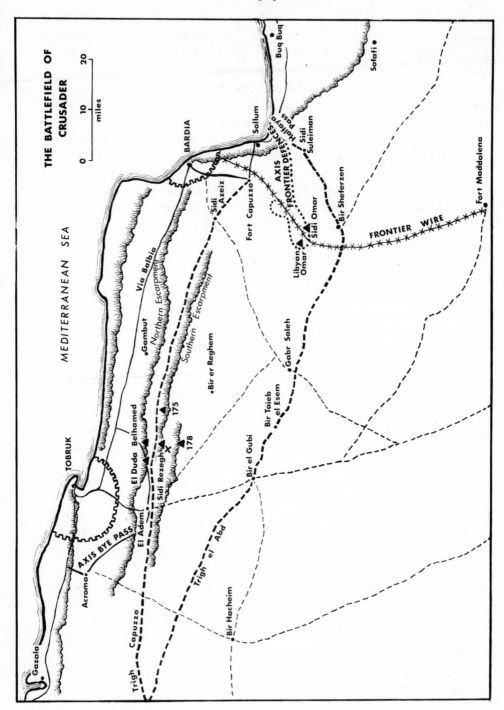

MAP 3 The battlefield of Crusader

of watching the great arc of open flank curving from Bir el Gubi round to the frontier defences. Evidence about Rommel's stocks is conflicting and obscure, but the hard fact seems to be that enough fuel and ammunition had been built up to sustain the short sharp assault on Tobruk which was contemplated, yet not enough (without substantial resupply) to see the *Panzergruppe* through an unexpected mobile conflict fought at great intensity over a period of three weeks. There was nothing, however, in either the dispositions or the logistic state of the Afrika Korps to prevent it meeting a major attack with a powerful, concerted blow.

Power was in Cunningham's hands also, at the outset, but the likelihood of its being applied in a concerted effort disappeared before the two armies had even engaged. The object of his armoured 30 Corps was to destroy the Afrika Korps 'on the ground of his own choosing'. He chose, as an opening gambit, to push it down the Trigh el Abd as far as Gabr Saleh, due south of Gambut, a spot whose only significance, as the South African History observes, 'seems to have been that it presented a convenient landmark on which to rally in a featureless desert'. Here there was to be a pause, to await Rommel's reactions: a curious piece of military thinking, since the elementary requirement for a commander wishing to draw the enemy on to his guns is to occupy ground for which he knows that his opponent *must* fight. In justice to the much-maligned Norrie, one must observe that he pointed this out to Cunningham and argued strongly for an immediate drive to Sidi Rezegh and the Tobruk outskirts, which would certainly have stimulated an instant reaction from Rommel. But he was disregarded. Lacking the authority and experience in armour which Vyvyan Pope would have been able to assert, had he lived, Norrie bowed to the bad plan of an inept Army Commander. If Rommel had been sufficiently alert, they might between them have lost CRUSADER within 24 hours of the arrival at Gabr Saleh.

But Rommel was suffering from myopia. In spite of 8th Army's advance during the 18th, he opposed the recommendations of all his senior commanders for a vigorous response. At Afrika Korps HQ Crüwell and Bayerlein were uneasy. Von Ravenstein proposed moving the armour of 21 Panzer – 5 Panzer Regiment – to the north of Gabr Saleh with the object of hitting the enemy in his flank. Agreeing with this, Crüwell also sent 15 Panzer the code-word *Ebbe*, which instructed Neumann-Silkow to move the division inland from the coast, to the Trigh Capuzzo area south of Gambut. All these sensible arrangements were cancelled by Rommel when Crüwell telephoned him at Gambut at ten o'clock that night: 'The enemy,' he argued, 'intended merely to harass us. It was unnecessary to put 15 Panzer on the alert. We must not lose our nerve.' Far from losing his nerve, Crüwell kept his head and allowed 15 Panzer's instructions to stand. In the meantime what might have been clinching evidence was already available: the War Diary at HQ Afrika Korps noted that at 2300 hours 'the German Liaison Officer with *Savona* Division reported results of the interrogation of an English soldier captured at Sidi Omar'. The prisoner, a gunner from 4 Indian Division, had revealed enough to confirm a general forward movement by 8th Army. But at *Panzergruppe* this intelligence was discredited as a 'plant'.

While the immediate commanders of the DAK can thus be observed reacting in an entirely correct and professional manner, by contrast with their Group Commander, there is this to be said for Rommel. On the night of the 17th/18th a storm of exceptional violence raged over the desert. Its viciousness was noted on both sides. The war correspondent Alexander Clifford, for example, recalled

> The most spectacular thunderstorm within local memory. . . . The thunder mumbled and murmured and roared in long growling cadences, and burst overhead with a crack like a bomb. *

And his colleague Alan Moorehead remembered the downpour, 'squalls of bitter sleet'. It is this sudden, torrential rain which figures most vividly in Afrika Korps reminiscences, for it caused both damage and death. Falling most heavily along the coastal region where so many DAK units were disposed, the tempest sent great surges of water racing down the wadis where men slept in hollows tunnelled into the normally dry water-course's side, and either drowned them or swept their equipment away. More to the point, it turned the airfields of the *Luftwaffe* into sodden blotting-paper. Flight was impossible during the 18th, and in consequence Rommel was denied the air photographs which might have convinced him. This denial actually had a direct effect, for the staff at *Panzergruppe* under-valued the sighting reports sent in by the armoured cars of Group Wechmar on the ground that neither air reconnaissance nor radio intercepts supported them. (The absence of intercepts was, of course, due to the strict wireless discipline observed by the British.)

On the morning of the 19th, therefore, 8th Army was left free to squander its strength. 7 Armoured Division, having reached its first objectives as an integrated force, but without sight of an enemy to 'destroy on ground of its own choosing', broke into three disconnected parts. Gott, its commander, despatched 22 Armoured Brigade to Bir el Gubi to deal with the Italians. 7 Armoured Brigade shot off to the table-land of Sidi Rezegh, whither Norrie had wished to send the whole division. Meanwhile 4 Armoured Brigade was held back at Gabr Saleh, for one of the anomalies in Cunningham's plan was

---

* *Three against Rommel*, p. 127.

his surrender to the insistence* of the infantry generals in 13 Corps that this brigade should be held available to protect their southern flank.

At Bir el Gubi on the 19th the Italians fought a successful defensive action against an enemy as innocent as themselves. 22 Armoured Brigade, new to the desert and short of training, ignored the advice of those veterans, 11 Hussars, and moved in on the fixed positions of *Ariete* without artillery preparation or infantry support. Italians surrendered readily but, when they saw that there was no one on foot to take them over, returned to manning their guns. Twenty-five of the new Crusaders were lost – for nothing, since the 34 Italian tanks destroyed made no difference to the true balance of power, and *Ariete* remained in control at Bir el Gubi. Here is a reminder that, for all the contempt justifiably felt by both German and British, some Italian units on some occasions could acquit themselves well. During the battle *Ariete* was not always where it was wanted – perhaps because Gambara wanted it not to be there – but in general it proved a valuable ally for the Afrika Korps, as did the Italian infantry, intermittently, when close-quarter fighting developed around the Tobruk perimeter.

The gallant but fruitless charge by the 22 Armoured Brigade against *Ariete*'s defences illustrates to perfection how for many months the Afrika Korps was able, in one respect, to retain a qualitative superiority. This brigade, which had only disembarked in October, consisted of three Yeomanry regiments, 2 Royal Gloucestershire Hussars and 3 and 4 County of London. Since the British, unlike the Germans, had failed to evolve an up-to-date and firmly imposed doctrine for armoured warfare, volunteer cavalry regiments like these were denied the thorough technical training which might have purged them of the ethos of peacetime, the hunting-shooting-fishing mentality of the rural middle and upper classes. So terms and attitudes of the horsed cavalry still lingered long after mechanisation, and the subtle techniques of manoeuvre already practised and perfected by DAK were outside the mental limits of 'yeoboys' whose ideas about tactics had not advanced beyond Balaclava. They had but a small conception – for they had not been taught it – of co-operation between all arms. The infantry was a lower order. Since gunners – particularly the RHA – had some identification with horses they were more acceptable. Given time and training, there was actually nothing to prevent an effective conversion, for the basic qualities of both men and officers were admirable, and units like 11 Hussars or 12 Lancers, who had been mechanised in the '30s and applied themselves professionally to their new trade, were outstanding. Nevertheless, broadly speaking, these ex-cavalry regiments (both regular and

---

* This almost hysterical insistence is a striking instance of the psychological dominance already achieved by the panzers of the Afrika Korps.

territorial) – of whom a good many would reinforce 8th Army – displayed all the characteristics of the social segment they represented: they were brave but anti-intellectual, slow to learn and conscious cultivators of their own *apartheid*.

The poet Keith Douglas, who served in just such a regiment from Alamein onwards (and whose *From Alamein to Zem Zem* is one of the desert classics), noted these characteristics with affectionate objectivity in his poem 'Aristocrats'.

> *The noble horse with courage in his eye*
> *clean in the bone, looks up at a shellburst:*
> *away fly the images of the shires*
> *but he puts the pipe back in his mouth . . .*
>
> *How can I live among this gentle*
> *obsolescent breed of heroes, and not weep?*
> *Unicorns, almost,*
> *for they are falling into two legends*
> *in which their stupidity and chivalry*
> *are celebrated. Each, fool and hero, will be*
>
> *an immortal . . .*
> *It is not gunfire I hear but a hunting horn.* *

The point is that such a poem, with all that is implicit in it, would be inconceivable in relation to the Afrika Korps. Closely knit together by the effects of German military training and discipline, and suffused with the class-less spirit of National Socialism, it contained neither units nor sub-units which held themselves apart because of their peacetime background or a divisive sense of class superiority. In DAK the aristocrats were in fact also the efficient men – von Wechmar, for example, or von Ravenstein. For the Afrika Korps homogeneity was an immense benefit in comparison with the fissiparous tendencies of 8th Army, which suffered not only from differences of class attitudes within its British formations but also from the varying and sometimes abrasive characteristics of the Commonwealth troops, Australian, South African, Indian, New Zealand. In the *Panzergruppe* the real split was racial, not social: between German and Italian, rather than between German and German.

7 Armoured Brigade was more fortunate than 22.† As it pressed on to Sidi Rezegh it was unimpeded except by the sodden ground. Reconnaissance Unit

---

* From *Collected Poems*, by Keith Douglas, Faber, 1966.

† Though not in the experience of its commander, Brigadier Davy, who only took over the brigade in October, a Hussar who had previously neither commanded nor even served in an armoured unit!

33 fell back, conforming to its advance and facing similar problems, since South African armoured cars working with the brigade 'came on a number of bogged and abandoned enemy vehicles – (20 lorries, 1 ambulance, 4 staff cars and 1 four-wheeled armoured car)'. During the late afternoon the South Africans and 6 Royal Tank Regiment (so soon to be decimated) had an exhilarating time dashing about the airfield and accounting for 19 aircraft.

This little tableland, about three miles wide and rising gently eastwards, was the heart of the main killing-ground in CRUSADER. Its southern edge was formed by what the Afrika Korps called the *third* escarpment, on which the trigonometric Point 178 was a salient feature. Along its northern rim the ground falls away down a *second* escarpment, marked at its eastern end by the trig. Point 175 and to the west by the distinctive white tomb of the prophet, Sidi Rezegh. Along the flats north of this rocky ridge the Trigh Capuzzo passes, flanked by a further escarpment, the *first*, which, following the line Zaafran–Belhamed–El Duda, was the last of these features before the defended areas encircling the harbour of Tobruk.

The unexpected appearance of 7 Armoured Brigade caused great alarm among the Axis troops on Tobruk's perimeter. The *Afrika* Division and *Pavia* were particularly affected: their dispositions, of course, were all north-ward-facing, and now a tornado had struck their rear. In fact they were safe enough, since no infantry accompanied the British armour. Nevertheless, at Point 175 two battalions of Regiment 361 had to hold off a tank attack with a single infantry gun, and the second escarpment looked wide open. Here was an early example of the Afrika Korps's good fortune, for this easy initial success of 7 Armoured Brigade suggests that if Norrie had possessed enough authority to persuade Cunningham to send the whole of 7 Armoured Division *ventre à terre* up to Sidi Rezegh, 8th Army might have achieved a commanding position within 48 hours – a position Rommel would have been compelled to assault on Cunningham's terms.

Instead, back at Gabr Saleh 4 Armoured Brigade now remained in isolation. During the morning its armoured cars and 3 RTR scurried off to the NE in a pointless chase of the hovering Reconnaissance Unit 3, which got stuck in a salt marsh and had a battering from the nimble Stuarts. However, it dis-entangled and escaped northwards over the Trigh Capuzzo, while the Stuarts, after their long run, were almost out of fuel. And now, about 1400 hours, the call came for a return to the Trigh el Abd, where their fellows of 4 Armoured Brigade 'were being attacked by enemy tanks east of Gabr Saleh'.

The reason was von Ravenstein. During the morning he and Crüwell appreciated the significance of what was happening around Gabr Saleh and along the Trigh el Abd. By mid-day Crüwell extracted from a reluctant Rommel permission for von Ravenstein to take action, as he desired. A battle group from 21 Panzer was to tackle the armour harrying Reconnaissance Unit 3. At the same time, 1145 hours, warning orders were sent to 15 Panzer to link up with 21 Panzer, SW of Gambut, by 1800 hours. But Rommel was still not bending his mind to the realities, for six o'clock in the desert evening was after sundown, so that although the principle of concentrating Afrika Korps was correct, in practice these orders meant that it would be unable to operate in unison until next morning.

Many valuable comments on CRUSADER from the German viewpoint are to be found in the first volume of *Feldzug in Nordafrika*, a record of the campaign prepared for the US Army by captive German officers after the war. The CRUSADER volume was the work of Colonel Rainer Kriebel, operations staff officer (German *1a*, British *G1*) of 15 Panzer.* On these mid-day orders issued to DAK Kriebel comments:

> To have the armoured group of 21 Panzer operating towards Gabr Saleh during the afternoon of 19 November, with orders to perform certain tasks, was a dangerous gamble. The battle group had no means of protecting its flank and rear. It would have been better to use the whole division for the operation. It was a lucky coincidence that the British had also split up their forces. . . .

It was also a lost opportunity. The consequences might have been enormous if DAK had moved as a whole, since here was a supreme moment to begin the destruction of 8th Army's armour in detail which Cunningham's dispositions had made possible. In the event the battle group, though powerful, was not quite strong enough to obliterate the isolated 4 Armoured Brigade. Colonel Stephan (an able officer, later killed) had in his group the whole of his 5 Panzer Regiment, the armoured core of 21 Panzer, comprising 85 Mks. III and IV and 35 light Mk. II, and he was strengthened by a regiment of twelve 105 mm gun-howitzers and four 88s. To meet him, when the clash came during the afternoon, 4 Armoured Brigade had available just one regiment, 8 Hussars, for 3 RTR could not return in time from their dash to the north and 5 RTR only joined in after the fight had started. Thus Cunningham's notion of destroying the enemy on ground of his own choosing was now reduced, at the point of his own selection, Gabr Saleh, to an unequal struggle by one dis-organised brigade. And the paradox is that if Cunningham had stuck to his plan, and kept 7 Armoured Division together until Rommel reacted, it would have been 8th Army to whom the chance would now have been given of

---

* Many telling translations from Kriebel's narrative are to be found in Agar-Hamilton and Turner, *op. cit.*

beginning a piecemeal destruction of DAK.

Both sides, in fact, had missed a trick, and the result of the engagement seemed inconclusive. As darkness fell 4 Armoured had lost 23 tanks – of which a dozen were repaired and in action within 48 hours. Stephan suffered a total loss of two Mk. IIIs and one Mk. II. But apart from the tactical disorder of the British, there were several features which boded well for DAK. The Germans remained on the battlefield while 4 Armoured withdrew into night leaguer – that conventional and pernicious practice of the British which, while it enabled them to replenish and reorganise in peace, allowed their opponents to recover the damaged tanks of both sides, or alternatively to blow up British armour before its owners could recover and repair. And too often this comfortable British habit left the Afrika Korps in a position of tactical advantage when the next dawn renewed the battle. It was noticed, moreover, that during the engagement the DAK's drill for recovering tank casualties in mid-battle – an important development in which the Germans consistently outshone their opponents – was working smoothly. Above all, Stephan's use of his mobile 105s and 88s to protect his flanks was an effective answer to the dashing Stuarts. In retrospect it is evident that DAK had won the first mobile action in CRUSADER.

The good luck of 4 Armoured Brigade continued throughout the 20th, for though Crüwell now had the whole of DAK in hand he wasted time and fuel in a futile attempt to destroy the 'force' which had chased Reconnaissance Unit 3 on the previous day. After much beating of empty ground 21 Panzer ran out of fuel. 'Frantic appeals', as von Mellenthin puts it, for petrol to be flown forward could not be answered, and half DAK's armour was thus immobilised until after dark. So Crüwell only had 15 Panzer in action when, towards the end of the afternoon, 4 Armoured Brigade was encountered in a good defensive position with the sun behind it. (22 Armoured Brigade, summoned up from Bir el Gubi, where the South Africans now kept an eye on *Ariete*, arrived too late to make any difference.) The previous day's pattern was repeated, for another 26 Stuarts were destroyed. Though Brigadier Gatehouse of 4 Armoured claimed 30 panzers, there is in fact no record of a single German loss. Such exaggerated claims, beginning to build up at Cunningham's HQ, were an important factor in sustaining far too long an unjustified optimism. Von Mellenthin, nevertheless, was dissatisfied:

There is no doubt that we missed a great opportunity on 20 November. Cunningham had been obliging enough to scatter 7 Armoured Division all over the desert, and we had failed to exploit his generosity. If Afrika Korps had concentrated at Gabr Saleh on the morning of the 20th, it could have wiped out 4 Armoured Brigade; on the other hand, if it had moved towards

Sidi Rezegh, it could have inflicted a crushing defeat on the British forces there.*

During the next two days the little strip of land beneath the tomb of Sidi Rezegh powerfully asserted its magnetic force. In Cunningham's case this was because misleading figures of German losses, compounded by RAF reports that the enemy was 'streaming westwards' from the frontier, led him on the evening of the 20th to have the long-awaited code-word signalled to General Scobie in Tobruk, ordering him to begin the break-out the following morning. Simultaneously the Support Group of 7 Armoured Division, under Brigadier Campbell, was to force its way over the second escarpment to within a few miles of el Duda, a potential point of linkage with Scobie's thrust. Skirmishing and re-adjustment of positions had gone on all through the 20th in the airfield area and along the second and third escarpments, but by evening the situation was still in balance, with the infantry of the *Afrika* Division gradually extending its control over the escarpments while the British occupied the ground between – exposed, among other discomforts, to the heavy shells of Böttcher's artillery group at Belhamed. Still, Cunningham was confident. Put simply, therefore, on the 21st the British had to strike north beyond the second escarpment, get on to the Trigh Capuzzo and make contact with Tobruk's garrison before the panzers of the DAK could attack them in the rear.†

But Rommel had come to life. During the evening of the 20th he endorsed Crüwell's proposal to break away from the British armour around Gabr Saleh and direct both panzer divisions to Sidi Rezegh. Realisation had dawned that the 8th Army's operations were a genuine attempt to relieve Tobruk – an insight almost certainly sharpened by the BBC's 9 p.m. news on the evening of the 20th:

> 8th Army, with about 75,000 men excellently armed and equipped, have started a general offensive in the Western Desert, with the aim of destroying the German–Italian forces in Africa.

'This particular release,' the South African history observes, '*may* have been intended to alarm and dishearten the Axis forces, but it gave Rommel the vital information for which he was waiting.' Some of his colleagues, and other critics, have felt that he might well have interpreted the battle picture much sooner. However, the driver was now in his seat, and it is fascinating to ob-

---

* *Op. cit.*, p. 63.
† To assist this process a South African infantry brigade was supposed to move north from Bir el Gubi, pass through the airfield and join in the attack on the second escarpment. It never arrived.

serve the difference a committed Rommel could make. So far, through no fault of its regimental soldiers, the part played by DAK in CRUSADER had been aimless, inconclusive. Overnight it acquired a decisive assurance. Rommel's orders to Crüwell reveal his mood:

> The situation in this whole theatre is very critical. In addition to the strong enemy force south-east of Tobruk, 500 or 600 enemy vehicles are moving through the desert towards Benghazi from the south-east.* On 21 November Afrika Korps must begin moving in good time and follow the enemy tanks which have advanced towards Tobruk. Objective the airfield at Sidi Rezegh.

Whenever it received orders that it must 'begin moving in good time', the Afrika Korps knew that Rommel had taken personal charge of the battle.

A cumulative sequence followed. On the morning of the 21st the two British brigades at Gabr Saleh failed to prevent DAK from breaking contact and rolling westward behind its usual rearguard of anti-tank guns†, so that even before an attack could be launched northwards from Sidi Rezegh to link up with Tobruk's garrison word came in from the watching armoured cars that a strong force of tanks was approaching from the south-east. The *Panzergruppe*'s situation was suddenly enviable, for though, about 8.30 a.m., Brigadier Campbell thrust the infantry of his Support Group successfully northwards and seized a two-mile stretch of the second escarpment between Point 175 and the prophet's tomb, when 6 Royal Tanks of 7 Armoured Brigade tried to exploit further the battalion was decimated. Böttcher's artillery group at Belhamed, assembled for the assault on Tobruk, now switched to the south and took a heavy toll. Rommel, typically, was on the spot and to check the breakthrough sent in 3 Reconnaissance Unit with four 88 mms. (Unlike the British reconnaissance regiments, Units 3 and 33 each contained a special anti-tank company of five 50 or 37 mm guns.)

Thus while his 6 Royal Tanks were being eliminated Brigadier Davy simultaneously learned of the approach of the Afrika Korps and was faced with a hard decision. He tried to deploy his two remaining units, 7 Hussars and 2 Royal Tanks, to hold off the enemy, but while 15 Panzer contained the tank battalion with its anti-tank screen the armour of the whole DAK con-

---

* This was *Oasis Force* – 29 Indian Brigade with South African armoured cars – which, with a stock of dummy tanks, was intended to create the appearance of a major outflanking move via the southern oases. In spite of Rommel's signal, it had no appreciable effect on CRUSADER.

† Optimism about German losses the previous day led to the belief that this quick westward move was a retreat, and partially accounts for the success of DAK in disengaging. The short-range Stuarts also ran out of fuel.

centrated on 7 Hussars. Very swiftly the colonel was killed and all but 12 tanks put out of action: these too, Davy painfully recalled, were in a sorry state. Through being allowed to deal with 'penny packets' the Afrika Korps had once again achieved a critical success.

For now it could give almost unimpeded attention to the support company and headquarters of 2 Rifle Brigade, positioned at the eastern end of the third escarpment and backed by a battery of 60 Field Regiment and the anti-tank guns of 3 RHA. 21 Panzer handled the matter surgically, picking off the guns one by one and then sweeping the infantry posts with fire. Ward Gunn's posthumous VC was the typical 8th Army award for unquenchable courage in the face of unnecessarily hopeless odds. The battle had, indeed, been a test so far not simply of courage, or even equipment, but primarily of tactics and technique. Rommel's decision to rush DAK to Sidi Rezegh had achieved superiority at the key points, while his opponents' strength had been dissipated. The well-tried drill of the Korps had proved consistently effective – both in holding off British armour and in attack. 'The enemy tanks were accompanied and in some cases preceded', Brigadier Davy noted, 'by anti-tank guns which were not at first recognised as they were mingled with British tanks and lorries. Some of the guns were very boldly handled and scored hits before their presence had been noticed among the other vehicles.' Such subtlety was beyond their opponents' grasp. Yet when, after the morning's actions, DAK pulled out to re-supply, and a South African armoured car troop enticed two dozen panzers towards a squadron of 2 Royal Tanks lying hull-down, the result was the destruction of five and damage to six more, without loss to the British. 'It was an object lesson,' comments the South African history, 'in what could happen if the British tanks caught their opponents without their regular anti-tank screen.' An object lesson also, it might be said, in what happened when 8th Army fought with DAK's professionalism.

As the day ran on further, confused fighting, mainly around the third escarpment, eroded the British strength still further. 'Apart from the 7th Hussars (nine tanks) now on the opposite side of the enemy,' Davy observed, 'the only "runners" in the 7th Armoured Brigade were one of the 7th Hussars, six of the 2nd Royal Tanks, one of the 6th Royal Tanks and three of Brigade Headquarters, and most of these had been hit more than once.' Yet as evening fell neither Rommel nor Crüwell felt comfortable. Events in the north had thrown a threatening shadow. And this in spite of the fact that, as the severe but perceptive South African history points out, 'the tactics which the Germans had painfully acquired and rehearsed during the summer's lull, with their emphasis on artillery and the use of 88s in particular, had been abundantly justified'.

Rommel's mind was clouded by personal experience. For him the critical events of the day had not been the activity of his armour, but the attempt at a break-out by the garrison of Tobruk. Matching the costly northward thrust by Campbell and 6 RTR, infantry and tanks fought fiercely through the morning and early afternoon of the 21st to clear a path amid the minefields and defended posts with which the *Panzergruppe* had encircled the perimeter. An advance of 4,000 yards was purchased with heavy casualties in men and armour: the impetus then died, as a link-up with 7 Armoured Division was not yet feasible. But over 1,000 prisoners were taken – half of them German – and Rommel had been thrown off balance for a second time that day. Kriebel recorded how his commander

> scraped together all the reserves of the Division 2bV *Afrika*, Army Artillery, anti-aircraft artillery, and all the signals personnel he could lay hands on and ordered Reconnaissance Unit 3 to move up by forced marches. At the head of these troops he halted the enemy by midday. . . .

Crüwell, for his part, was less impressed by his victories than by the position of his troops, which he saw as being a layer in a complicated sandwich. From north to south ran, first, the aggressive Tobruk garrison; then the Germans and Italians on the perimeter; next, between the tomb and Point 175, a strip divided between Germans and British: then the area dominated by DAK: and finally, around Crüwell's flanks and rear, the menace of 4 and 22 Armoured Brigades as well as the still uncommitted South Africans. Far from feeling expansive, Crüwell was afraid of a squeeze.

And so, while the multi-decker-sandwich effect of the troops' dispositions looked like a Staff College nightmare, the reactions of the different commanders that evening were equally remarkable. Here is an interesting case-study in the psychology of war, for there was only one battle, yet the orders of three of the principals during the evening of the 21st show that each had made an interpretation incompatible with that of the others. But each was wearing different spectacles. At 8th Army HQ, 80 miles from Sidi Rezegh at Maddalena, Cunningham's optimism was enlarged by false reports that his armour had surrounded DAK, south-east of the airfield plateau which was still in Campbell's hands. His orders were aggressive: push on out of Tobruk, start attacks by 30 Corps on Rommel's frontier outposts, set the New Zealand Division moving westwards. Crüwell's pessimism produced the instinctive response of a prudent armoured commander: he wanted room to reorganise, replenish and think again. The DAK War Diary records that his plan was to regain 'freedom of manoeuvre', and to that end the whole of Afrika Korps was instructed to move during the night to the old base area of Gambut.

Rommel's concern, however, took a more active form. At 2240 Crüwell received his master's orders – he appears not to have repeated his own to *Panzergruppe*. 'On 22 November DAK in conjunction with *Pavia* Division will hold the area reached today as well as Belhamed. The Korps will prevent enemy tank forces on its front from pushing through to Tobruk. . . .' In effect this meant establishing a secure hold on the whole debated area round Sidi Rezegh while keeping the two panzer divisions available as a mobile striking force. Crüwell, however, nullified this proposition by still sending 15 Panzer to Gambut and only obeying Rommel by switching 21 Panzer to Belhamed. He had lifted his head out of the noose, but implicit in his splitting up of DAK was the offer of the airfield plateau to the 8th Army.

Nevertheless, at 1545 on the 22nd the Diary of the Afrika Korps noted: 'Panzer Regiment 5 reported having taken Sidi Rezegh airfield.' As the last light died Gott met his three brigadiers, Campbell of the Support Group, Gatehouse of 4 Armoured and Scott-Cockburn of 22 Armoured, and 'decided to withdraw from the Sidi Rezegh position, which was half captured and no longer tenable'. In a battle of many surprises this was a notable *bouleversement*. How had it occurred?

The seeping rain of a cold winter's night had turned the surface of the desert to 'the consistency of cold cream'.* By midday on the 22nd, however, 15 Panzer had withdrawn to the east, retiring behind the usual gun-screen which fended off 4 Armoured Brigade. At Belhamed 21 Panzer began to improve the defences against a sortie from Tobruk. In the airfield area, now left for the taking, 7 Armoured Division was at last beginning to concentrate its battered units. The South Africans had been ordered to move north on to the plateau, and from the east 6 New Zealand Brigade was pressing forward from 30 Corps along the Trigh Capuzzo. It looked as though Cunningham's hope, expressed to Norrie that morning, might be implemented: 'He told me that, as the operations were developing, it appeared to him that it would become more and more an infantry battle. . . .'

This tranquil scene in which, as von Mellenthin observed, 'the British position was very favourable', was suddenly and brutally transformed by an event which illustrates to perfection the way that Rommel's dynamic leadership from the front, and eye for the tactical advantage, made the Afrika Korps at its best so beautiful a military machine. There was an air of relaxation. That was no good for Rommel. About mid-day he visited von Ravenstein at Belhamed and ordered him to mount an attack southward over the second escarpment, with his infantry supported by his own and Böttcher's artillery, while the tanks of 21 Panzer made a detour to the north of Belhamed, then turned south-west down the Axis by-pass to El Duda, worked further south,

---

* Alexander Clifford, *op. cit.*

1   Rommel and the road to Cairo

2   A world of sand

3   The mobile 88 mm: tractor-towed and in action

4 Behind the lines

5　Anti-tank guns: the towed German model contrasts significantly with the captured British 2-pounder *portée*

6　Observation post. The clarity and magnification of German equipment far surpassed the British

7　Command from the front. Rommel issues orders with his *Storch* standing by

8a   Hours of ease

8b   Hours of ease

9 The battle's toll. A British gunner has fought to the last: his opponents lie in their graves

10 Artillery-men

11 Road-making: possibly the Tobruk by-pass. Compressor-driven drills were essential for digging positions in the rocky ground which was so large a part of the battle-area

12   A typical infantry position

13 Heavy gun in action

14   Rommel and Kesselring

15 The panzers. The price of victory was vigilance

16 Rommel's character, strong and direct, is admirably reflected in this memorial erected to their leader by the veterans of the Afrika Korps

and finally drove eastwards for the airfield. This challenging new initiative, and Rommel's presence, inspired von Ravenstein's weary men.

During the early afternoon the panzers struck with a shock effect, taking the British off guard and fighting with great *élan*. The remains of 7 Armoured Brigade, and then 22 Brigade, were sucked into a conflict which raged over the plateau in blinding clouds of dust. The British field artillerymen served their guns to the last, and it was now that Brigadier Campbell earned his VC, scurrying about the airfield in an open car to rally his troops. When 4 Armoured Brigade arrived on the battlefield about 1530, confused by what an officer of 11 Hussars called 'a vast synthetic sandstorm', Campbell was to be seen banging on the sides of their tanks to attract attention and leading them against the enemy, still in his vulnerable car, and waving a red flag. To no avail. By early evening 21 Panzer was running short of ammunition and just beginning, as its War Diary reveals, to think that it had had enough when Gott's conference decided the issue. The British fell back on the line of the third escarpment.

Towards dusk the last remaining guns of a troop of 60th Field Regiment and a troop of 3rd RHA seemed doomed. The advancing German infantry were almost on them. Firing at point-black range, with apparently no hope of survival, these indomitable men still fought their guns. Suddenly a troop of light British tanks roared out of the gathering bloom, charged straight into the German infantry and, firing with every weapon they had, halted the enemy attack long enough for the gunners to hook in and pull out.

The final scene was awe-inspiring enough. In the light of burning vehicles and dumps our guns slipped out of action, leaving the field to a relentlessly advancing enemy, who loomed in large, fantastic shapes out of the shadows into the glare of bursting shells. *

Many first-hand descriptions exist of this epic afternoon: but the salient point is that out of the apocalyptic struggle between gun and tank, amid the wreathing smoke, the scream of solid shot and the crump of shells from Böttcher's heavy artillery, it was the indomitable men of the Afrika Korps who emerged as victors. This can be illustrated statistically. DAK's qualitative superiority in armour had now become quantitative, for at the end of this bitter day the two panzer divisions reported a joint strength of 173 operational tanks as opposed to the 144 still remaining in 7 Armoured Division.

There was a final turn of the screw. During the afternoon Crüwell had set a replenished 15 Panzer in motion again, and by early evening it was seeking to take in the flank the British withdrawing from the plateau. About four miles

---

* Brigadier Hely, *The Royal Artillery Commemoration Book*, p. 189.

to the south-east of the airfield it suddenly encountered a large group of
vehicles – around 1700 hours according to the Division's War Diary, which
describes what followed:

> The battalion commander recognised the vehicles as English tanks at ten
> yards. He burst through the enemy leaguer in his command vehicle and
> ordered No. 1 Company to go round to the left and No. 2 Company round
> the right to surround the enemy. The tanks put on their headlights and the
> commanders jumped out with their machine-pistols. Thus far there had
> been no firing. A few tanks tried to get away, but were at once set on fire by
> our tanks, and lit up the battlefield as bright as day. While the prisoners were
> being rounded up an English officer succeeded in setting fire to a tank.

For three-quarters of an hour there was a wild scramble with hand-gun and
grenade, but into the bag went the headquarters of 4 Armoured Brigade and
a substantial portion of 8 Hussars – 35 tanks (by 15 Panzer's reckoning), an
ACV, 17 officers and 150 other ranks. The second-in-command, a full Colonel
with red-banded hat, was assumed to be the Brigadier, but Gatehouse was on
his way back from Gott's conference and avoided capture. This brief episode
was nevertheless critical, for during the action next day there was a paralysis
of communication to, from and within 4 Armoured Brigade, while Gatehouse
was reduced to establishing his headquarters in a chair strapped to the top of
his tank.

But the desert, always unpredictable, had in reserve an even greater shock
for the Afrika Korps itself. During the night 6 New Zealand Brigade was
advancing by forced march to the aid of 7 Armoured Division, under orders
from Freyberg which told it to get to Sidi Rezegh. 'You will receive no further
orders but you will start fighting. . . .' About dawn on the 23rd the brigade
halted for breakfast and discovered it was in a hornet's nest, the headquarters
of DAK, at Bir el Chleta just south-west of Gambut. 200 prisoners, vehicles,
and other equipment were captured, but the main haul was virtually the complete cypher staff and wireless trucks of the Afrika Korps. 'General Crüwell
and I,' Bayerlein recalled, 'escaped this fate by a hairsbreadth.' But a severe
communications problem remained, particularly as Rommel, now weaned
from his obsession with Tobruk, had decided to eliminate the 8th Army's
Schwerpunkt once and for all.

Morning mists on the 23rd heralded a day of clouded skies and chilling
winds – the day which, in Kriebel's words, 'was to see the fiercest battle of the
entire campaign and which will remain unforgettably in the memory of all
Afrika Korps warriors as the "Bloody Sunday of the Dead"'. This Sunday
before Advent imprinted itself because its name in the Lutheran calendar,

Totensonntag, seemed in German minds to match by its overtones the gruesome quality of what was to follow.

Already, at 2230 the previous night, Rommel had issued detailed orders to confirm an intention he had expressed during the afternoon. They began, 'On 23 November *Panzergruppe* will force a decision in the area south-east of Tobruk, by means of a concentric attack by DAK and parts of Corps Gambara'. The object was to squeeze the remains of 7 Armoured Division between DAK descending from the north and *Ariete* advancing from Bir el Gubi in the south. However, transmission and de-coding delays meant that Crüwell did not receive the full text until 0430 the following morning, by which time he had issued his own instructions to DAK, based, it must be assumed, on his general impression of what Rommel had in mind.

Crüwell's plan was clinical and supremely confident. DAK now held all three escarpments. During the night 21 Panzer was in leaguer on the airfield and 15 Panzer just south of Point 175. Here Crüwell set up his HQ, and at 0645 issued his executive orders. Leaving its infantry, along with *Afrika* Division, to keep a firm hold on the escarpments, 15 Panzer, joined by Panzer Regiment 5 from 21 Panzer, was to strike south and east of the enemy's rear. Having cut the communications of 30 Corps and linked up with *Ariete*, the massed panzers were then to turn through 90 degrees to the north and simply roll over the opposition.

This was but weakly knit together. On the open ground south of the third escarpment lay 5 South African Brigade, with the rump of 22 Armoured Brigade (some 30 tanks) guarding its western flank. The last of 7 Armoured Brigade and the Support Group covered the east. 4 Armoured Brigade, disorganised by the previous day's fighting and the loss of its headquarters, was incapable of making a significant contribution. And immediately south of these positions, as if no attack were anticipated, hundreds upon hundreds of supply and administrative vehicles, the 'soft' transport, were scattered over a wide area. Beyond them, uncertain and uneasy, lay 1 South African Brigade.

By 0800 hours 15 Panzer, with Crüwell and Bayerlein to the fore, had struck this amorphous mass like a thunderbolt. The German reports refer constantly to 'vast supply columns' scattering in wild confusion as shell and bullet set vehicles on fire. 'Complete chaos and disaster were very close at hand,' says the history of 11 Hussars, 'when Jock Campbell for the second time in the battle performed one of his prodigious feats.' Seated on top of his ACV (with 23 men inside it!) he rushed about waving red and blue flags for Stop and Go, scraping together whatever units he could muster for a counter-attack and issuing at one moment his imperishable instructions to a troop of guns: 'Expect no orders. Stick to me. I shall advance soon!' The speed of the British armour was now invaluable, and it was used with a self-sacrificial ferocity. As the morning ran on, therefore, Crüwell decided that it would be better to await *Ariete*'s arrival before risking further losses. Great damage had been done to the British in this savage, tempestuous action, but the immediate psychological advantage was theirs. DAK therefore disengaged.

By 1235, however, contact had been made with the main body of *Ariete*. Crüwell was not a cavalier spirit like Rommel. One has the impression of a personality at once severe, ruthless and unbending. And now, having started the day with a Rommel-like sweep, he proceeded to launch an attack which is, perhaps, unique in the Afrika Korp's history.* It was as if he had grimly determined to get it all over. Facing his whole force to the north, he set in the front line *Ariete* on the left, Panzer Regiment 8 (with 120 tanks) in the centre and Panzer Regiment 5 (with 40 tanks) on the right. Behind them the infantry of Rifle Regiment 115 were to ride in their trucks, the orders being that 'the tanks were to act as a support force and enable the infantry to break into the enemy positions'. Unorthodoxy was justified by the need for speed. 'The infantry brigade,' its commander stated, 'will remain in transport as long as possible and will not debus until it comes under heavy infantry fire.' This great body was now drawn up and aligned almost as if it were on a Prussian parade-ground. Then – *Ran an den Feind, voll einsetzen!*

Crüwell completed his prinking by mid-afternoon. At about 1500 hours the whole phalanx rolled forward at speed, assisted by its own artillery and the guns in the north. Both sides were aware that it was a matter of all-or-nothing. British, South African and German records, both unit and personal, emphasise the volume of fire with which DAK's Juggernaut was received. In the German records one detects, too, an immense pride in the devotion of the troops – particularly the infantry in their vulnerable lorries – as they drove steadily forward to a highly predictable death. Colonel Cramer, commanding Panzer Regiment 8, 'personally led the regiment forward, and at every sign of faltering spurred it on by brief exhortations over the air'. Colonel Zintel, of Rifle Regiment 115, stood upright in his vehicle at his regiment's head until he died from the machine-gun fire in front of his objective. That sense of fatalistic gallantry which inspired men of both the Afrika Korps and the 8th Army in desperate situations seems to have driven this extraordinary charge onward. Heinz Werner Schmidt, now commanding a heavy company in Regiment 115, photographed the scene in his memoirs:

We headed straight for the enemy tanks. I glanced back. Behind me was a fan of vehicles – a curious assortment of all types – spread out as far as the eye could see. There were armoured troop-carriers, cars of various kinds,

---

* Von Mellenthin noted that 'an attack of this sort was an innovation in German tactics'.

caterpillars hauling mobile guns, heavy trucks with infantry, motorised anti-aircraft units. Thus we roared onward to the enemy 'barricade'.

I stared to the front fascinated. Right ahead was the erect figure of the colonel commanding the regiment. On the left close by and slightly in rear of him was the major's car. Tank shells were whizzing through the air. The defenders were firing from every muzzle of their 25-pounders and their little 2-pounder anti-tank guns. We raced on at a suicidal pace.

The battalion commander's car lurched on and stopped suddenly – a direct hit. I had just time to notice the colonel steadying himself. He turned sideways and dropped from the car like a felled tree. Then I had flashed past him. The major was still ahead.

As the bedlam died away the battlefield had a special atmosphere of desolation which few who were present readily forgot. But for DAK the result seemed favourable. 5 South African Brigade was virtually destroyed and its sister brigade hard hit. As night fell German armour penetrated to the escarpment area and linked up, as planned, with the infantry of 21 Panzer. The day's work, in which Bayerlein had participated, seemed to justify his summary:*

Twilight came, but the battle was still not over. Hundreds of burning vehicles, tanks and guns lit up the field of *Totensonntag*. It was long after midnight before we could get any sort of picture of the day's events, organise our force, count our losses and gains and form an appreciation of the general situation upon which the next day's operations would depend. The most important results of this battle were the elimination of the direct threat to the Tobruk front, the destruction of a large part of the enemy armour and the damage to enemy morale caused by the complete ruin of his plans.

But Bayerlein's assessment, though understandable, is nevertheless out of true. In fact it does not mention the two most important consequences of *Totensonntag* – still less that each of these carried the seeds of defeat for the Afrika Korps. The most direct effect of the day's fighting was on Cunningham's confidence. Wild reports reached him early in the day that the 8th Army now had only 30 or 40 cruiser tanks left and he began to turn to Auchinleck for advice and reassurance. *Totensonntag* darkened his mood.† We are already moving towards that moment later in CRUSADER when Auchinleck takes over

---

* In *The Rommel Papers*, p. 162.

† All contemporary evidence indicates that during his meeting with Auchinleck at Maddalena on the evening of the 23rd Cunningham, as his Chief of Staff, Brigadier Galloway, recorded, 'thought the battle was lost and laid much emphasis upon the necessity of getting out of the area and back to where it would be possible to save Egypt'.

himself, and at last gives his army the firm direction and impetus it had lacked from the start. In this sense what the Afrika Korps did on 22 and 23 November was to throw up its own antibody.

And the British armour had been less reduced than was at first supposed on both sides. But the loss ratio in DAK was intolerably high: out of the 162 panzers available at dawn, 72 had gone by nightfall. In both panzer and rifle regiments, as might be expected from a direct assault bravely driven home, the casualties were severe – and heaviest among the experienced battalion and company commanders. Afrika Korps could not afford such a butcher's bill. The meagre reinforcements of men and armour trickling over the long supply-line from Italy were wholly inadequate to keep DAK up to strength, whereas its opponents were already feeling the refreshment of *matériel* and replacements flowing forward from the Delta. Crüwell had cut the heart out of the Afrika Korps, and however the graph of success might rise or fall during the continuing battle, by a remorseless process the balance of power must increasingly tilt in Auchinleck's favour. The implications of the parameter of supply were inescapable.

6

Roundabouts and swings

'It was not long before Rommel was hounding DAK on to
further exertions, and it speaks very highly for their efficiency
that they were able to respond so quickly.'
The Mediterranean and The Middle East, Vol. III

Auchinleck's attempt at the Maddalena meeting to stiffen Cunningham's
morale was followed next morning by an uncompromising order: 'Continue
to attack the enemy relentlessly using all resources down to the last tank.'
Specifically, Cunningham was instructed that it was essential that he should
'recapture the Sidi Rezegh–El Duda ridge at the earliest possible moment'.
But even as the British commanders conferred on the evening of the 23rd
Rommel was giving an entirely new focus to the conflict, an act which would
finally demoralise his opponent and eject him from the field.

During *Totensonntag* Rommel had been out of touch – either dealing with
the consequences of the capture of DAK's HQ, or assisting in the heavy
fighting which, during the day, failed to prevent 6 New Zealand Brigade from
reaching and establishing itself on Point 175. Certainly he was ignorant of the
realities of Crüwell's charge. He believed, in fact, that the British had been
beaten in a 'battle of annihilation', and his mood was euphoric. He got back to
Panzergruppe HQ that night in what von Mellenthin called 'a state of excited
exaltation', and his midnight report to Berlin declared two simple intentions:
a.) To complete 7 Armoured Division's destruction. b.) To advance to the
frontier.

The reasons for this dramatic decision have never been fully established.
Unfortunately the part of the Rommel *Papers* filled in by Bayerlein omits the
whole of CRUSADER. Bayerlein himself recalls – and he was, of course, an eye-
witness – that when Crüwell made his own way across the darkened battlefield
and finally contacted Rommel in the early hours of the 24th, his commander
gave as objectives the destruction of the New Zealand and 4 Indian Divisions
in the frontier area, the cutting of the 8th Army's communications and supply

routes, and capitalising on 'the shock effect of the enemy's defeat'. Rommel's failure to strike for the huge British dumps south of Gabr Saleh, 62 and 65 Field Maintenance Centres, is often mentioned, but von Mellenthin and Bayerlein make it clear that their location was known from captured documents and did not enter into Rommel's plan. The basic truth seems to be that a cavalier had seen a chance to draw his sabre, spur on his steed, and charge.

Certainly the spur was applied to the DAK. Both panzer divisions leaguered that night around and above the eastern end of the third escarpment, summoning up ammunition, fuel, water, ambulances and sorting out their disorganised units. At 0845 on the 24th a staff officer brought orders from Korps HQ for them to be ready to move at 1000, straight overland for Gabr Saleh and then eastwards along the Trigh el Abd. Object: to trap the enemy attacking the Sollum front. (Rommel seems not to have appreciated the full significance of the New Zealand movement towards Tobruk.) At 1040 Rommel, losing patience with his weary divisions, set off with his Chief of Staff and the spearhead of 21 Panzer. 'The Commander-in-Chief put himself at the head of the division: speed increasing all the time!'* 15 Panzer made a start by mid-day, and then also moved fast. And so, as General Jackson put it, 'Lieutenant-Colonel Westphal was left in charge of Panzer Group HQ while the three most senior German generals in Africa – Rommel, Gause and Crüwell – went charging off down the British lines of communication to win CRUSADER and possibly start the invasion of Egypt.'† By the end of the afternoon Rommel had reached the frontier wire near Sheferzen, and pushed von Ravenstein onward with a small group in the direction of Halfaya, where the indomitable Major Bach still reigned. The main body of 21 Panzer leaguered for the night a few miles short of the wire at about 1800: 15 Panzer lay up a few miles further west. 21 Panzer was dry of fuel, and in a running engagement with 7 Armoured both divisions had lost tanks en route. Only about 60 in all came in to leaguer.

Yet this manoeuvre, as unexpected by Rommel's army as it was by their opponents, had an extraordinary initial effect. Its centre-line ran roughly down the lines of communication of 30 Corps. In its track was Gott's headquarters, where both Cunningham and Norrie happened to be. Apart from the constant traffic between front and rear, very large numbers of soft vehicles were spread peacefully over the desert without any significant protection – the normal scene, in fact, far behind the front line. But suddenly the Trigh el Abd had itself become the front line, as the panzers raced eastward. Eye-witnesses on both sides, as well as subsequent historians, have competed in describing the

---

* War Diary, Afrika Korps.
† Jackson, *op. cit.*, p. 171.

stampede that followed – the famous 'Matruh Stakes'. 'The moral effect of Rommel's blow was enhanced by the tendency of almost every group to persist in retreating along the exact route which had been chosen by that undeviating personality for his own advance.'*

The most telling damage, however, was done not to Cunningham's army but to his mind. The rearward-racing rabble, so often described, consisted mainly of non-combatant behind-the-lines troops in a panic. The supply columns of the fighting formations on the whole retained or recovered cohesion, and Norrie is on record as stating that 'in spite of these mishaps Q services and supplies functioned smoothly'. DAK itself, and particularly its own supply columns, were also in some disarray after being harried up to and after nightfall by 7 and then 4 Armoured Brigade. And Crüwell, when he at last joined Rommel around 1700, was disturbed to find that his Korps was in bits and pieces between Halfaya and Gabr Saleh.

Still, the psychological shock had been great, and not least for Cunningham. Knowing his pessimistic state of mind, one has only to read the oft-quoted account† by the New Zealander Brigadier Clifton (Chief Engineer 30 Corps) of the Army Commander's escape to gauge its impact. Driven from Gott's threatened HQ across country at high speed, amid shot, shell and bullet, he just reached in time the landing strip where his aircraft's engines were already running. 'Off she bumped, clearing a crossing three-tonner by inches.' As he flew east Cunningham could observe beneath him what must have seemed like the signs of imminent disintegration.

That the 8th Army did not in the end fall apart may be ascribed not so much to the shortcomings of the Afrika Korps as to those of Rommel. It is usually agreed that if his 'dash to the wire' had proved successful it would have won fame as a stroke of military genius. This is unquestionably so: though it left behind as an open question the situation around Tobruk, the profit-and-loss account for the first day's venture by no means ruled out the possibility of a decisive success. But for that the initial thrust of the spear had to be pushed home.

Instead, Rommel lost his grip. This was perhaps symbolised by the melancholy episode during the night of 24/25 November, when his truck broke down on the way to *Panzergruppe* HQ. So Rommel, Crüwell, Gause and Bayerlein waited in the 'Mammoth' until dawn amid the transport of 4 Indian Division – an unpleasant reminder for Crüwell of *Totensonntag*, during which his stationary ACV was apprehended by a British tank, only to be saved by the timely fire of a German gun. And the simple fact is that for the next 48 hours

---

* Agar-Hamilton and Turner, *op. cit.*, p. 291.

† *The Happy Hunted*, p. 131.

Rommel's mind remained adrift.

This was hard on the Afrika Korps, which had responded to Rommel's call with a remarkable resilience. It demanded high and professional qualities to absorb all the punishment inflicted during the airfield battle and *Totensonntag*, and then, with the minimum warning, to move 50 or 60 miles through enemy-occupied territory, constantly harassed by detachments of British armour and artillery – and to end up as a force whose lack of cohesion was largely due to its commander's own orders. Brave and enduring though it was, there is no doubt that on 24 November 7 Armoured Division would have been incapable of making a similar move in such conditions or of arriving at its destination more or less in one piece.

But the panzer General had an obsession. Convinced that the bulk of 13 Corps was still in the frontier area, menacing *Savona* Division and the various German-manned posts, he decided to box it in and destroy it. Without an intelligence staff, he was blind to the fact that bodies of 2 New Zealand Division had already moved or were moving westwards, or that 4 Indian Division was no longer accessible in open country but had already taken over some of the Italian defences. Indeed, the Division had been warned by the events of the 24th and was actively preparing to stand its ground.

The record of the next two days is therefore one of profitless individual engagements on the part of the two panzer divisions in an attempt to make Rommel's chimera a reality. The men were very tired. What had begun as an adventurous gallop seemed aimless. All that remained on the frontier from 2 New Zealand Division was 5 Brigade at Sidi Azeiz and Capuzzo: it and 7 Indian Brigade were hammered but not broken, though at Sidi Azeiz (early on the 27th) 5 Brigade HQ and one New Zealand battalion had to surrender, with 700-odd lost in dead, wounded, and prisoners. The most savage aspect of these two days was the duels to the death between groups of panzers and 25-pounder troops as batteries defended their naked infantry. 1 Field Regiment so protected 7 Indian Brigade at Sidi Omar, and a vivid account of the action is given by its commander, Lieutenant-Colonel Dobree, in that rich source for evidence about the North African campaigns, *The Royal Artillery Commemoration Book*.

Since it was during CRUSADER that the technique of DAK for dealing with the 25-pounder field artillery, its deadliest enemy, reached its full elaboration, a pause for analysis is necessary. At its best the system was something like this. Once a gun position had been identified there would be a preliminary softening-up by HE from the Mk. IVs, and by any accompanying guns or mortars. The panzers would then roll forward in open order and engage. If this first assault failed, the tanks drew off – if possible to a hull-down position – and gave the guns a further treatment. Then they would move in again for the final kill, getting right among the guns and crushing their trails. In the ideal attack the panzer's main body would engage the guns' attention from the front, while other tanks were pushed out on either flank to take the gun position in enfilade and pick off the gun crews with machine-gun fire. It was the technique of the Zulu *impi* – the encircling half-moon.

Since the field artillery was the most efficient element in the 8th Army (during *Totensonntag* even the guns of the South Africans, who were not otherwise notably effective, did great execution), such actions were not always successful or even favourable for DAK. The gunners of the 8th Army evolved their own techniques in reply – holding fire and keeping the disciplined crews prone on the ground until the last nerve-wracking minute. In the clash between Panzer Regiment 5 and 1 Field Regiment on 25 November the British lost 18 killed and 44 wounded during a close-quarter conflict, but though five guns were knocked out they were repaired and in action next day. Panzer Regiment 5 (already down to 25 tanks and having just lost its commander, Colonel Stephan) was reduced by another eight tanks destroyed. Seven more were soon lost at Sidi Omar to the guns of 25 Field Regiment in another direct clash.* And the real target of the panzers, 7 Indian Infantry Brigade, had been preserved.

But it was not always so. Often the pendulum would swing in the panzers' favour, and in any case a deeper truth is to be discerned behind such actions. The armour of the Afrika Korps had achieved such a psychological superiority over the British infantry, at all levels, that the field artillery had to be dissipated for its protection down to troops or batteries. There were not enough 2-pounder anti-tank guns, and those available were distrusted. By the permanent threat it offered to its opponents' infantry DAK thus prevented the British field artillery from being employed in its proper role – for the magnificent 25-pounder was wasted as an anti-tank gun. It was not until the late summer of 1942 that the guns of the British really began to fire *en masse*.

The good fortune of the Afrika Korps in receiving an injection of first-class staff officers when General Gause arrived was now dramatically demonstrated. Colonel Westphal, left by Rommel to hold the fort at *Panzergruppe* HQ, became progressively concerned during the 25th about developments around Tobruk and realised that the 'dash to the wire' was eccentric, in the literal sense. He therefore started to send signal after signal urging the return of DAK to the west. But neither Rommel nor Crüwell could be reached directly by radio, and an aircraft despatched with situation maps for Rommel was shot

---

* This, it should be noted, was an incompetent attack handled by Stephan's replacement, Major Mildebrath. An advance across a minefield against dug-in artillery was not in DAK's best style. The Afrika Korps War Diary says the attack was ordered by Rommel personally: it is characteristic of his thoughtless desperation during this phase.

down. 'Huddled in our greatcoats,' von Mellenthin recalled, 'in the wooden huts which served as our headquarters at El Adem, Westphal and I viewed the situation with increasing anxiety.'

During the 26th, as DAK continued to be committed to piecemeal attacks for no good purpose, Crüwell himself began to urge a return. Gradually, by using 21 Panzer as a link, Westphal began to get his signals through. Indeed, in two short sharp messages about 0600 on the 27th he actually *ordered* DAK to withdraw. Some hours later Rommel, after much myopia, had grasped reality, and the remnants of both panzer divisions, refreshed with captured fuel, were beginning to head westward. DAK owed Westphal a considerable debt.

His initiative rescued them from a situation coldly summarised in the South African history.

> The impression left by the German accounts of 26 November is of tired troops scattered inconsequently in isolated fragments about the frontier area and pre-occupied mainly with getting petrol, water and food – and ensuring their own survival. From time to time Rommel would dash up to one or other of them, cancel the orders they had received from one of his subordinates, and sting them into some sort of offensive action. But as soon as his vehicle had disappeared, the disillusioned troops would revert to the more practical task of finding sustenance for men and tanks.

Kriebel (who was, it will be recalled, the chief staff officer in 15 Panzer), decided that 'Rommel's advance to the Sollum front appears in retrospect as an evil dream'. That it might with luck have proved to be a triumph is another matter: Kriebel was a realist.

Luck had in fact swung the wrong way. Auchinleck remained watchfully at Cunningham's HQ throughout the 24th: by the time he reached Cairo again on the 25th, it was evident that both he and his airmen, Tedder and Coningham, had lost confidence in Cunningham's will for victory. This was no time for a pessimistic commander who had accepted defeat in his mind. On the afternoon of the 26th, therefore, Auchinleck's Chief of Staff, General Ritchie, took over command of the 8th Army. The chips had fallen wrong for Rommel and DAK. During *Totensonntag* and the 'dash for the wire' they had psychologically wounded Cunningham, but the effect was a substitution of Auchinleck's right-hand man, indoctrinated with his thinking and totally committed to his policy of continuing the battle down to the last tank. Ritchie alone was inadequate for high command: but he was an opportune channel for Auchinleck's will.

Apart from this re-invigoration of the 8th Army's command (where, it must be added, all the evidence forcibly indicates that no senior staff officer or the commanders of corps or divisions had weakened in resolution) the battle would now be continued on terms increasingly adverse for the Africa Korps. Westphal's fears were justified, since by dawn on the 27th the two New Zealand brigades, 4 and 6 (whose westward movement perturbed him), had linked up with the Tobruk garrison at El Duda and recaptured both the second escarpment and the airfield area beyond it. Moreover, the 'dash to the wire' had provided the shattered armoured brigades of 30 Corps with a priceless pause for rest, replenishment, re-organisation and the replacement of losses. The New Zealanders had indeed suffered severely in the cruel fighting along the escarpments – where they noted the outstanding bravery of the Bersaglieri – but, broadly speaking, an exhausted and depleted Afrika Korps was about to undertake the second battle of Sidi Rezegh in the face of a refreshed enemy and at a tactical disadvantage.

It was first necessary to reach the new battlefield. About midday on the 27th 15 Panzer's westward march along the Trigh Capuzzo was detected, and Gott ordered 22 Armoured Brigade to head it off while 4 Armoured Brigade attacked its southern flank. The young 22 Brigade, whose skill seemed to grow with experience, organised an ambush which evoked the Germans' admiration, concealing their guns and observation posts along the escarpment and giving the impression, quite false, of a superior strength. 4 Armoured Brigade, after a 20-mile run, entered the fray in late afternoon. The *brio* of the engagement is reflected in the record of Artillery Regiment 33:

> A group of enemy tanks attacked the supply vehicles in the rear of the division. They burst right into the middle of the column and fired shells and machine-gun bullets into the vehicles, which were pushing forward at full speed. *Batterien* 6 and 8 immediately swung their guns round, but the dust was so thick that they could see nothing, until suddenly an enemy tank appeared in a cloud of dust about fifty metres in front of the gun positions of *Batterie* 6. We immediately opened up our open sights. The tank burst into flames. Another tank just behind it was knocked out. In a very short time the *Batterie* destroyed ten more tanks at point-blank range and thus beat off the attack on the division's rear. Just after that two heavy bombing raids took place, causing very heavy casualties in men and equipment.

21 Panzer, which had been moving along the Via Balbia, was unable to grope up the first escarpment in time to assist. By nightfall the situation seemed serious. It was Rommel's 25th wedding anniversary.*

---

* The Rommels were unlucky on these occasions. Lucie's birthday fell on 6 June – and therefore on D-Day, 1944.

But the British now made him an entirely unnecessary present. Slavishly keeping to the drill-book, they fell away to a night leaguer. As Kriebel acidly observed, 'the enemy withdrew to the south in spite of their superior numbers'. Once again a contested field was left to DAK, and the consequence was that 15 Panzer merely pushed on during the darkness. A most promising opportunity to cut off the German armour from its hard-pressed infantry around Tobruk had been thrown away, and as 15 Panzer settled down for the night it was perfectly placed for a link-up next day. Ritchie, calling on his troops to stop the enemy 'escaping westwards', had entirely misread DAK's intention – though his cry makes even less pardonable the generosity of his armoured brigades in leaving the door to the west wide open.

For the anniversary of his wedding night Rommel's circumstances were lacking in amenity. Crüwell and Bayerlein reported to him at his forward HQ near Gambut. A long search in the dark revealed a British lorry. Inside it, Bayerlein recalled,

> were no British troops, but Rommel and his Chief of Staff, both of them unshaven, worn with lack of sleep and caked with dust. In the lorry was a heap of straw as a bed, a can of stale water to drink and a few tins of food. Close by were two wireless trucks and a few dispatch riders. Rommel now gave his instructions for the next day's operations.

Here is a perfect vignette of the 'Feldherr of the front line'. And his orders, contrary to Ritchie's assumptions, were wholly aggressive.

Rommel had recovered his mental poise – he was even to admit that Westphal's recall of DAK was justified – and he now grasped the essential point. The two New Zealand brigades, 4 and 6, which straddled the airfield plateau and its escarpments, must be cut off from the salient created by the Tobruk garrison, surrounded and eliminated. Operations during the next few days revealed that his diagnosis may have been right but his weapon was too frail, for the Afrika Korps, having already caused the retirement of a British Army Commander and 7 Armoured Brigade, so damaged the New Zealanders that Freyberg later insisted on removing the remnants right out of the battle. * But DAK exhausted itself in the process.

'The Cauldron' is immortalised as a description of the area where fighting during the Gazala battle was most bitter. But DAK had already begun to apply the German equivalent, *Kessel*, to the blood-soaked cockpit of Sidi Rezegh. It was not easy, at command level, to start stirring the *Kessel* again.

---

* This was no reflection on a gallant division. Dominion commanders like Freyberg had a special responsibility to the home government for keeping their divisions in being, and the problem of reinforcements for the New Zealand division was formidable.

Because of the capture of his headquarters Crüwell was still functioning without an operations or intelligence staff, or even a clerk. All his wireless traffic, according to the War Diary, was carried by one Korps set and one belonging to 15 Panzer. Command and control were inhibited. Rommel, for his part, was unable to fly back from his advanced HQ at Gambut to *Panzergruppe*, with all its staff and facilities at El Adem, until the 28th, two of the aircraft despatched for him having been shot down.

'Evil communications corrupt good manners' – and good generalship: for the feeble co-ordination of DAK's operations on the 29th surely derived from this source. Rommel ensconced himself on the third escarpment with Crüwell, Bastico and other German and Italian notabilities, to watch 15 Panzer launch in the early afternoon an attack on the El Duda front held by the Tobruk garrison. Sustained until after midnight, the operation was an unmitigated failure. 'Our defensive positions were fought to a standstill one after the other by the English tanks', 15 Panzer War Diary noted, 'and their weapons and ammunition destroyed.' One of the two battle groups committed was overrun: the second had to withdraw.

The fact is that the habit of dividing instead of concentrating the forces available, for which the British are so severely and so soundly criticised, was not confined to them. Rommel had done this earlier in CRUSADER and so, on his own initiative, had Crüwell. On the 29th Rommel did so again, for while 15 Panzer was being rebuffed 21 Panzer (now down to a handful of tanks) was pressing without much appetite against the New Zealanders' flank in the distant area of Point 175 and the Trigh Capuzzo. Practically speaking the attacks had no logical connection.

But logic had gone out of the window that day, for it was on this front that each side achieved a major success entirely by chance. *Ariete*, who also distinguished themselves on the 29th by preoccupying the British armour, moved north during the afternoon against Point 175, where the New Zealand 21 Battalion had already repulsed two German attacks. The Battalion was expecting relief from the south by a South African brigade: *Ariete*, as it approached, clearly identified the enemy as friends. In a confusion of mutual mis-identification the Italians comfortably over-ran the position, collecting 200 prisoners and a field hospital containing, they claimed, 1,000 patients and 400 staff.

Earlier in the morning, however, this same battalion had achieved a scoop by picking up von Ravenstein, who missed his way to a meeting with Crüwell. 'It was terrible,' he told Desmond Young after the war, 'because I had on me the Chief of Staff's map with all our dispositions and had no time to destroy it. When I saw that there was no way out, I determined to call myself Colonel Schmidt and hoped that they would not notice my rank badges.' However, he gave himself away and was taken back to Cairo. This conversation explains, perhaps, the reference to a captive General Schmidt who appears in various contemporary documents, including a letter to Churchilll from Auchinleck of 12 January 1942.*

In this Auchinleck referred to evidence that the enemy was hard pressed, as disclosed in Ravenstein's daily conversation, because of the way those over-heard spoke freely 'of great losses in recent fighting, mismanagement and disorganisation, and above all of dissatisfaction with Rommel's leadership'. Von Ravenstein, a hard-bitten fighter but an aesthete and an intellectual, was scarcely *en rapport* with Rommel (how could he be with a man who, when they emerged together from the opera in Rome, immediately started to discuss an infantry position?) and he was speaking in the aftermath of the 'dash to the wire'. Still, it may be that these words were his last service to the Afrika Korps, since there is no doubt that in mid-January they powerfully supported the view in Cairo that DAK had shot its bolt – DAK, which, under Rommel, would within a few months have rushed through the gates of Egypt.

The recording of von Ravenstein's views was neatly executed. Brigadier Shearer, Auchinleck's Director of Military Intelligence, was much criticised at the time for inviting the captive general to tea. The purpose, however, was to remove him unsuspecting from his tent. During his absence the lighting fixture was 'bugged'.† Perhaps von Ravenstein's suspicions were lulled because he expected to be treated in style: certainly he lived in a style far different from the average soldier, if the account in 21 Battalion's history of the contents of his car is evidence. Among a variety of provisions it contained 'a tin of Aulsebrook's biscuits, some cartons of South African cigarettes, a case of Crosse and Blackwell's tinned delicacies, a bottle of Greek brandy'.

The short supply of senior officers available for fighting commands in the Afrika Korps is well illustrated by the consequences of von Ravenstein's capture. When CRUSADER began General Böttcher, as has been seen, was in charge of the heavy artillery. Later he had to take over, in addition, an *ad hoc* infantry group on the third escarpment. Now he was transferred again, to take temporary command of 21 Panzer. Meanwhile Colonel Mickl of Infantry Regiment 155 was switched to Group Böttcher.

Rommel's orders for the 30th, predictably, were to complete the encircle-ment and destruction of the New Zealanders, and Mickl in his new command responded enthusiastically. 'At 10.30 a.m.,' 26 New Zealand Battalion re-corded, 'the enemy began the longest and heaviest shelling of the battle. For over five hours enemy gunners plastered the western end of the Sidi Rezegh

---

* The real officer was General Schmitt, captured on the frontier in the New Year.
† Personal communication to the author by Brigadier Shearer.

feature . . . it was too dangerous to lift a head over the level of the slit trench.' And it was Mickl's group which, in the afternoon, under Rommel's eyes and backed by 15 Panzer, finished off 6 New Zealand Brigade in a direct assault on the Sidi Rezegh or second escarpment, so that by the evening tanks of 15 Panzer had thrust north to the Trigh Capuzzo. Their victims were now reduced to a Brigade HQ, the field regiment, a machine-gun platoon and a company of engineers. 600 prisoners had been taken.

At dawn next morning 15 Panzer kept up its pressure by attacking the last New Zealand brigade, 4, in its positions at Belhamed. An early mist helped. By breakfast-time one of its battalions had surrendered, helpless before the panzers, and Freyberg's own headquarters were almost captured. As the remnants of the division withdrew to the east 4/22 Armoured Brigade (now a composite, but with over 100 tanks) moved in to rescue them. The British tanks had a marked psychological effect on the Germans, and some swift surrenders occurred. But both sides were now losing the taste for battle, and nothing major developed.

'Freyberg's fight,' Field Marshal Sir Michael Carver has rightly observed, 'was over. Once again it looked like disaster; but the losses he had inflicted on Crüwell's command had decided CRUSADER in Ritchie's and not in Rommel's favour.' An intimation of defeat was, indeed, already permeating the DAK. During the 30th 21 Panzer should have pushed hard against the New Zealand Division's eastern force in support of Mickl's group in the south. Instead they complained about heavy opposition, and Böttcher actually proposed a with-drawal to Rommel. Crüwell soon stamped on that, signalling to a new com-mander obviously infected by the atmosphere around him: 'You are under my command exclusively. Wireless messages to *Panzergruppe*, particularly in clear, are forbidden. You are to hold on at all costs. Take up all-round positions with Div. HQ in the middle.'

But no draconian *Diktats* by Crüwell or Rommel could disguise the fact that DAK was now in decline. On the morning of 1 December the future General Sir Howard Kippenberger, then a battalion commander, was in the dressing station at Point 175 captured by *Ariete*. The attack on Belhamed and his own battalion was in progress.

I watched sadly and anxiously from the edge of the wadi and had an odd conversation with a German artillery officer. He came up and said: 'We have taken Belhamed and our Eastern and Western Groups have joined hands.' I expressed regret. 'But it is no use; we have lost the battle,' he went on. 'I am glad; it has been a pleasure to meet you. You have fought well', I said. 'That is not enough. Our losses are too heavy. We have lost the battle', he answered – and went on his way.

The South African history also quotes a letter from W.E. Murphy, the New Zealand historian, who was an anti-tank officer in CRUSADER and was captured, wounded, in the same dressing station as Kippenberger. He noted that German troops passing through the station 'were practically sleepwalkers and certainly did not regard themselves as victorious. . . . I think their morale was very near breaking point. . . . The German officer [see above] was by no means an exception. . . . I heard many similar remarks from other ranks with whom I chatted.'

But Rommel, as Bayerlein commented on 1 December, 'could not allow his troops the rest they so badly needed'. And so, for the next week, we observe the Afrika Korps hopelessly bleeding to death while the British, with Auchinleck at Ritchie's side, prove unable to make such effective combinations out of their growing superiority as to deliver a *coup de grâce*. Tobruk is finally relieved: 8th Army holds the field: but in view of the desperate character of the fighting during the middle phase of the battle CRUSADER may be said to have begun at half-cock and ended in a sort of anti-climax.

Rommel's refusal to accept the inevitable is vividly illustrated by the message he issued to his *Panzergruppe* during 2 December. Having emphasised the enemy's great losses and announced that the first round had been won, he continued: 'Soldiers! This magnificent success is due to your courage, endurance and perseverance. The battle, however, is not yet over. Forward then to the final knockout of the enemy.' But his orders for the 3rd revealed that in fact the battle was as alive as it ever had been, since the three areas he specified for attention had long been foci for intensive fighting. These were the frontier regions, where the stranded Axis garrisons must be relieved: the El Duda positions where the Tobruk troops were always menacing: and the open ground to the south, along the Trigh el Abd, where the British armour, regrouping and reinforcing, offered a continual threat.

Crüwell wanted a massive drive to the frontier with DAK *en masse*, but Rommel insisted on Neuman-Silkow taking a battle-group from both panzer divisions without the panzers, and making for the frontier while the rest of the *Panzergruppe* tackled the other two problems. Yet Crüwell was right: a policy of too little in too many places was now fatal. On the 3rd, and again on the 4th, Neumann-Silkow was punished and halted by New Zealand and Indian troops. On the El Duda front Sümmermann (whose *Afrika* Division had now become 90 Light), stated on the 3rd that his command was 'no longer in a condition to fight'. On the 4th an attack from the south by Group Mickl and supporting units was contained by heavy fire. In any case, Rommel decided that afternoon to cut his losses in respect of Tobruk and the frontier, concentrating instead on the third and what now seemed the largest problem – the British armour.

He was approaching desperation. And blow after blow was to fall between the 2nd and that extreme moment on the 8th when, in an altercation with Bastico, Rommel 'like an over-bearing and uncouth boor yelled that he had struggled for three weeks to win the victory and had now decided to take his division to Tripoli and have himself interned in Tunisia'. (Or so the Italian Official History maintains!) Until the evening of the 6th the pattern is one of confusion . . . confusion compounded by a lethargy or indifference which seems to have prevented either side from establishing the location or strength of the other. The pivotal point was Bir el Gubi, round which DAK and 4 Armoured Brigade side-stepped, intermingled and occasionally snapped at one another. On the evening of the 6th Neumann-Silkow was killed by a shell – the second of DAK's original divisional commanders to go, with Sümmermann soon to follow. But already, on the 5th, the bell had tolled.

From the Italian High Command in Rome came Colonel Montezemolo, to inform Bastico (on the 4th) and Rommel (the following evening) that apart from bare essentials nothing could be carried over the Mediterranean, by way of reinforcements, supplies and equipment, until at least the end of December when *Luftflotte* 2 would start making sorties from Sicily. DAK now had 40 tanks: the British over 100, with replenishment of all kinds flowing in. Even Rommel could not ignore the inevitable. Bastico screamed, pretended he had been kept in the dark, but had to agree. *Panzergruppe* must withdraw.

If no general can be reckoned a complete commander until he has stood the test of defeat and retreat, the same may be said of an army. By this criterion the Afrika Korps was about to demonstrate once again its professional skill and invincible morale, for though it had now lost many of its best officers and men, and a large proportion of its equipment, and though a temporary weariness had affected minds as well as bodies, during the long haul from the environs of Tobruk to the Gulf of Sirte it retained both cohesion and the will to fight. Unlike the British, as they scampered before the infant DAK in the spring of 1941 (and would shortly do again) the Afrika Korps showed that far from racing to the rear it could turn, stand its ground and inflict numbing wounds on the enemy.

Before it was too late much of the stores and depot material in the Gambut area was extricated and set moving westwards. The heavy artillery group came out of action and departed down the Via Balbia. Unit transport was thinned out and withdrawn. Though it was not a copybook exercise, the departure of DAK from the field of CRUSADER was effected with a poise and control in marked contrast to the atmosphere of the Matruh Stakes or any of the other gallops in which the 8th Army indulged. There was little poise, however, in the relations between the Axis commanders. The Italians passionately desired to cling to positions as far forward as possible for as long as possible. Indeed, one of the reasons for the violent altercation between Rommel and Bastico on the 8th was because the panzer General's orders to withdraw *Pavia* from the Tobruk outskirts had been countermanded by Gambara: during the night of the 7th, in consequence, *Pavia* was mauled by the British.

By the 11th a semblance of stability was achieved. For ten miles or so, southwards from the sea at Gazala to the usefully defensible Alam Hamza, Navarrini got his infantry divisions into line, with Gambara's armour and mobile troops guarding his right. DAK, with its last 40 tanks, covered the open flank. In case Oasis Force tried to cut off the *Panzergruppe* (which was unlikely, as it was weak and under surveillance from the *Luftwaffe*), or in case the 8th Army copied O'Connor and pushed a task force across the base of the Jebel Akhdar (which was equally improbable), the battered 90 Light withdrew to form a backstop at Agedabia, losing its commander, Sümmermann, during an air raid *en route*. As it was not fully motorised, the division had to be ferried in whatever transport was available, or it marched.

So a 'Gazala line' had been established: but though its northern end rested on the sea, the southern was in the air – unprotected except by a skeleton DAK. It was a situation which skill and drive could have decisively exploited, but the British were now tired, muddled and cautious. By an inexplicable decision Ritchie had placed the mobile advancing elements under Godwin-Austen and the HQ of his infantry-orientated 13 Corps, while Norrie and his 30 Corps HQ, practised in mobile operations, were left to handle the subjugation of Rommel's frontier posts. It is not surprising that in this Alice-through-the-looking-glass atmosphere the 8th Army's attempts to break or encircle the Gazala position were foiled.

There were several actions up and down the line, but always most fiercely around the central and dominating feature of Alam Hamza. Here on the 13th and 14th the old struggle at pointblank range between panzer and 25-pounder was savagely renewed – 25 Field Regiment, on the 13th, claimed 12 tanks for a loss of seven officers and 58 men, an eloquent equation. Then, on the 15th, during another engagement at Alam Hamza the Buffs of 4 Indian Division were destroyed by 15 Panzer, losing over 1,000 men, mainly as prisoners. Their futile attack was meant to distract the *Panzergruppe* from an outflanking move by 4 Armoured Brigade, which that day slipped round the southern tip of the line, turned north to disrupt the *Gruppe*'s rear – and ran out of petrol. Neither then nor on the 16th was any practical advantage taken of the 8th Army's exceptional opportunity. It was left to Rommel, never more lynx-eyed a realist than when things were at the worst, to recognise the true situation. DAK's brilliant achievements of the last few days were essentially meaningless. As he advised *Comando Supremo* on the 16th: 'the fighting power of the troops – despite superb individual achievements – is showing signs of flagging, all the more so as the supply of arms and ammunition has completely dried up'.

And so, when Cavallero, Kesselring, Bastico and Gambara called on him late that night in a high-pressure attempt to block a further withdrawal Rommel simply shouted them down and carried on as he had always intended to do. During the night Crüwell began to move DAK and the Italian mobile troops due westward across the base of the Jebel, while Navarrini's infantry made for safety down the Via Balbia. The 8th Army proved as powerless to prevent the retirement as was the Desert Air Force, which in spite of a comfortable superority seemed comatose. 'The result was,' as Air Vice-Marshal Coningham reported sadly, 'that for nearly three days the enemy's troops in the comparatively small area south-west of Gazala had not one bomb dropped on them.'*

By the beginning of the New Year the *Panzergruppe* had been completely extricated from the Jebel Akhdar and established in conditions of substantial security around the El Agheila bottleneck. Before the withdrawal was completed two further credits and one large debit had been added to the balance-sheet. Loss of the frontier ports was an inevitable price for an unavoidable retreat: under pressure from the two South African divisions, therefore, Bardia surrendered on 2 January, bringing another German General, Artur Schmitt, into the bag, while the last stand of the *Panzergruppe*, at Halfaya, continued until the 17th, when Major Bach at last gave in along with another of those Italians whose spirit recommended them to their allies, General de Giorgis.† Of the 29,900 'missing' from the *Panzergruppe* during CRUSADER no less than 13,800 were troops captured in these frontier surrenders.

But as Rommel wrote in his *Rules of Desert Warfare*, 'the armour is the core of the motorised army. Everything turns on it, and other formations are mere auxiliaries.' In this vital area DAK had made two quick gains. Before Benghazi was evacuated the merchant ship *Ankara* had docked on 19 December, landing 22 tanks for 15 Panzer. The rest of the convoy went to Tripoli, where *Monginevro* also off-loaded 23 tanks which were shortly in 15 Panzer's hands. Though two other ships had been sunk in passage, on 13 December, and a further 45 panzers lost, these reinforcements were of critical value to the impoverished DAK, particularly as an intelligence miscalculation in Cairo dismissed the landing of tanks at Benghazi as a total impossibility because of what was assumed by the Royal Navy to be the effective blocking of the quays. Thus it was a surprised 22 Armoured Brigade which ran into the Afrika Korps at the end of the month, as it covered the last lap of the withdrawal to El Agheila. In two sharp engagements with a DAK of unsuspected strength and resilience it lost 37 tanks on 28 December and another 23 on the 30th, exactly

---

* *The Mediterranean and the Middle East*, Vol. III, p. 83.
† The three CRUSADER captives, von Ravenstein, Schmitt and Bach may be seen together in a photograph reproduced in *The Foxes of the Desert*, by Paul Carell.

two-thirds of its complement. Here was ominous evidence that the Afrika Korps was back in business.

From the opening days of CRUSADER it had never, in truth, been a force that could safely be discounted by 8th Army – such, indeed, was the moral superiority achieved by the panzer regiments that it never *was* discounted, either by its adversaries in the front line or by their senior commanders. It is evident, in retrospect, that the Korps itself had few reasons for self-criticism. The dominating parameter had been that of supply and reinforcement. Between July and October 1941 the monthly average of general military cargoes and fuel reaching North Africa had been 72,000 tons – and even that was inadequate. But in November the figure was 30,000 tons (the remains of an appalling 62 per cent loss *en route*), and in December only 39,000 tons were disembarked. No army, however gallant, could sustain a prolonged and fast-moving battle with its throat choked: yet the Afrika Korps fought and survived CRUSADER in a condition of strangulation. All the techniques evolved in training had worked in practice – the many subtle uses of anti-tank guns, the swift recovery of damaged panzers, the drills for dealing with field batteries. The courage shown during *Totensonntag* and the almost daily conflicts, the endurance of hard weather and harsh conditions had persisted to the end. The Korps emerged from CRUSADER unbroken in spirit (for all its temporary drop in morale) because it was abundantly evident that on even less than equal terms it was still superior.

Certainly there had been moments when it was led astray. Both Rommel and Crüwell made tactical errors so grave that an efficient opponent must have profited. But each had displayed a great ability to compensate for faulty judgement by energetic and correct decisions. Both the panzer General and DAK's commander were fortunate that they could rely on so well-drilled and well-tempered an instrument. Fortunate, too, that an enemy no less courageous or enduring, and better supplied, was led by men even more prone to error. Leadership, in the end, was the key. 'The greatest weakness on the British side lay in their inability to bring all their forces to bear to achieve their primary aim. . . . Rommel made many mistakes, but there was no doubt who was master and who it was that appeared at the decisive moment. So far the British had not found their own type of Rommel.'*

---

* Sir William Jackson, *op. cit.*, p. 182.

7

The cauldron boils

'Troops must be able to carry out operations at top speed
and in complete co-ordination. To be satisfied with norms
is fatal.'

Rommel, *The Second Battle for Tobruk*

During the fall-back from Cyrenaica the Afrika Korps had, in large measure,
restored its fortunes by its own efforts. Now their results were compounded
by events elsewhere. The first was Japan's attack on Pearl Harbour, whose
consequences for the African campaign were as direct, and as favourable to
DAK, as had been those of the German invasion of the Balkans in the previous
spring. Suddenly, in the Far East, a vast segment of the British Empire was
now threatened but naked. The few counters available had to be switched to
the opposite side of the board. Almost immediately, therefore, 6 and 7
Australian Divisions left the Middle East for New Guinea. The hardened
7 Armoured Brigade sailed with its tanks for Burma, to become the steel shaft
in the famous retreat. 18 British Division, already in convoy, was diverted
from Suez to Singapore, and 17 Indian Division, also ear-marked for North
Africa, went off from its homeland to Rangoon and the start of an historic
career. In this way both the actual and potential strength of the 8th Army was
diminished.

At the same time the immediate prospects for the *Panzergruppe* improved
sensationally. *Fliegerkorps* 2 had arrived in Sicily and Kesselring was orches-
trating from Rome a joint air/sea offensive against Malta and British operations
in the Mediterranean. Two dozen U-boats were at work or on the way.
Already, in November, they had sunk the aircraft-carrier *Ark Royal* and
battleship *Barham*. On 18 December a cruiser and a destroyer went down in a
minefield, and next morning two Italian frogmen penetrated the harbour at
Alexandria, putting out of action for months the two battleships *Queen
Elizabeth* and *Valiant*. Within a few weeks the Royal Navy had sustained the
kind of damage to be expected in a disastrous fleet action. The gradual allevia-

tion for the Afrika Korps, during the coming months of Malta's purgatory, can be seen from a single figure. In April the combined monthly tonnage of stores and fuel safely disembarked had soared to 150,000, representing a loss in passage of only 1 per cent.

Churchill's second sight and the pervasive optimism of Cairo are illustrated in an exchange of notes between the Prime Minister and Auchinleck early in the New Year. Churchill signalled: 'I fear this means that the bulk of seven-and-a-half enemy divisions have got away round the corner. . . . I note also that nine merchant ships of 10,000 tons are reported to have reached Tripoli safely. . . . I am sure you and your armies did all in human power, but we must face facts as they are. . . .' In reply, on 12 January, Auchinleck laid great stress on the depressed tone of the overheard conversations between Ravenstein and Schmitt, and buoyantly declared that 'I am convinced the enemy is hard pressed more than we dared think perhaps'.

This was a piece of self-deception. Auchinleck knew, for example, how his 22 Armoured Brigade had only recently been taken apart. He knew, for ULTRA had told him, that in the convoy which docked at Tripoli on 5 January were 54 tanks with their crews, a stock of armoured cars and a consignment of fuel. What he did not know was that 15 Panzer had received those extra 22 tanks at Benghazi. Still, this was not the moment to write off the Afrika Korps.

Nor did Rommel's staff think so, for on the very day of Auchinleck's letter, the 12th, von Mellenthin, supported by Westphal, suggested that *Panzergruppe* had a fleeting moment of superiority over the opposition. After some doubts, Rommel accepted the proposition of a spoiling attack with enthusiasm, increased as the intercept service brought evidence of British disorganisation on the Agheila front. Intense security was imposed – night moves, tanks camouflaged as lorries, no intimation of intentions either to the Italians or – more daringly – OKW. Unit commanders were not briefed until the last minute. When the operation began, about 8 a.m. on 21 January, the Afrika Korps had 84 tanks and the Italians another 89.*

Within four days Auchinleck was rushing up from Cairo once again to 'restore the situation' – but this time it was one created by a commander of his own choice, and Ritchie's decisions had reflected an optimism which Auchinleck himself shared. What Ritchie had failed to see was that an operation which, as he rightly dignosed, had begun as a limited thrust was developing its own dynamism. The reason, in effect, was a similarity between the opposition Rommel was now meeting and that which had faced him in the same place in

---

* So the British *Official History*. Here is a good instance of the difficulty of establishing exact figures for armour in the desert campaigns. Von Mellenthin's editor gives 117 German, 79 Italian. Bayerlein in the *Rommel Papers* gives 111 German with 23 in reserve. Sir Michael Carver in his *Tobruk* says 'about 100 German tanks and nearly as many Italian'.

the previous year – too few troops forward, too many small units too far apart, too many inexperienced troops, and too much dissension among the British senior ranks. This was the sort of opportunity which Rommel and the Afrika Korps were quick to exploit.

In the first forward move on the 21st *Ariete* and *Trieste* advanced from Mersa Brega astride the main road, accompanied by a typical *ad hoc* Group under Colonel Marcks (two motorised infantry battalions, one each from 21 Panzer and 90 Light, plus some artillery and reconnaissance elements). DAK thrust further inland, along the northern rim of the difficult Wadi Faregh. The British outposts, 200 Guards Brigade by the Via Balbia and the frail, inexperienced Support Group of 1 Armoured Division on the Wadi, fell back, the latter in particular losing many guns and vehicles in the soft going which even caused problems for 15 Panzer. By next morning Group Marcks was at Agedabia.

This was the day when the Axis troops were formally rechristened *Panzer-armee Afrika*,* and during it Rommel devised a neat army operation. Group Marcks smashed north, scattering British transport, and reaching Antelat by 1530. Turning east, it reached Saunnu before evening. That night, as von Mellenthin records,

> The Italian Armoured Corps was to hold the Agedabia area, the Afrika Korps was to try and establish a cordon along the line Agedabia–Antelat–Saunnu, and Group Marcks was to move south-east of Saunnu, and endeavour to close a ring on the eastern flank.

A glance at the map makes clear that these manoeuvres would have boxed in the British – the Guards, and the Support Group and 2 Armoured Brigade of 1 Armoured Division. But staff work at DAK HQ was fumbled. 21 Panzer failed to take over Saunnu after Marcks departed: there was a hole in the side of the box, and the British, with further losses, escaped.

Nothing, however, was going to halt Rommel – even a visit on the 23rd by Kesselring and Cavallero, conveying a directive from Mussolini which required a stop to offensive operations and consolidation back at Mersa Brega. When the dust of argument had settled, Rommel 'pressed on regardless' – to some tune on the 25th, when a concerted attack by the Afrika Korps shattered 2 Armoured Brigade whose scramble to Msus and beyond von Mellenthin witheringly describes as 'one of the most extraordinary routs of the war'. (In charity he also added – as was the case – that the British tank units apparently

---

* Some 12,500 Germans and 25,000 Italians: DAK and 90 Light, 10 Corps with *Bologna* and *Brescia*, 20 Corps with *Ariete* and *Trieste*, and 21 Corps with *Pavia, Trento* and *Sabratha*. 37,500 men in 10 divisions – the figures reveal how far below war establishment most units had fallen.

had no battle experience.) This repetition by Britain's 1 Armoured Division of the performance by 2 Armoured Division, in the same place and in face of the same enemy, underlines one of the important factors which made for DAK's cohesion and efficiency as compared with the amateur lack of solidarity among the British. The British system tended too much towards replacement of one complete unit by another. The Afrika Korps retained its units, which were fed by individual reinforcements, so that the unit's 'know-how' and *esprit de corps* were transmitted and perpetuated. There is an analogy, here, with the organic development of the panzer through a very limited number of Marks. The British system had its manifest advantages, but the German method at least ensured that it was the exception, rather than the rule, for a completely inexperienced unit to be thrust into the firing line, just as the Afrika Korps never had to fight with an untried type of tank.

The next phase was decisive. By moving 90 Light, the Italian XX Corps and Marcks Group north and north-west towards Benghazi, and at the same time making a menacing feint towards Mechili with DAK (which the RAF spotted) Rommel threw the minds of the British command off balance. He already knew from his intercept service that his enemy was unhappy. Now, in quick succession, General Tuker – one of the wisest of all British divisional commanders (whose 4 Indian Division was shielding Benghazi) – advocated an evacuation of Benghazi: Godwin-Austen his Corps commander approved: Ritchie, supported by Auchinleck, countermanded the order on the assumption that Rommel was overstretched; there was a continuing argument between 8th Army HQ and the field commanders about maintaining the fight: and finally, on 6 February, the British fell right back to *Panzerarmee*'s old line running from Gazala south to Bir Hacheim.

Rommel, who was promoted to Colonel-General, received Mussolini's permission to enter Benghazi on the day he entered, a perfect symbol of the ambivalence in the Italo–German relationship and of the parameter of frustration, at the higher politico-strategic level, which was a constant impediment for the Afrika Korps. As for the operation itself, Bayerlein's contemptuous summary in the Rommel *Papers* is justified: 'two mixed combat groups, neither very strong, attacked frontally through Cyrenaica and retook this great territory by 6 February'. It had been a partridge drive. 'I have a most uncomfortable feeling that the Germans out-wit and out-manoeuvre us as well as out-shooting us', Auchinleck had written to Ritchie on 1 January after DAK had turned and savaged 22 Armoured Brigade. This was the simple truth – in spite of the lessons supplied by nearly a year of conflict. In the recovery of Cyrenaica the Afrika Korps exhibited once again its total professionalism – a driving energy, the ability to fuse rapidly into effective task forces, the avoidance of gross tactical errors and, as usual, magnetic leadership by Rommel at the right place in the battle. Technically speaking, this was a very difficult combination to overcome by an enemy who somehow lacked the time, the will or the imagination for the kind of training that evolves a common doctrine universally understood – an enemy, too, lacking the unity of command essential if such a doctrine is to be imposed. The British were not short of material. 4 Indian Division at Benghazi was a good infantry division by any standards. But as its commander 'Gertie' Tuker used to preach, if the 'approach to battle' is wrong the battle itself will not be right.

And now, ironically, more misguided approaches to battle in the spring of 1942 drew the Afrika Korps and the 8th Army towards a further conflict which, from the German point of view, occurred in the wrong place and from the British at the wrong time.

It requires no hindsight to observe that for both sides Malta was the key to a sound strategic posture in the Mediterranean. In 1942 Admiral Raeder saw this clearly, and he pushed Hitler hard towards an agreement with the Italians that Malta must be taken. Kesselring's *Fliegerkorps* 2 effectively neutralised the island and its seaways as the spring advanced – but would not the *Luftwaffe* be switched back to Russia? Rommel, happy enough to have Malta put out of action, was nevertheless single-minded in his urge to capture Tobruk and the Delta, so that for him reinforcement of DAK and a hunter's licence were the outstanding priorities. Hitler, haunted by his airborne losses on Crete, was ambivalent – and for the *Führer*, as for the high priests of OKW and OKH, Russia was always dominant. Italian policy over Malta was a mixture of desire and doubt.

Out of the running debate over Operation HERKULES – an assault on Malta – which enlivened the command posts and cabinets of the Axis during the spring of 1942 it is therefore not surprising that a fatal compromise emerged. Though Rommel met with a cool reception when he flew to Hitler's headquarters in March, and though pressure from Raeder and, indeed, Cavallero led to a firm plan for HERKULES to be implemented in June,* a further review by Hitler, Mussolini, Kesselring and Cavallero at Obersalzberg towards the end of April gave Rommel (now supported by Kesselring), what he wanted. There was to be no HERKULES until he had attacked the British in their Gazala line, and completed the conquest of Tobruk. Then he was to turn to the defensive, and Malta would be the next objective.

Hindsight here comes into its own, for we now see that by shifting its eyes from the true strategic target the German High Command threw away perhaps its last hope of retaining a presence in North Africa. In May/June 1942, with a

---

* Very detailed plans were made, envisaging an Airborne Corps of two Italian and one German divisions with supporting troops: but HERKULES is always faintly reminiscent of a 'tactical exercise'.

strong *Luftwaffe* and a feeble Royal Navy in the Mediterranean, it was not beyond the bounds of possibility for long-suffering Malta to have been captured by the Axis, and it is certainly difficult to assess the full range of benefits that the availability of the island, as a base for U-boats and bombers, might have produced. Still less is it easy to imagine how, without Malta, the British could have re-established a significant interdiction of the *Panzerarmee*'s supply lines. At the end of May, therefore, when Rommel attacked at Gazala, the Axis had committed itself to battle in the wrong place – and when the Afrika Korps went on to take Tobruk the psychological effect of success was such, as will be seen, that Hitler and Mussolini dropped HERKULES with hardly a pang. This was self-mutilation.

For Auchinleck the Gazala battle occurred at the wrong time simply because his correct and considered judgement was that the 8th Army was not yet ripe for further action. The battle was untimely also because he had not been planning a defensive engagement; all his preparations were for a British offensive, and Rommel's forward move caught the 8th Army on the wrong foot. The reasons are simple: Malta, once again, and Churchill.

Though the Prime Minister occasionally mistook the real strategic focus – in his obsession over Norway, for example – during the prolonged debate between London and Cairo which proceeded in parallel with the arguments of the Axis about Malta, Churchill never lost sight of the little island. The immense and sustained pressure which, with the full backing of his military advisers, he brought to bear on Auchinleck was always with the object of making the 8th Army advance westward at the earliest moment, so as to secure the forward airfield, from which aid could be given to Malta and the relieving convoys. 'We are unable to supply Malta from the west', signalled the Chiefs of Staff on 26 February. 'Your chances of doing so from the east depend on an advance in Cyrenaica.' All the contentious exchanges that followed revolved round this central point, with Auchinleck using every plea – the need to build up his armour, to train his troops, to cover the northern flank of his theatre – so as to avoid a premature operation for which he knew that the army was unready. He lost. Churchill's signal of 10 May (endorsed by the War Cabinet, the Defence Committee and the Chiefs of Staff), was final. 'We are determined that Malta shall not be allowed to fall without a battle being fought by your whole army for its retention.' Auchinleck could only resign or, as was instinctive in him, obey orders. He committed himself, with profound misgivings, to an offensive.

Thus for many reasons, and as a result of intense discussion in the highest places, a situation was created which, at the end of May, would launch the Afrika Korps against that very Gazala line where, after CRUSADER, it had found a temporary and uneasy lodging, and from which its opponent was on

the verge of debouching. In the meantime talk at the top allowed for some rest
in the ranks. Perhaps the main refreshment lay merely in not fighting, in being
alive, in having time to write letters and seek out friends. There were few
'welfare' alleviations of the kind familiar to the British in Cairo or Alexandria.
A cinema in bombed Benghazi, the *Oasis* news to read, an egg bartered from
an Arab, some fresh greens from the cultivated parts of the Jebel, a change of
clothes, a bathe in the sea and some draughts of *vino* – for all but the lucky few
who reached Italy or home this was about the measure of relaxation. There
was always training and, as the Tripoli convoys increased their deliveries,
more equipment to absorb. Battle-worn panzers had to be re-invigorated, and
by the eternal process of cannibalisation captured vehicles had to be brought
into condition again. In No-man's-land the usual bickering continued between
armoured cars and other light forces – and here, unfortunately for von Mellenthin and the intelligence staffs, the 8th Army seems to have maintained an
effective veil.

To be unaware of the presence in the line of one tank brigade and four
brigade groups (one armoured and the other three infantry), is a considerable
failure in Intelligence, yet all these units were missing from the 8th Army's
forward order of battle as reconstructed at *Panzerarmee*. Additionally, the full
scope and southerly extension of the enemy minefields had not been estimated,
nor the presence of 150 Brigade Group in its box dominating the 'mine marsh'
between the Trigh Capuzzo and the Trigh el Abd. In his memoirs von Mellenthin is quietly apologetic, saving his face by saying 'perhaps, fortunately, we
underestimated the British strength, for had we known the full facts even
Rommel might have baulked at an attack on such a greatly superior enemy'.
In intelligence jargon, this is a remarkably defence of negative information!

But Rommel and his staff were equally ignorant of the enemy's self-imposed
problems. They appreciated that the 8th Army was preparing an attack, but
not that for this operation, named BUCKSHOT, both the water pipeline from the
east and, more particularly, the railway had been extended to Belhamed, thus
enabling an immense stockpile to be built up outside Tobruk * – it was called
No. 4 Forward Base – from which a great drive across the neck of the Jebel
could be sustained. When the *Panzerarmee* attacked, the existence of this
treasure-chest would gravely limit the freedom of maneouvre open to Ritchie
and his corps commanders. But it was not a factor in the Axis plan.

And there was another vital fact withheld from Rommel as he put the final
touches to Operation VENEZIA – his intentions were known in Cairo with
considerable accuracy. It seems virtually certain that from the ULTRA intercepts

---

* For example 1,500,000 gallons of fuel had been accumulated.

of signal traffic between *Panzerarmee* and OKW Auchinleck knew when the attack would occur. Nor, at least in its initial stages, was that attack particularly well devised or handled. As on other occasions, the unflagging professionalism and resilience of the officers and men of the Afrika Korps were needed to extricate Rommel from a near-disaster of his own making and provide him with space and time in which his military genius, aided by the errors of his opponents, could re-assert itself and create the conditions for victory. It is in the Gazala battle, perhaps pre-eminently, that one sees how Rommel and the Afrika Korps were complementary. As Wellington said to Creevey in Brussels before Waterloo, pointing at one of his soldiers, so Rommel might have said before Gazala, pointing at one of his panzer-grenadiers: 'It all depends upon that article whether we do business or not.'

The peace of recent months, and the recovery of control over the eastern Mediterranean, were reflected in *Panzerarmee*'s present strength. By the end of May DAK had 332 tanks as 'runners' with 77 in reserve, though mainly the old Mk. III (H) with its short gun. The frontal armour had now been thickened on most of them, however, and 19 (all in 21 Panzer) carried a new long, high-velocity 50 mm gun. A similarly up-gunned Mk. IV was in the pipeline, but the four which had been delivered played no part in the opening phase of the battle, as there was no ammunition. In June, von Mellenthin says, 'this excellent tank began to arrive in increasing numbers'. There were 228 Italian tanks. More importantly, Rommel now had 48 of the 88 mms as well as some Czech 76 mm anti-tank guns and his normal complement of 50 mms. His army was rested and reinforced. On the evidence of the past, its prospects were good.

As in the past, however, the British had the preponderance of strength. They too had been re-equipping steadily, and Ritchie now faced Rommel with 843 tanks and another 145 coming up from the east. Moreover, 167 of those at the front and 75 of the reserves were the powerful American Grant, with its thick armour and 75 mm gun which at last gave the British a tank weapon that could fire high explosive shell – so critical against the 88s. *Panzerarmee* knew of the Grant as early as 20 May: but neither side could fully appreciate until battle was joined that its low-hung gun, with a small traverse, was a grave weakness, for the Grant was a tall tank and had to be mainly exposed to enable the gun to be fired. Still, it was a new factor and would cause more concern to the Afrika Korps than anything since the Matilda. With his two armoured divisions, 1 and 7, plus sundry independent tank brigades, the two South African Divisions, 50 Division, the Free French in the Bir Hacheim Keep, and several other mobile brigade groups Ritchie, on paper, presented the *Panzerarmee* with a formidable problem.

His opportunity was dissipated from the start in what General Jackson has

mordantly described as 'a cumulative progression of avoidable disasters'. Von
Mellenthin was overcalling his hand when he wrote: 'The fact that within
three weeks of the launching of our offensive this magnificent British Army
was reduced to a state of complete rout must be regarded as one of the greatest
achievements in German military annals.' Still, Gazala was a spectacular
victory, and the reason, once again, must be found in Tuker's 'approach to
battle'. Auchinleck was clear-sighted: since it was obvious that Rommel's
main threat must come through the centre of the line or round the desert flank
past Bir Hacheim, he urged Ritchie to clutch his two armoured divisions
together, around the Trigh Capuzzo, so that they could strike *en masse* against
DAK's *Schwerpunkt* once it was disclosed. Ritchie, clouded in his own mind
and swayed by the contradictory appreciations of his subordinates, ignored
the advice of his Commander-in-Chief and held his divisions apart. It is true
that Auchinleck wanted the armour too far north; it is true that Ritchie and
his generals were reasonably afraid of bunching the armour in case Rommel
spotted it and took avoiding action; it is true that some plans were made for
concentrating the British tanks in certain eventualities. But in practice, as in
CRUSADER, once the armoured divisions had been separated the British at
Gazala were never able to mount a single fully co-ordinated attack in which the
whole weight of the armour was applied.

Opposition along these convenient lines was more than Rommel was
entitled to expect for his VENEZIA plan, in which the leading role was naturally
assigned to the Afrika Korps. (DAK was now commanded by Nehring, 90
Light by Kleemann, 15 Panzer by von Vaerst and 21 Panzer by von Bismarck
– such were the changes wrought by the stress of war under Rommel's command.) D Day was 26 May. As an opening distraction the two Italian infantry
corps, stiffened by two regimental groups from 90 Light, began to lean on the
main north-south Gazala line, under the overall command of Crüwell who got
back from leave the previous day. Meanwhile, beneath the moon and in a state
of high tension, Rommel led DAK in a great sweep south of Bir Hacheim and
then northwards – the panzer divisions having been ordered to crash through
the British and penetrate to distant Acroma, far away on the Axis by-pass
outside Tobruk, while Kleemann with 90 Light (and trucks fitted with aero-
engines to create dust-clouds) turned north-east for El Adem and Belhamed,
partly as a diversion and partly to seize supplies and check the transfer of
reserves from Tobruk. 'The move of this column of several thousand vehicles', *
von Mellenthin recalled, 'had been prepared in minute detail; compass bear-
ings, distances and speeds had been carefully calculated; dim lights concealed

---

* Rommel in his *Papers* put the figure for the VENEZIA striking force at 10,000 vehicles.

in petrol tins indicated the line of march, and with the smoothness of a well-oiled machine the regiments of the Afrika Korps swept on to their refuelling point south-east of Bir Hacheim.'

By the following evening, however, the well-oiled machine was creaking. VENEZIA involved too many risks. Originally Rommel intended that DAK's advance should roll over the French at Bir Hacheim; instead, he left the job to *Ariete*. But the French remained undisturbed. Thus, unless Rommel achieved instant victory, all the fuel and supplies to maintain his momentum must travel on the exposed route south and then north and east of the Hacheim pivot. And instant victory was improbable, for objectives like Acroma were too distant (remembering that much of the 8th Army stood in the way), while by fanning out his forces and sending 90 Light on a secondary mission towards Tobruk Rommel was dividing instead of concentrating.

Late on the 27th, therefore, the situation looked serious. After eliminating 3 Indian Brigade and savaging 7 Motorised Brigade, DAK had fought intense actions with large or small groups of British armour, expensively for its opponents (who could afford greater losses), but punishingly for itself. A third of its panzers had been lost. 15 Panzer, up on the Rigel Ridge above the Knightsbridge track-intersection, had only 29 runners while 21 Panzer, not far away to the west, had 80. 90 Light with Reconnaissance Units 3 and 33 were detached to the east. Rommel was out of touch with *Panzerarmee* HQ. The psychological and material impact of the Grants had been immense. As General Messe was to say later about the Wadi Akarit battle: '*non e stata una bella battaglia*'.

As Rommel on the 28th persisted with his northward thrust towards Acroma (using 21 Panzer only, since 15 Panzer was halted, dry, on the Rigel ridge) the armoured divisions of the Afrika Korps were in grave danger, at this stage in the battle, of being cut off and destroyed. Without fuel and ammunition they must have withered. Salvation came from both the British and the Italians. During the 28th and 29th Norrie made many stabs at DAK with his own armour – there was vicious fighting about Bir el Harmat before nightfall on the 28th, and at Knightsbridge on the 29th conflicts like those of CRUSADER – but the classic anti-tank screens were lethal as ever, and the truth was that the British seemed incapable of knitting together a comprehensive and effective plan. They had field guns and now the Grants' HE with which they should have neutralised the 88s. 'There was too much "motoring",' Field Marshal Sir Michael Carver has observed with the authority of one who was on Norrie's staff at the time. Rommel in his *Papers* put it mercilessly: 'This dispersal of the British armoured brigades was incomprehensible.'

But if it was the British who, fundamentally, prevented the Gazala battle from turning into the Waterloo of the Afrika Korps, it was the Italians who

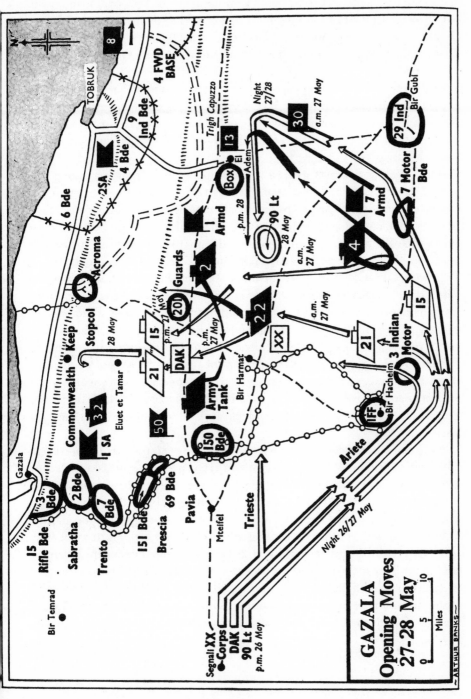

MAP 4 Gazala: opening moves

first found the key to victory. *Trieste* had gone astray on the opening night and
butted into the minefields around the Trigh el Abd. Here, by the 29th, they had
cleared a path to the east. It was to become a lifeline. One of the famous
Rommelei had occurred during the day, when the Colonel-General personally
and at great risk led a supply column across the battlefield to relieve his panzers.
Yet though, in the evening, he had nevertheless to admit that VENEZIA in its
initial form had failed, and though he desperately pulled together the whole of
DAK into a tight defensive semi-circle, backing on to the minefields and
splayed, roughly, across the Trigh Capuzzo, it was only the end of the
beginning.

   Heinz Werner Schmidt gives a vivid account of the fighting during this
opening phase. Leading his company in 2 Battalion of 115 Rifle Regiment, the
mobile infantry of 15 Panzer, after many alarums he reached the approaches to
Acroma. While waiting there he shot a gazelle,* which his men began to roast
over a fire of petrol and cleaning-rags. Suddenly his sergeant-major dropped
dead, shot through the head, and the familiar cry went up, 'Tanks on the right'.
They were Grants – 60 or more. Schmidt watched with horror the shot from
the German 50 mms bouncing off the Grant's armour, and the high-explosive
from the enemy's 75 mm tank guns exploding, a new spectacle, amid his own
infantry. The position was over-run and the battle moved on. Schmidt survived, to gnaw the half-roasted venison. 'I can still remember the feeling of
the juice running down from the corners of my mouth. It was good to be
alive.' But of 350 who had gone into action only 30 remained: the colonel was
a prisoner and Schmidt the sole officer left from 2 Battalion. (A little later, after
Tobruk fell, he had another stroke of luck: he was flown back to Germany for
leave.)

   But in spite of such local successes, and such material strength, the persistent
optimism of Ritchie and his subordinates from now on increasingly lacked
justification. They failed to realise what CRUSADER should have taught them,
that nothing was more to be respected than Rommel and the Afrika Korps
with their backs to the wall. If VENEZIA itself was ill-judged or too daring,
Rommel had now completely recovered the finger-tip feel which made him,
at his best, so brilliantly assured and decisive a field commander. Aware, at
last, of 150 Brigade's dominating presence in the minefields, he saw that the
trick was to hold off the British in the east, eliminate 150 Brigade, clear a viable
route through the mines for his supply columns and then, by destroying the
French at Bir Hacheim, set free his desert flank. With the energy of a man who

---

* One envies the frequent references to gazelles in the records of the Afrika Korps. The author, who
served with 8th Army from Alamein to Tunisia, never saw a single one – alive or dead!

knows just what to do, and the assistance of his opponents, he achieved his objectives.

For the British never made up their minds. The contrast between 'a Montgomery battle' and Gazala is pathetic. Trivial and inept attempts to relieve 150 Brigade simply left the position to be held by its defenders, unsupported, in a brave fight carried on for two and a half days against a concerted assault by DAK led by Rommel himself. Leadership from the front was exacting its price. Crüwell had already been taken prisoner, shot down in his Fieseler Storch over this very position.* Von Vaerst had gone, and it was during the elimination of 150 Brigade (complete by dawn on 1 June) that both Gause and Westphal were wounded. Nevertheless, what was now known as the Cauldron had been firmly secured, with 21 and 15 Panzer holding the ring to north and south, the intrusive 150 Brigade removed, and a safe supply route to the west established.

All previous British attempts to tap into or through the Cauldron's rim failed, whether with armour or infantry. Nevertheless, after much debate and delay a 'major' effort was mounted. This was ABERDEEN, a fiasco which surely compares with the disasters of Black Week in the Boer War. The facts speak for themselves. At dawn on 5 June 32 Army Tank Brigade with infantry support attacked 21 Panzer on the Sidra Ridge: caught in the minefields, some 58 tanks were lost out of 70 and 21 Panzer was unscathed. Meanwhile 9 and 10 Indian Brigades, with 22 Armoured Brigade, sought to advance westwards through the heart of the Cauldron into the area once held by 150 Brigade, and thus block again the *Panzergruppe*'s supply route. The infantry went to the wrong place, its artillery support fell in the open desert, and the armour abandoned the Indians to fight a private battle with 8 Panzer Regiment. In a swift *riposte* Rommel himself led 15 Panzer out of the Cauldron: 5 Indian and 7 Armoured Division's headquarters were over-run, as well as those of 9 and 10 Indian Brigades. In the paralysis of communication and command that followed nothing was done for the four battalions and four field regiments left behind in the Cauldron.

Of the 5,000–6,000 men who had fought in the Cauldron, there was one officer who escaped, and he returned six months later on the crest of the Eight Army's successful advance. He found the battlefield untouched. The guns were still in position surrounded by burnt-out vehicles. The gunners lay where they had fallen, the faithful layers still crouched over their sights.†

---

* Kesselring, who was visiting *Panzerarmee*, took over Crüwell's command. Crüwell was repatriated in 1944 because of asthma. As the British Official History says of his capture, 'there passed from the desert stage one of its outstanding figures'. This good soldier was a great loss to the Afrika Korps.

† 'The Stand of the South Notts Hussars', in *The Royal Artillery Commemoration Book*.

In coping with the clumsy and, once again, unco-ordinated ABERDEEN attack the Panzer Divisions had not been greatly stretched (90 Light had already made off for Bir Hacheim). The tanks on either side were now approaching parity, which, granted DAK's qualitative superiority, was ominous. In field and anti-tank guns 8th Army had lost heavily – and whole regiments of gunners, irreplaceable as functioning units, had melted away. It was hardly evident to the Germans, moreover, that in ABERDEEN their opponents were showing signs of learning their trade, and trying to mount an 'all arms' attack in which artillery, infantry and armour were fused (though such had been the British purpose) because the attack had simply disintegrated. Rommel was entitled to a certain euphoria as he tackled his next objective.

There was, in fact, no reason why he should have felt any concern about Bir Hacheim. Recollections of Dakar or Syria might have reminded him that Frenchmen, whether Vichy or Free, could still fight. But when he despatched Kleemann down to Bir Hacheim early on the 2nd, with 90 Light and *Trieste*, he was not being unjustifiably optimistic in assuming that this little local difficulty would be resolved within a day. How could Rommel or Kleemann guess that Koenig's small force was inspired by the spirit of Verdun, or that it would still be *in situ* on 10 June in spite of concentrated bombardment by the *Luftwaffe*? By now Rommel himself was on the spot, and aid from 15 Panzer and the heavy artillery Group had arrived.

Once the strength of the defences had been appreciated the problem to be overcome was one which affects armoured formations at all times and which particularly affected the under-manned DAK – to break into a fortress you need quantities of infantry. DAK's infantry was always in short supply and particularly vulnerable in an open battle like Gazala: Heinz Werner Schmidt's experience is a good instance. But weight of metal finally told. Almost miraculously – in view of the open ground about Bir Hacheim – 2,700 of its 3,600 defenders were extricated by 7 Motor Brigade, and by the night of the 10th all was over. An embarrassment had been removed, and the delay caused by Koenig's epic stand was of far less consequence than it might have been, since the British frittered away the freedom they enjoyed on the rest of the front in 're-organisation' and fruitless small-scale attacks by the South Africans in the north.

The fall of Bir Hacheim was the beginning of the end. 'Now our forces were free,' Rommel recalled, and he had certainly travelled far from that point during the opening phase when he confessed to a captured British officer that lack of water might soon compel him to capitulate. The next stop must obviously be the defeat of the British armour *en rase campagne*; granted that, Tobruk must drop into his hands and the path to the Delta was open. The task was carried out by the Afrika Korps with clinical efficiency, so that on 15 June

Rommel could already write to his wife: 'the battle has been won and the enemy is breaking up'.

The method was simple – though for the tired panzer units its execution was a dreadful strain. Ritchie had committed another error – which Rommel reprobated in his *Papers* – by failing to draw back towards Tobruk the infantry elements (1 South African Division and two brigades of 50 Division), which lay dangerously exposed in the northern sector of the Gazala line. Starting on the afternoon of the 11th, therefore, Rommel launched a series of continuous attacks on or about the key sector of the British front – the Rigel Ridge and Raml escarpment, running east–west between the Knightsbridge box held by 201 Guards Brigade and the El Adem box held by 29 Indian Brigade. For Ritchie the loss of this line would involve a double menace – to the infantry in the Gazala salient, and to Tobruk itself. Its security was vital: here his armour must fight, if necessary to the death. Another formulation would be to say that Rommel had completely recovered tactical initiative for the Afrika Korps, who now could call the tune. (Ritchie, it must be remembered, was steadily losing his freedom to manoeuvre as the battle drew closer to No. 4 Forward Base.)

Both sides were nearing exhaustion. But while the British still retained all their armoured brigades and had replenished them with tanks, the true situation was less impressive. The price for using a wide variety of types – Grants, Crusaders, Stuarts, Valentines – each requiring a different skill in its crew, different spares, different ammunition, was an immense difficulty in restoring coherency and efficiency to 8th Army's battered units. For the panzer regiments of DAK, which in any case had suffered less damage, the problem of reinforcement was eased by the family relationship of the Mk. III and Mk. IV, for which a few replacements (including 6 Mk. IVs with the long gun) had reached the front. The infantry in DAK was now slight – perhaps a thousand riflemen in 90 Light – but what followed was not an infantry affair.

After a slow start on the 11th the battle flared on the 12th, with 15 Panzer pushing from the south towards Knightsbridge while 21 Panzer came in from the west, a division of strength which Norrie tried to exploit. Instead, inevitably, counter-orders bred confusion. Messervy, commanding 7 Armoured, was nearly captured by 90 Light and took shelter in a water-tank, leaving his brigades without direction or control. Rommel was able to turn weakness into strength, and use his separate divisions to strike converging blows beneath which 7 Armoured Division was destroyed piecemeal. By nightfall the British had lost about 100 tanks. The Cauldron, then Bir Hacheim, then 12 June were the turning-points of the Gazala battle. And once again the Afrika Korps had the inestimable benefit of an Army commander in the front line, for throughout the day Rommel and Bayerlein (who had replaced Gause as *Panzergruppe* Chief of Staff) shuttled between 90 Light and 15 Panzer, bombed, shelled, sometimes pinned down, but surviving and *aware of what was happening.*

This was certainly not the case in Cairo. Auchinleck, who had just returned there from a visit to Ritchie, signalled to Churchill on the evening of the 12th a report of inexplicable confidence, yet it is now evident, as he surely should have seen at the time, that 8th Army was in grave peril if not already defeated. The premises had been established for a logical sequence of events which now occurred with a *Blitzkrieg* effect. On the 13th the Guards abandoned Knightsbridge, after a stand which evoked a heartfelt commendation from Rommel, and the British armour, shattered in the day's fighting, was reduced to half that of DAK.* 70 tanks, of which only 50 were cruisers, offered a thin shield behind which to evacuate the Salient and protect Tobruk. And so, with the usual argument (this time between Gott and Pienaar of 1 South African Division) during the 14th Ritchie set in train the process which sped 8th Army back to Egypt and placed Tobruk in Rommel's hands.

The contentiousness and contradiction which still vitiated British direction of the desert war now flourished at the highest level. Ritchie allowed his Salient divisions to disentangle themselves and disappear to the east. At the same time, while paying lip-service to Auchinleck's requirement that a defence line should be established outside Tobruk from Acroma to El Gubi, he was ambivalent over his Commander-in-Chief's basic demand, that he must not allow a force to be surrounded and besieged in the fortress itself. Simultaneously Auchinleck, not fully aware from Cairo of the speed at which 8th Army was disintegrating, was put under irresistible pressure by Churchill to ensure that Tobruk should not be surrendered in any circumstances whatsoever. It was sad for Rommel that there was no German equivalent to ULTRA. The British trumpet was giving an uncertain sound, and he and his staff would have enjoyed listening to it.

Not that it mattered. During the early morning of the 15th elements of 15 Panzer had thrust north across the Via Balbia to the sea, cutting off Tobruk to the west, and by nightfall 21 Panzer had reached the familiar acres of Sidi Rezegh in the east. The El Adem box still defied 90 Light, but the ring was closing, and already Auchinleck's dream of maintaining a stable line outside Tobruk had been dissipated. The departure of the El Adem garrison during the night of the 16th/17th, and the last fight of 4 Armoured Brigade the following evening (when it met 15 and 21 Panzer near the old Rezegh airfield and lost 32 out of its scratch assembly of 90 tanks) were conclusive. A few hours later 21 Panzer cut the Via Balbia near Gambut, and the investment of

---

* So Sir Basil Liddell Hart in the Rommel *Papers*. Sir Basil also points out that command of the ground where fighting had raged during the last few days enabled DAK to recover many of its damaged panzers for repair. This was a vital advantage to DAK in mid-battle, since its flow of replacements was so limited.

Tobruk was complete. Theoretically the Afrika Korps would still have to work fast: within 48 hours preparations for HERKULES were due to be put in hand, a deadline which assumed the collapse of Tobruk.

In sheer physical terms the Afrika Korps on the 18th was in no condition for an *attaque brusquée* on a fortress which, in the previous year, had withstood a prolonged siege: only the fortunate fact that the fortress itself was now in no condition to sustain such an attack prevented DAK from finishing the Gazala battle in anti-climax. For exhaustion had sapped its vitality. As early as the night of the 14th/15th, during the thrust for the Via Balbia in the west, the truth was disclosed.

> Rommel had been trying all night to drive his DAK to cut the road, but the fierceness of the struggle to reach the escarpment had exhausted them, and they slept where they had stopped at nightfall. Even when the dawn broke and most of the South African division was still driving along the Via Balbia, neither panzer division stirred. It was not until eight o'clock that they reached the escarpment, and nine before their artillery was in action against the road.*

This and similar episodes raise an important question for the historian. Suppose the British had been able to stabilise a defensive ring around Tobruk and fend off a flagging Afrika Korps already short of fuel, ammunition, and human energy – suppose the second siege of Tobruk had been prolonged – would Hitler in frustration have turned against Malta? Would Roosevelt have handed over the Shermans and self-propelled guns which were so critical from Alamein onwards? It is certainly obvious that the swift surrender of the port had incalculable consequences. But for Rommel it is to be doubted whether the future then counted. All that mattered was that Tobruk was in his grasp and that he was determined to seize the prize swiftly, ruthlessly and scientific-ally. Taking for granted the ability of the Afrika Korps to make a final effort, he wasted no time on the 18th and issued orders for an assult to begin at dawn on the 20th.

Everything was in his favour. Though both Ritchie and Gott were satisfied about Tobruk's defensibility, they were misled by superficial factors and blind to the cruel truth. Certainly there were plenty of stores – 3 million rations, 7,000 tons of water, $1\frac{1}{2}$ million gallons of petrol, thousands of rounds of ammunition in all categories. But the garrison of 2 South African Division, 32 Army Tank Brigade, 201 Guards Brigade and 11 Indian Infantry Brigade was a casual miscellany under the South African Major-General Klopper.

---

* Michael Carver, *Tobruk*, p. 222.

They had no time to learn one another's ways or to concert and practise counter-attack plans. The artillery in Tobruk, not inadequate, was nevertheless another unco-ordinated miscellany. Many of the perimeter mines had been lifted, ditches and trenches had silted up and defence posts deteriorated. Overall, no comparison was possible with the taut, alert, educated posture of the Australians during the earlier siege – and Klopper, suddenly overburdened with responsibility, was no Morshead.

Rommel, by contrast, had a well-articulated plan and an experienced team. By deceptive movement of troops around the perimeter he concealed his intention, which was to apply the ideas he had long worked out for the assault on Tobruk in November 1941 which was pre-empted by CRUSADER. Preceded by a massive air and artillery bombardment 15 and 21 Panzer, accompanied by *Ariete*, were to smash their way beyond the mines and anti-tank defences in the vulnerable south-east corner, and then tear through the heart of the fortress down to the harbour. Kesselring, as eager to finish with Tobruk as Rommel, brought in every bomber available in the Mediterranean theatre – from Greece and Crete as well as Africa – and it is worth remembering that just as DAK had learned much about the techniques of siege warfare during the previous year, so the *Luftwaffe* pilots had by now discovered from experience a great deal about the special skills required for close-support bombing in the open desert. Putting together the Afrika Korps and the *Luftwaffe* of 1942, it may be said that if their acquired *expertise* had been available a year earlier even the Australians would probably not have kept them out of Tobruk.

This was evident as the attack went in early on the 20th. The air-strikes, beginning at 5.20 a.m., were accurate, concentrated and devastating. Compared with DAK's amateur efforts of the past, the organisation of the engineer assault groups was efficient and effective – so much so that both 15 and 21 Panzer were through the minefield and across the anti-tank ditch by about 0830. For many, of course, the lie of the land was familiar. Captain Schmidt, waiting with his company before dawn in a wadi near El Duda, watched his men shivering under their blankets and recalled that the sector where he was about to attack was precisely the one where, in April 1941, he had crawled for several hours on a night reconnaissance.

The details of and reasons for the lightning collapse of the Tobruk garrison, the opaque communication between Auchinleck, Ritchie and Klopper, the agonising blow to morale – all these are part of the histories of Great Britain and South Africa. From the point of view of the Afrika Korps the fact of immediate significance was that by dawn on the 21st a white flag of deafeat had been raised, 32,000 men fell into the hands of the *Panzergruppe* – and one should emphasise the group achievement, for though DAK had provided the armoured spearhead which tore Tobruk's defences apart, the Italians – *Ariete*, *Trieste*, *Brescia*, *Pavia* – had played an important supporting role. 'The operation . . . was a masterpiece of rapid improvisation and ruthless determination to succeed. It also showed what good soldiers can do when buoyed up by success, however tired they may be.'*

For both the Afrika Korps and the Italians, as for all soldiers, the strategic, political or other more refined consequences of a stunning victory were as nothing compared with the riches of the loot. (Even as late as 1944, in his château on the Seine, Rommel used to recall for his aides the delights which Tobruk added to his table.) Caccia-Dominioni was there with his war-worn sappers. He describes the 'entire villages' of warehouses:

> There were stacks of tinned beer; huts bursting with pure white flour, cigarettes, tobacco and jam; gallons of whisky; priceless tinned food of all kinds; and tons of khaki clothing – that magnificent khaki, which looked so heavy and was so light and cool to wear. The first-comers (armoured detachments of *Ariete*, 15 Panzer Division and *Trieste*), swiftly hit on a vast store of shoes – gorgeous shoes, just like those that had occasionally been seen on prisoners; soft, elegant suede shoes with thick rubber soles.†

It has often been observed that a distinctive trait of the German is his capacity for envy. Further, contemporary observers frequently noted how, during the great advance of March 1918, German troops were not only seduced into indiscipline by the booty they captured but also shaken in morale by the disparity between their own *ersatz* equipment and the quality and quantity of their enemy's *matériel*. There is no evidence that the treasure-house of Tobruk had any such effect on the men of the Afrika Korps.‡ How could it, as they read Rommel's triumphant Order of the Day? '. . . We have taken in all over 45,000 prisoners and destroyed or captured more than 1,000 armoured fighting vehicles and nearly 400 guns. During the long hard struggle of the last few weeks you have, through your incomparable tenacity, dealt the enemy blow upon blow. . . . Now for the complete destruction of the enemy. . . . During the days to come, I shall call on you for one more great effort to bring us to this final goal.'

---

* Jackson, *op. cit.*, p. 235.

† Caccia-Dominioni, *op. cit.*, p. 28.

‡ Instead, as Schmidt records, they took the practical line of sending home parcels of Australian bully beef. 'It was regarded in Germany as a luxury.'

8

Advance without security

'A plan with a chance of success – a try on.'
Rommel

It was not a matter of the days to come, but of the day after tomorrow. During the 21st Kesselring arrived at *Panzerarmee* HQ. Now that Tobruk had fallen and the RAF had been driven from its forward airfields, he was eager to set HERKULES in motion – which, as had been specified, required Rommel to halt at the Egyptian frontier. But the new* Field-Marshal was afire. 'I was determined,' he wrote in his *Papers*, 'at all costs to avoid giving the British any opportunity of creating another new front and occupying it with fresh formations from the Near East.' In other words, HERKULES or no HERKULES, he was going to bounce the British out of Egypt. In fact he could have little hope of success if HERKULES was implemented, since this would have involved a withdrawal of the *Luftwaffe* from his support. So Kesselring strenuously argued.

But the issue was soon resolved. A liaison officer flew to Hitler, an optimistic signal was sent to Mussolini, and Rommel had won his point, 'in spite of the reasoned and powerful objections of the Italian General Staff, the German Naval Staff, Field Marshal Kesselring, and also General von Rintelen, the German military attaché in Rome'.† Three opportunists, the *Führer*, the Duce and the Axis field commander, had in effect destroyed the last chance of retaining a presence in Africa – for the deferment of HERKULES until September, as now agreed, was in practice a postponement until the Greek Kalends.

---

* Actually it was on the 22nd that Rommel heard of his elevation to the highest rank at the age of 49. He told his wife he would rather have been given a new division, and forgot to wear his appropriate shoulder badges until he reached Alamein and was fitted out by Kesselring. But this was mock modesty. Rommel cared about rank and awards more than he disclosed.

† Von Mellenthin, *Panzer Battles*, p. 118.

The Afrika Korps did not complain. Although it was set on the move immediately, to such effect that its advance guards were crossing the frontier on the 23rd, its morale, as eye-witnesses registered, was buoyant – in spite of a long, wearisome battle and many losses. (The seizure of a well-stocked fortress and the pursuit of a defeated enemy have injected adrenalin into exhausted troops throughout the centuries.) One instance will suffice. A high proportion of *Panzerarmee*'s wheeled vehicles now consisted of captured British transport. As the forward troops moved east of the frontier the men of Rommel's headquarters guard amused themselves by mingling unobserved with the retreating enemy. This was not the act of soldiers in low spirits, but Rommel and von Mellenthin refer to it and Caccia-Dominioni has a lively description:

> Captain Kiel, the commander of Rommel's *Kampstaffel*, invented a new sport for the entertainment of his men: tall and fair as they were, dressed in British khaki, bare-headed in accordance with the fashion current in both armies, and driving captured vehicles that still bore their original markings, they would infiltrate among the enemy rearguard, tag along quietly for a while – and then suddenly reveal their true identity with the merry rattle of machine-gun fire! Any number of prisoners had been rounded up in this way.

Nevertheless, the parameter of instability at the highest level of politico-strategic control, which so often affected the fortunes of DAK, can here be observed in operation – and operating, too, in the most deleterious fashion. If Rommel may be pardoned, or at least allowed a large plea in mitigation, for wanting to dash to Cairo as he had dashed to the wire, by what military rationale did Hitler and the great staff minds of OKH and OKW grant him permission to do so – short of armour, short of men, with a job lot of transport, out-running his air cover and extending his over-long supply lines with every mile he marched towards the Delta? Yet authority *was* granted, and in that sense the *Führer* and his High Command were as committed as Rommel to his advance-without-security. Nevertheless, having so committed themselves, and having allowed their Field Marshal to race into the distance, they fail – as will be seen – to sustain him with the material support implicit in their *Vorwärts*! The decision of the Axis leaders to allow their African army to cross the Egyptian frontier was in fact the beginning of the end for the Afrika Korps. Surviving by quality rather than quantity, and by never quite being defeated, it would always, hereafter, lack the strength for a decisive blow. Much of the travail it would undergo must be laid at the door of its masters in Germany.

And those masters had abundant evidence to tell them that American supplies were now flowing to the Middle East and must increase in volume. It needed no *Schwarze Kapelle* or other spy ring in the White House, reporting to them that the capture of Tobruk had had a fatal consequence (the immediate hand-over by Roosevelt of the 300 Sherman tanks), for them to realise that 8th Army was not finished and must be expected to grow. Indeed, the simple and significant fact is that even after its defeat at Tobruk 8th Army could call on more men, more tanks, more guns, more aircraft, more reserves and more supplies than Rommel. His advance looked insecure both in terms of the support he might expect from Germany and Italy and the scale of opposition that might be presumed as he drew close to the Delta.

But it took time before the potential weight of opposition could register. The British had distracting problems. Until they had fallen back to Alamein there was nowhere for their infantry divisions to find a safe lodgement. Their armour, though statistically considerable, was mechanically exhausted, or in the hands of composite units, or in workshops and depots and convoys. Their artillery was disorganised. But the main disorganisation was at the top and middle levels of command. After Tobruk fell it was not until Auchinleck took over personally – and then not immediately – that some kind of rationale emerged and the British established a semblance of order and control. 'Rommel was to show, once again, by his lightning advance to El Alamein, that there were circumstances in which mobility alone, compounding the confusion "on the other side of the hill", could be decisive in its own right.'*

The 'loosely knit' character of 8th Army during this phase of defeat and recovery made its commanders at the time (and most subsequent historians) feel that in the forward areas it presented at first merely a thin red line. From the viewpoint of the Afrika Korps the situation was very different. We may take as a test-date 26 June, the day when the *Panzerarmee*'s eastward drive brought it up against the areas of resistance which Ritchie and Gott were cobbling together in and around Mersa Matruh. That morning the tank strength of DAK was about 60 (with 40 odd of the feeble Italian tanks in *Littorio*). The British had some 155 cruisers at the front plus 19 infantry tanks – with nearly 50 Grants still in action. Matruh was garrisoned by 10 Indian Division and the headquarters of 10 Corps. At Gerawla, a few miles to the east, were the two remaining brigades of 50 Division. Due south, on the escarpment at Minquar Quaim, lay the refreshed New Zealand Division, and further south and west spread the two brigades of 1 Armoured Division, 4 and 22, with 7 Motor Brigade covering the open desert flank. DAK, by contrast, was as comparatively short of infantry as it was of armour. In addition, the Desert Air Force ruled the sky. On the 24th DAK's War Diary notes, 'no sign

* Carver, *op. cit.*, p. 261.

of the *Luftwaffe*', and Caccia-Dominioni observes that bombing during the night of the 25th–26th was 'hell'. Valuable supplies, perhaps for ten days, had been picked up in Tobruk – where, as elsewhere, British demolition had some effect – and *Panzerarmee* noted that 500 tons of fuel and 930 of food were seized at Capuzzo. But incessant air attack on the lines of communication was a sinister omen. The Afrika Korps could hardly expect a walk-over.

Though Auchinleck had in fact relieved Ritchie on the 25th, since it was evident that the new fluid situation was beyond his capacity, the immediate effect of personal control by the Commander-in-Chief was, if anything, even more deliquescent. The result of his firm decision not to allow an investment of Matruh, combined with his declared policy 'to keep the 8th Army in being', tended to make his subordinates look over their shoulders and, rather than fight today, prefer withdrawal and the hope of fighting some other day. Since Matruh was in any case only thinly mined to the west and south, the units of 8th Army were prepared neither materially nor psychologically when, late on 26 June, the *Panzerarmee* attacked.

It should have mattered greatly, but in such a situation it mattered little that von Mellenthin's intelligence was astray. (The New Zealand Division, for example, had been placed in Matruh instead of at Minquar Quaim.) By the evening of the 26th 90 Light was through the western minefields, and next morning 21 Panzer followed by *Littorio* began to push east below the Minquar Quaim escarpment while 15 Panzer took on 1 Armoured Division to the south. In theory Afrika Korps was now at risk. The New Zealanders were in a strong and comfortable position. Against their anvil 21 Panzer should have been hammered, for 15 Panzer could not break through to its aid while 90 Light – not much over 1,600 men – was out of touch and itself pre-occupied by the Matruh garrison. But another British failure of nerve or judgement occurred. During the evening of the 27th Gott ordered 13 Corps – 1 Armoured and 5 Indian Divisions – to break away and fall back to Fuka, while the New Zealanders were left without clear instructions, fighting their way out during the night in an epic charge through 21 Panzer's leaguer. By the 28th all the desert wasteland as far as Alamein had the air of a disturbed ant-heap, and early that morning 90 Light, supported by a Reconnaissance Regiment and *Kampstaffel* Kiel, had penetrated to the *enceinte* of Mersa Matruh.

The gains were enormous. Apart from supply-dumps saved from burning, and 40 tanks (presumably in workshops), Rommel calculated that the *matériel* captured was enough to equip a division. The struggle had been too open, and *Panzerarmee* too stretched, for a large haul of prisoners, but 600 were taken in spite of the determined break-out of the garrison. Matruh was the last unqualified victory of the Afrika Korps. Rommel, however, was in no mood to halt for celebration – he could, indeed, only hope to succeed by maintaining a forward momentum. So the advance continued under a hard master who felt no sympathy for the yearnings expressed in the War Diary of 90 Light – 'to have a swim in the sea, and to sleep its fill after the heavy fighting for Mersa Matruh and all the hardships of the preceding days'.

A climax impended. Either Auchinleck must carry his policy of 'an army in being' to its logical conclusion and extract his troops from Egypt, whether up the Nile or into Palestine, or sooner or later an action must be fought which would indicate to both sides that a decision had been reached. Though it was perhaps more evident to Rommel than to Auchinleck at the time, most military students have subsequently judged that this moment of truth occurred on 1 July. Two days later Rommel wrote to his wife, 'resistance is too great and our strength exhausted'. Von Mellenthin's feeling was that 'we had just failed'. Nevertheless, the vultures had assembled: Mussolini, Cavallero (now a Marshal) and von Rintelen all flew over on the 29th to be in at the death of 8th Army, but the Duce was not going to ride his white horse into Cairo.

Gazala and the return to Tobruk had been for the Afrika Korps a kind of equivalent of the return by their fathers to the Old Front Line during the great advance in the spring of 1918. They knew the terrain: even ammunition was waiting for them (as is recorded) where they had stored it in 1941. But this battleground east of the Egyptian frontier was *terra incognita*. Short of time, Rommel risked a conflict without the careful reconnaissance that was mandatory – a precaution about which DAK was normally so skilful and so professional. The critical action of 1 July was therefore fought in ignorance of the ground. Moreover, haste produced a repetition of the intelligence failure at Gazala and Mersa Matruh, for the location and the character of 8th Army's units were miscalculated.

In the 'box' defences running from the Mediterranean shore around the immortal rail-halt of El Alamein von Mellenthin had placed the remnants of 50 Division instead of, as it turned out, an alert force of South Africans. 1 Armoured Division was located far to the south of the Ruweisat Ridge (along with – correctly – the New Zealanders and 5 Indian Division). In fact the British were strong in armour outside the Alamein Box – and von Mellenthin had made one further oversight which, in the event, was to prove disastrous.

Rommel's final plan was for his favourite manoeuvre – the bomb-burst. The Afrika Korps was first to make a breach between the Alamein Box and the Ruweisat Ridge. While the Italians (now about 5,000 riflemen) held the gap 90 Light would swing north and cut the coastal road behind the Alamein garrison, (the Matruh technique), and the two panzer divisions would hurtle southwards to take the New Zealanders and Indians from the rear. Rommel's colour-pencil sketches on a map could make such a plan seem vibrant and dramatic. In perspective, one remarks that 55 German and 30 Italian tanks, plus 500 odd motorised infantry in the panzer divisions and about 1,000 in 90 Light, were the executants for this elaborate enterprise – and few had been out of battle or slept more than two or three nights in one place since the beginning of VENEZIA.

Not surprisingly, the avoidable occurred and the unexpected caused disruption. The panzer divisions got entangled during the night of the 30th, 90 Light hit instead of missing the Alamein Box, and because of a late start and confusion DAK found itself advancing into the morning sun and concentrated artillery fire. 90 Light was saved by a dust storm, but when visibility improved in the early afternoon not even Rommel's presence could prevent it breaking as the *Trommelfeuer* was renewed. This is one of the rare occasions when even German sources use the word 'panic' of the Afrika Korps. And worse was to come. As the panzer divisions tried to swing south during the morning they discovered just to the west of the Ruweisat Ridge a wholly unsuspected defended locality in the Deir el Shein depression. Here 18 Indian Brigade, fresh from Iraq, with 23 field guns from three different regiments and 16 6-pounder anti-tank guns which their users had only possessed for a fortnight, held out until the evening in one of the most remarkable actions of the campaign. The panzers had been stopped in their tracks long enough for the British armour to re-group and counter-attack. The great bomb-burst had proved to be a squib. By nightfall DAK could only count 37 tanks. The Suez Canal, which Mussolini had set as the limit for Rommel's advance, now looked very far away.

For the rest of the month operations continued almost without respite, their arrow-heads, zigzags or blunt short thrusts making a complicated arabesque which threw its pattern over the whole 40-mile gap between Alamein and the Qattara wilderness. It was a broken terrain, this battle-ground so unfamiliar to the Afrika Korps; here was a safe, hard tank-run, there an unpredictable patch of powdery sand. Small lifts of ground and even the occasional depression had a disproportionate tactical value, and both sides soon discovered that dominating all was the spine whose east-west dorsal bisected the front – the blood-soaked promontory of the Ruweisat Ridge. The conflict during these weeks was between a *Panzerarmee* that had fought to the finish and an 8th Army that was seeking to make a fresh start. Auchinleck, in other words, began to pick up the initiative which in any important sense had dropped on 1 July from Rommel's hands.

All the same, it is an astonishing fact that when August came the Afrika Korps and its dwindling Italian allies were still in contention at approximately the same place. The transfusion of life-blood into 8th Army continued steadily, and the more rapidly since base and front line had drawn so close together. 9 Australian Division arrived at the beginning of the month, fit and refreshed after its garrison duties in Syria. The fighters and bombers of the Desert Air Force had a virtual monopoly. The nerve of those behind the British lines was certainly unsteady – the famous 'Ash Wednesday', the reported intention of the Fleet to abandon Alexandria, the evacuations, the rumours, the back-biting have an unsavoury flavour when contrasted with the realities of the *Panzerarmee*'s capability. And the many accounts by his country-men of Auchinleck's resolute and single-minded conduct of the July battles must be qualified by the documented reports in Commonwealth Official Histories – both Australian and New Zealand – which reveal men like Mors-head expressing views well summarised in a letter to Freyberg by the New Zealand General Inglis on 11 July: 'Information from aloft is scanty and late. I get most of ours personally from Gott, and they seem to leave him a bit vague. . . . I feel very much that we need a commander who will make a firm plan. . . .' All the same, Auchinleck's personal direction of the Army, whatever its limitations, was an immense additional strength, as Rommel himself generously registered in his *Papers*. The feeling in Cairo may have been faint-hearted, but at the front, in weight and leadership, the British in July were winners – on paper.

The *Panzerarmee*'s existence was now hand-to-mouth. A measure of rein-forcement continued. By 5 July 2,000 Germans had been flown from Crete to Tobruk, and the leading elements of 164 Light Afrika Division began to arrive during the month. (A disadvantage, however, was the need to use aircraft to protect the Cretan route, thus cutting the numbers available for Egypt. On 3 July, for example, Allied airmen made 900 sorties in relation to the battle, four times as many as the *Luftwaffe*. When several Stuka attacks were made next day on the New Zealanders, it is significant that DAK's morale was lifted by the unusual spectacle.) Tanks also dribbled in: after intensive fighting DAK could still muster 42 and the Italians 50. But the Italian infantry was ground to powder, and though Cavallero promised the first-rate parachute division, *Folgore*, to be followed by *Pistoia* and *Friuli*, in the Roman way these would not arrive in a rush. Yet Auchinleck's broad strategy in July, which Rommel's lack of offensive power left him unable to prevent, was to concentrate on the weaker links in the Axis chain and destroy the Italian units remorselessly.

Auchinleck could call the tune. By the 7th he had drawn DAK down to the south by a genuine but abortive attempt to push round the right flank of the *Panzerarmee*. He was well primed by ULTRA about Rommel's straitened supplies and could profit by making him use up fuel. He therefore set up an operation in the north, for 0330 on the 10th, whereby the Australian and South African Divisions from the Alamein Box were to eliminate *Sabratha* and *Trento*. This would bring DAK north on the run. The result on the 10th was disastrous for the Axis army – but at least it lacked humiliation. That had already occurred.

'In their varied experiences from Greece to Trieste the New Zealanders saw many odd incidents, but rarely one so entertaining and instructive as the enemy's full-scale attack on the empty Kaponga Box on 9 July.'* The Kiwis' Official Historian is describing an extraordinary episode during which, under Rommel's express and reiterated orders, 21 Panzer and *Littorio*, supported by Stukas and heavy artillery, carried out a copybook attack against an empty patch of desert which had been occupied but evacuated by a New Zealand Brigade. (DAK HQ had in fact argued, on the evidence of patrol reports, that the 'stronghold' was undefended.) So far in the desert campaign it is the British who have been mainly castigated for their follies. It is just, therefore, to register the most unsoldierly of all the actions of the Afrika Korps – the supreme irony being that although Rommel (as has been seen) had already checked Auchinleck's effort to outflank him in the south, he was convinced that the 'fall' of this 'stronghold' constituted his culminating stroke. Rommel was a man of mercurial temperament, prone to off-the-cuff decision and sudden intensities of belief. In this respect the Kaponga Box was his masterpiece. (There is another ironic footnote. The New Zealanders thought the affair was merely a 'cosmetic' attack by vainglorious Italians against a position known to be unmanned.)

If Auchinleck had planned (which he didn't) to use the vacated Kaponga Box as a deceptive lure he could not have had a greater success, for Rommel, thinking that he had found a gap, began probing eastwards with 90 Light and the Reconnaissance Units in the hope of rounding the British left flank in the old style of Bir Hacheim. During the afternoon of the 9th he met von Bismarck, to discuss how exploitation by 21 Panzer could 'bring about the fall of the Alamein line'. Instead, at about 0500 next morning he was roused by the thump of *Trommelfeuer* in the north. News soon followed that an attack from the Alamein Box had shattered *Sabratha*.

The writing on the wall was clearly legible. The Australians and South Africans, attacking respectively the useful features of Tel el Eisa and Tel el Makh Khad (just to the west of El Alamein and south of the coastal road) had indeed put to flight an indifferent Italian formation and broken into its gun line. Only 'panic stations' brought some stability. Von Mellenthin had to scrape together a battle group from *Panzerarmee* headquarters and the newly arrived 382 Regiment of 164 Division, which was in process of flying in from Crete. Rommel immediately abandoned his plans for an out-flanking manoeuvre (not to be renewed until the end of August), and rushed to the northern front with his *Kampstaffel* and a task force from 15 Panzer. But savage counter-

---

* Scoullar, *op. cit.*, p. 199.

attacks during the next few days produced no more than the decimation of *Trieste*, and Rommel described in his *Papers* how 'I was compelled to order every last German soldier out of his tent or rest camp up to the front, for, in face of the virtual default of a large proportion of our Italian fighting power, the situation was beginning to take on crisis proportions.'

Here was a promising recipe for the British. Hard blows carefully aimed at the Italians, de-synchronised over different parts of the front, and delivered by the most ardent elements now in 8th Army, the Australians and New Zealanders, would have a cumulative effect which ought to be decisive if, as at Tel el Eisa, they were supported by artillery at last used *en masse*. Tel el Eisa had shown how, by skilful use of the initiative, Auchinleck could force Rommel into switching the Afrika Korps pell-mell across the whole front to rescue their crumbling allies, thus wasting precious fuel and making it impossible to prepare and mount a full-scale and properly organised assault by *Panzerarmee*. But there was another 'if'. In the open country to the south where, unlike the crowded acres by the coast, there was a certain room for manoeuvre, decisive results could only be expected if the British armour displayed the same *élan* as the Commonwealth infantry. For the remainder of the July operations – now generally termed First Alamein – Auchinleck would discover that the armour was in fact the Achilles' heel of his army.

If this was not already evident, the truth became manifest in the course of successive attempts by Auchinleck (the second under strong pressure from Churchill) to make a breakthrough along the Ruweisat Ridge* and start the pendulum swinging, once again, to the west. The first attempt, made during the night of 14 July by one Indian and two New Zealand brigades, was a sensible continuation of the policy whereby Auchinleck struck left-right-left like an adept boxer. The immediate object, once again, was the Italians, for *Brescia* and *Pavia* guarded the Ridge. Before the New Zealanders, so able in a night assault, *Brescia* and *Pavia* melted. In the advance, however, a handful of tanks from 8 Panzer Regiment and a few German infantry posts were overlooked. At dawn the panzers stirred, the panzergrenadiers cut off the New Zealanders' anti-tank guns, and by a combination of apathy, incompetence and failure of communication 22 Armoured Brigade, which should have been up with the assault troops at daylight, failed to appear. With no difficulty, therefore, the New Zealanders (defenceless against armour), were killed or captured. By the afternoon Rommel, as usual, had responded to the threat with constructive energy, sending in Nehring with elements from the whole DAK. They engulfed 4 New Zealand Brigade and recovered the western prow of the

---

* The Ridge runs east–west for several miles. In the main July battles the British held the eastern end and their attacks were aimed at the recovery of the western end from *Panzerarmee*.

Ridge. When the struggle guttered away on the evening of the 16th 2 New Zealand Division had lost 1,400 men and its confidence in the armour was at a nadir.

There was no excuse for such a situation in July 1942. British palliatives like 'all of us now are tired' carry no weight, for the panzer regiments of the Afrika Korps had fought as hard and as long as their opponents. (The sickness ratio of DAK, from jaundice, gastro-enteritis and other desert ailments, was now running high.) Their conditions of food and welfare had certainly not been better. If they had a superiority, it had almost always been in skill and equipment, not in numbers. Yet after Rommel took disciplinary action over a few of his panzer commanders in the early days of the campaign, there is nothing in the whole record of the Afrika Korps to compare with the abandonment of the New Zealanders, naked before an armoured attack, in the opening stages of this first Ruweisat battle. The Korps was simply too professional for that sort of thing.* And, as the British Official History observed in its comments on First Alamein, 'the German soldier always seemed capable of making one more supreme effort'.

To repeat what has been said before, it was a matter of training and indoctrination, and professional leadership at all levels. There was nothing wrong with the men in 8th Army. Rommel recognised this when he looked at his British and Commonwealth prisoners and when he subsequently wrote about them. The human quality was exceptional on both sides. But whereas in the case of the Afrika Korps one is never – even in a case like *Totensonntag* – affected by a sense of waste, of ardent young lives simply thrown away, until the arrival of Montgomery the record of the British too often haunts one with precisely that intimation of tragedy. 'There was a feeling,' the Official History recalls, 'that as our enterprises seemed to start well and end badly there must be something wrong with the machine somewhere.' There was indeed: and in the second battle of the Ruweisat Ridge a perfect demonstration would be provided.

The fighting between the 14th and 16th had drawn the Afrika Korps into the centre of the Axis line, forming a shield across the western end of the Ridge. Rommel now put DAK on the defensive, for his mood was pessimistic, as he revealed in a long signal to OKW on the 21st which, in effect, said that he could continue to scrape along unambitiously, but that the Italians were a weakening link, the continuing loss of his 'old Africa hands' was disturbing, and the Commonwealth troops and improved British artillery were performing skilfully. He harped, too, on a note which would become more strident as

---

* The Australian Official History does not mince words. 'German armoured formations almost always arrived when most needed, British almost never.'

the weeks passed: the Italians were obtaining a disproportionate amount of shipping space. Either from ULTRA or by tactical intercepts Auchinleck realised that Rommel had relinquished the initiative, and so, instead of continuing his policy of attacking Italians to throw the Germans off balance, on 21 July he went straight for the Afrika Korps, firmly intending to break and pursue a defeated enemy.

This was what Churchill was demanding, and on paper the prospect looked promising. 61 Grants, 81 Crusaders and 31 Stuarts in 1 Armoured Division alone (plus reserves) together with the 150 infantry tanks (6 Matildas and the rest Valentines) of the newly arrived 23 Armoured Brigade made a formidable total by comparison with the 42 German and 50 Italian tanks at the front. (100 panzers were in workshops. Of the 42 panzers available all but six were Mks. III and IV, but of those only eight were the long-gunned Specials.) And since *Panzerarmee* was about to undertake a defensive battle it is worth noting that in Rommel's report to OKW on the 21st he pointed out that half his anti-tank guns and much of his field artillery had disappeared.

A simple plan proved too complicated for 8th Army. During the night of the 21st a brigade of 5 Indian Division attacked due west along the Ridge (faced by 21 Panzer) while 6 New Zealand Brigade came in across the mine-fields somewhat further to the south, making for the El Mreir depression where 15 Panzer lurked. This was the main thrust, and by midnight all three of the New Zealand battalions had penetrated into the depression, over-running infantry posts and destroying tanks with sticky bombs – but not causing panic. From unit after unit situation reports flowed in efficiently to Nehring's command centre at DAK, enabling him to build up a picture. There were resolute men about. The New Zealand battalion had the misfortune to hit 3 Battalion of 115 Regiment, commanded since April by Lieutenant-Colonel Warrelmann; he had been commissioned in 1934 after 13 years in the ranks, and held the German Cross in Gold and two Iron Crosses. Nevertheless, in the early hours of the morning the New Zealanders felt comfortable – subject to the promised arrival of tanks from 22 Armoured Brigade at dawn.

Nehring, however, had been holding his hand. Realising that the struggle in El Mreir was the main threat, he too waited for the dawn as the time to release his armour – the difference being that in DAK's case the armour actually moved, and to an effective plan. It was at 0215 that Nehring ordered 21 Panzer to drive south in three hours' time against the New Zealanders' right flank, while 15 Panzer created a pincer effect by assaulting from the opposite direction. Then there was an ominous lull:

Around the lip of the depression and in positions on its floor German officers and non-commissioned officers of tank, anti-tank, artillery, machine-gun, mortar and infantry units were intent on the time. Their watches showed four o'clock, an hour behind British Army time, a quarter of an hour to zero. They knew approximately where the British forces lay in the depression and they had their guns laid roughly on the area. Five minutes, then ten minutes past the hour. How they watched the minutes. At the quarter, signal and illuminating flares burst into the air and down into the depression poured machine-gun and anti-tank tracer, solid and high-explosive shells and mortar bombs, into the congested mass of men and vehicles, anti-tank guns, machine-guns and carriers. . . . Then, with a flourish of Very signals, the tanks came over the northern rim of the depression, down the slope and into 6 Brigade's positions.*

But there were no British tanks. The pattern of First Ruweisat was repeated; through a mixture of misunderstanding, reluctance, indifference and, it may be supposed, war weariness the support from 22 Armoured Brigade never materialised. At the end of the day the New Zealanders had been wiped out by the concentrated and unimpeded strength of DAK: the casualty return for 6 Brigade sent in to 13 Corps that night reported losses as over 1,000 men, 12 two-pounder and 13 six-pounder guns, 29 carriers and 7 Vickers machine-guns. Meanwhile, with great difficulty, the Indians had reached their objective at the end of the Ridge, only to be compelled to withdraw by a disaster whose combination of courage and ineptitude has often caused it to be compared with the charge at Balaclava.

23 Armoured Brigade disembarked at Suez on 6 July, the forerunner of 8 Armoured Division. Its tanks, as usual, required much treatment in the Base Ordnance Workshops, and even when the last one was handed over on 17 July there was, in truth, a good deal that still required attention. Thus the Brigade had no opportunity to master even the minimal skills of desert warfare before it was assigned a key role in the Second Battle of Ruweisat. In the 8th Army plan, the intention was for the initial two-pronged advance by the Indians and New Zealanders to be followed by a lunge between them, on the part of 23 Armoured Brigade, which would drive an iron wedge into the German defences between Ruweisat and El Mreir. During the early hours of the 22nd, when news from both the flanking attacks was uncertain, and when it was therefore even less certain that the minefield in 23 Brigade's path could be cleared, Gott reviewed the situation at his 13 Corps HQ. He decided to go ahead – but with one important modification. In the original plan the Brigade was to move down the 278 grid line, which would have carried it north of El Mreir. Since it appeared as though the night's events had been squeezing the

---

* Scoullar, *op. cit.*, p. 352.

enemy into this area, Gott laid down a new axis for the Brigade, the 276 grid line which would carry it just south of the depression and into an area more favourable for exploitation.

Wireless communications failed. The vital signal was not received. In consequence, about 8 a.m. two* regiments of the Brigade, 40 RTR and 46 RTR, were observed 'thundering' – a word often used by eye-witnesses – down the original centre line, to be shattered on uncleared mines or, in the disorganisation that followed, by German tank or anti-tank guns. About mid-day the seven Valentines whose crews had gallantly forced them through to the objective were withdrawn, and a count revealed that in four hours two virgin regiments had lost 30 officers, 173 other ranks and, out of an original total of 87, 40 Valentines destroyed and 47 seriously damaged.†

After a final effort to impose his will on the enemy, made in the north on 26 July, Auchinleck now closed down for the summer – one of the chief considerations in his mind being that his troops needed training. The need went deep. This episode of 23 Armoured Brigade, for which the responsibility was shared at many levels, reveals that however desert-weary the men of the Afrika Korps may have been in these last days of July, there was still one mercy: their enemy might, as they recognised, possess all the soldierly qualities, courage, self-sacrifice, endurance, but he had not yet learned how to knit a battle programme together and implement it with a professional's certainty of touch. As each side began to settle down behind a progressively extensive network of minefields, the DAK (if not Rommel) could relax. For the present 8th Army had shot its bolt. Present peace was enough for the panzergrenadier – but the Field Marshal lived in the future.

And the future was drawing relentlessly nearer. The fact was that the Afrika Korps should never have been allowed to break into Egypt: having made its entry, it should have been expelled. Few of the elements necessary for achieving these objectives were missing in 8th Army apart from the essential of effective command and control. But by their very success in striking so far and sticking so firmly Rommel and his men threw up their antibody, for Alan-brooke and Churchill, sensing what was wrong, now initiated that famous series of consultations and conferences about the higher direction of the desert campaigns which led to the replacement of Auchinleck and his sub-stitution, in mid-August, by General Alexander as C-in-C Middle East and Lieutenant-General Montgomery as Commander of the 8th Army.

Nor was life entirely peaceful. It was a cruel summer. Something in the conditions of the Alamein line, as it gradually consolidated into two sets of

---

* The third regiment, 50 RTR had been detached to the Australians at El Alamein.
† More than the whole DAK's armour was thus written off in one profitless enterprise.

parallel defence works, was propitious for the ubiquitous fly – the savage sun, static positions, the adjacent unhealthy Delta. Whatever the reason, the troops on both sides were now suffering from fly-swarms so multitudinous that it was often impossible to raise food to the lips before it became black with intruders. For the Afrika Korps there was a further discomfort: its units were close to and sometimes intermingled with the Italians, whose peasant style of sanitation provided the fly with too frequent a paradise. And this was an extra danger, for at a time and in a theatre where the gastric ailments of the Middle East were eroding the strength of DAK only the strictest sanitary discipline, to which the Italians were strangers, could stave off an epidemic. The same was true for the British: any carelessness and indiscipline bred disease. 'Gippy Tummy' or jaundice were the consequence, and just as frequently men were troubled with the purulent desert sore. Very rapidly the slightest scratch would extend into a wide suppurating circle which might take months to heal, and even then could leave a memorial scar. Like their enemy, many men of DAK walked around with the rough bandages on arm or leg which were the badges of their desert service.

Still, when that most percipient of war correspondents, Alan Moorehead, rounded off *A Year of Battle* with a general analysis of the situation in August 1942 he concluded, 'In the German Army I saw no signs of any breaking in morale. . . . It must be conceded that their morale was higher than ours in the Middle East.' The morale he is talking about is that which derives from having a visible end in sight. The Afrika Korps still knew where it was going: the 8th Army, in Churchill's apt words, was brave but baffled. In part Moorehead ascribed this difference to one of propaganda. 'Where our men in the desert had not seen a newspaper for months, let alone any other reading to divert and encourage their minds, the Afrika Korps were abundantly supplied. Every one of their camps I saw was strewn with recent magazines and pamphlets. They were filled with good action photographs from all sectors of the war. The airmail came in several times a week. There were thousands of radio sets.' And Lily Marlene, the song-bird of the Balkans, the voice that sank a thousand tanks. But she, at least, was common property, there for any man's taking, British or German, like the street-girl whose lilt she wafted nightly across the Mediterranean.

Yet basically the reason was not one of newspapers or nostalgic ditties or regular mail. That sense of corporate identity which the Afrika Korps had so rapidly evolved and so firmly consolidated remained unbroken. Only those who have shared it can understand the feeling of contented fulfilment which arises from being a part of a well-functioning team. The old hands in the Korps had now experienced this satisfaction many times, and the new men could look forward to it. Infantry, panzers, anti-tank guns, signallers, engineers, artillery knew from the realities of action that each could rely on the other. *Brüderschaft continued.* There was little back-biting or distrust within DAK – compared with what prevailed on the other side of the minefields. Above all, faith in the guiding star remained undimmed. Some of his subordinates might grumble, and OKW rightly hint (as happened) that the Field Marshal was too brusque with his officers, but even in that hard summer the confidence of the Afrika Korps was still Rommel's – without reserve.

Rommel, however, was ill – weak in body and mentally distracted. The August letters from himself or his aide, describing to his wife the details of his physical malaise, which are reprinted in Liddell Hart's edition of his *Papers* are only a token representation of the accounts given in his unpublished correspondence or contained in formal reports transmitted to OKW (and known, through ULTRA, to the British). He was always less fit and often more edgy and indecisive than his driving will allowed him to appear. Now his will was losing control over his body. By the end of the month his consultant, Professor Horster of the University of Würzburg, a leading stomach specialist, advised that a Field Marshal who was having fainting fits and suffered from chronic gastric disturbance was unsuitable to command the next operation. Rommel asked OKW to send Guderian in his place, a brilliant choice, but Guderian was under a cloud. So Rommel soldiered on, and in so doing almost certainly preserved for the Afrika Korps that central element of admired and trusted leadership which enabled it to survive its coming tribulations.

During the weeks before he made this decision Rommel was haunted by time. A sinister clock ticked in his head. By about the third week in September, so he and his staff calculated, the great convoys which they knew to be on the way would have discharged at Suez – as they did – immense reinforcements of troops and, probably, weapons of improved design. In the Middle East 10 Indian Division was known to have recovered: 50 British and 1 South African Divisions had been re-built: the enemy air forces were increasingly effective – particularly over the lines of communication, as they, together with the Royal Navy, sank ship after ship. When supplies did arrive the larger proportion went to the least important of the Italians, so that while, for example, *Pistoia*, a division meant only for rearward duties in Libya, crossed with several hundred vehicles at the beginning of August, *Folgore* (a first-class fighting formation) and the German 164 Light had only a few dozen vehicles apiece. Airborne units, they had flown in without heavy equipment. Such lack of rationale increased Rommel's frustration (and did nothing to improve the lot of the Afrika Korps). Rommel, of course, blamed the Italians all along the line, and his *bête-noire* von Rintelen in Rome. He wanted OKW to put Kesselring in charge of the complete supply and reinforcement system for *Panzerarmee*: in his heart, however, he knew this was impossible, for so long as the

Axis held, even notionally, it was impossible for Hitler to insult Mussolini by such a reflection on the competence of *Comando Supremo* and the Italian Navy. The factor of time seemed inescapable, and in spite of the reasonable doubts of his staff Rommel decided that as Hitler's known attitudes made retreat unthinkable he had only one course of action – to strike what must be a final all-or-nothing blow with the Afrika Korps before the British recovery could reach its peak. This, effectively, meant the period of the full moon towards the end of August.

Unfortunately, the lunar timetable was equally obvious to the British. Moreover, at this period ULTRA was reading Rommel's signal traffic with speed and regularity. His fuel problems, his uncertainties and irritations, his health, his order of battle and even the place and date of his coming attack were all known with great accuracy to the small inner group which was allowed access to this authoritative intelligence. The last parameter of frustration was exerting its full force, and Rommel, by contrast, no longer enjoyed the Fellers intercepts or Captain Seebohm's invaluable contributions. In a situation where he himself declared that surprise and speed were the essentials for success, he was about to hurl the Afrika Korps against an enemy already awake and alert.

The point of attack was in any case predictable. Auchinleck and his Deputy Chief of Staff, Dorman Smith, had diagnosed it before Montgomery's arrival removed them from the scene. In a world like that of the desert campaigns, where there was only one open flank, you either hammered away through the hard centre of your opponent's line or swept round the open flank. Rommel is very definite in his comments at this time that he was above all anxious to avoid what he called 'position warfare', which in his view suited the stolid temperament of the British and in which their superiority in weight of metal must tell. This was not the *métier* of his beloved Afrika Korps, whose prime qualities were swift and disciplined manoeuvre, the ability to think and adapt on the move, the sustained drive of unfettered individual leadership. And so, in what was to be its last concerted effort to conquer Africa, he sent DAK round the tip of 8th Army's front, in a great wheel which, in theory, was to carry it through the enemy minefields north of the Qattara Depression and then, in a left hook, beyond the Alam Halfa ridge. By next morning DAK would be some 30 miles from its start-line, around El Hammam on the coastal railway, and 8th Army's divisions in the line would be cut off from their Delta bases. The date proposed was 30 August.

The more one examines the record of the Alam Halfa battle, which Rommel launched during the night of 30/31 August, the more clearly one sees that it was doomed from the start. The parameter of supply was, as usual, adverse. The historic 'Pedestal' convoy, whose relics had struggled through to Malta in the middle of the month, temporarily assured the island's survival and thus enabled attacks by air and sea on the life-line of the Afrika Korps to continue. The tally of Axis sinkings rose: 6 ships in June, 7 in July, 12 in August. Rommel's signals to Kesselring and the German authorities form a crescendo of complaint which intensifies as the date-line for battle approaches. He finally decided to attack on the basis of largely unfulfilled promises, but a Mk. IV could not be driven forward on hope.

The flow of repaired panzers and reinforcements had in fact raised the figures for Afrika Korps (still under Nehring's command) to about 200 including 97 Specials. On the Alam Halfa front 10 Armoured Division (under Gatehouse) had 210 tanks of which 164 were Grants, as well as the whole of a refurbished 23 Armoured Brigade which, with its Valentines, was available near to the Halfa ridge. (British reserves were far more abundant, and more accessible in the handy Egyptian base.) As for men, the arrival of units like *Folgore*, 164 Light and the Ramcke Parachute Brigade was obviously helpful – but not helpful enough, for the parachutists in particular, *Luftwaffe* troops, had loyalties and attitudes far different from those of the true Afrika Korps. They had a characteristic arrogance and self-sufficiency which, for all their fighting qualities, made them uncomfortable partners. Rommel disliked them. 'They keep wanting to be dropped from the sky,' he said to his Chief of Staff, Bayerlein, 'and I keep telling them they'll be dead before they land.'* Caccia-Dominioni has a contemptuous account of the harsh field-punishment inflicted down by Deir el Shein during 21 August on a young parachutist who had ignorantly drawn water without permission. (His company commander, Oberleutnant Trewerl, had survived Rotterdam and Crete.) This admirable Italian writes out of shock: such was not the ethos of the Afrika Korps.

But for DAK, which as usual was to make the main thrust, the most sinister aspect of the impending battle was the fact that, for the first time, the plan of attack was fully comprehended in advance by a general capable of making the correct dispositions to meet it and equipped with sufficient men and equipment. The old idea that Montgomery simply stole a visionary anticipation by Auchinleck and Dorman-Smith that Rommel would strike at Alam Halfa was never credible, and now seems a mere fantasy as we discover how ULTRA, thickened up by other Intelligence, kept him abreast of Rommel's intentions. But for the Afrika Korps on 31 August the really important question was, how had he applied his knowledge to create a system of defence? The fumbling of Cunningham and Ritchie, the stubborn strain in Auchinleck were familiar enough to DAK. What was Montgomery's style?

Bearing away north eastwards from the front line, the ridges of Alam Nayil

---

* Communication from Manfred Rommel to author.

and Alam Halfa formed one flank of a channel leading directly to the Nile and the Canal. The other flank was formed by the Qattara Depression. (Rommel's intentions, if he burst through the channel, are graphically illustrated by the 'bomb-burst' plan he drew on a map of Cairo, which is reproduced opposite page 285 of his *Papers*.) The mouth of the channel was blocked by British minefields now more elaborate than the *Panzerarmee* realised. Montgomery, in effect, converted this channel into a trap.

On Alam Nayil were the New Zealanders, a firm shoulder. On Alam Halfa stood two brigades of the recently arrived 44 Division whose presence seems to have escaped von Mellenthin. In the gap between these infantry localities Montgomery placed 22 Armoured Brigade, with pre-selected, dug-in battle positions and 23 Armoured Brigade on call as a reserve. Thus the northern side of the channel was solid. Its exit was blocked by another fresh formation, 8 Armoured Brigade, while the minefield mouth and the southern side were covered by 7 Armoured Division, now consisting of light mobile troops and motorised infantry. Once it entered the trap, therefore, DAK was exposed to the enemy in whatever direction it might move.

Vigorous air reconnaissance and stepped-up bombing during the last days of August made it plain that the British were alert. Fuel stocks were risible: to the last the news was more of sinkings, and promises from Kesselring and Cavallero, than of tangible deliveries. Rommel was manifestly ill – during the battle he could scarcely get in and out of a tank. His final exchanges of signals with OKW show him as irresolute and pessimistic. Yet when the clearing of minefield gaps began shortly before midnight on the 30th, and the panzers started to advance, it could scarcely be maintained that the programme for the Afrika Korps was unambitious.

The assault was to be made on a broad front. 90 Light, on the left, was to skirt the base of Alam Nayil. Then came the Italians' mobile formation, XX Corps. Then DAK. Finally, covering the flank down to the Qattara Depression, came the seasoned Reconnaissance Units 3 and 33. But the plan gave the Afrika Korps, as spearhead of the attack, what now seems the impossible task of making a night move over difficult and unfamiliar going (including the passage of a large minefield) and being formed up 30 miles to the east by 6 a.m. on the 31st, ready to sweep north to the coast. The shades of Gazala/Bir Hacheim were heavy over Alam Halfa.

Two hours after the clinching sweep of the Afrika Korps was supposed to have started Rommel wanted to stop the offensive – though he was persuaded by Bayerlein not to do so. The optimistic timings had not been maintained. Mines more copious than had been expected, effective delaying tactics by 7 Armoured Division and savage bombing by the light of flares had prevented DAK even from extricating itself from the minefields by dawn. Nehring had been wounded, and von Bismarck killed by a mortar-bomb. So Bayerlein, who temporarily took command of the Afrika Korps, carried on – but with a fatal alteration in his orders. Baulked of his great turning move Rommel decided that at least he should capture Alam Halfa. DAK was therefore instructed to wheel to the north much earlier than had originally been intended, in a 90 degree switch whereby it would head directly for the western end of the Halfa ridge – and the most powerfully defended point on the British front.

The inevitable result is soon described. An unco-ordinated attack by the two panzer divisions early in the afternoon caused the British some initial anxiety, but 22 Armoured Brigade, fighting from positions of its own choice (and stiffened by 23 Armoured Brigade, whose 100 Valentines were now in the line) resisted until nightfall when von Vaerst, who had moved from 15 Panzer to take over DAK, gave the order to withdraw. Great quantities of fuel had been consumed to no purpose: the Italian Corps had been laggard in its supporting advance: the enemy was organised and aggressive. Throughout the day, moreover, the Afrika Korps had endured two new experiences. The first was accurate, concentrated and continuous shelling by the British artillery. The second was 'Party Rally' bombing – the nickname given by the Korps to the groups of aircraft which sailed almost insolently overhead in the perfect formation of pre-war parades at Nuremberg.

The pattern bombing of these daytime formations was continued during the night by relays of planes which attacked accurately by dropping flares and flying in low. The War Diary of the Afrika Korps singles out the night of the 31st and the following nights as unique. There was no rest possible after the long day's battle. The sense of nakedness which comes from being bombed at night in the open produced its own stresses. Soft transport and armour were either destroyed or damaged. In any case the bombing imposed a scale of dispersal which prevented the companionship and ease of re-supply possible in the normal night-time leaguer.

There was no change on the morrow. 21 Panzer was stuck for lack of fuel. 15 Panzer, trying to edge round the eastern flank of 22 Armoured Brigade, was threatened by 8 Armoured Brigade but easily held off and taught a lesson to this tyro unit by setting up a routine anti-tank screen. Basically the story of 1 September and the following night is one of continuous bombardment. The Party Rallies floated overhead remorselessly – and Rommel noted how much damage was caused by stone splinters broadcast by the bombing: seven officers were killed on the staff of the Afrika Korps. To one watching like the author from the Alam Halfa ridge it seemed as though the Afrika Korps huddled below and mutely absorbing such punishment had, for the first time, truly lost the initiative. As the bombs and shells flashed and the great clouds of smoke and dust bellied up, there was something curiously passive about DAK. But

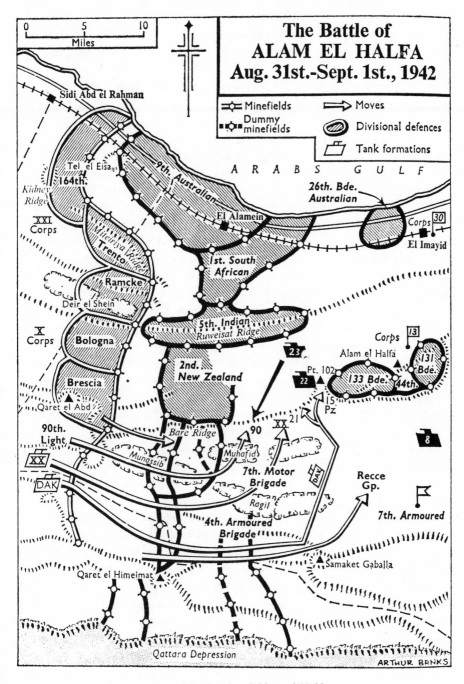

MAP 5   The battle of Alam el Halfa

then, as Heinz Werner Schmidt, now with 90 Light, observes: 'The truth of the matter is that our panzers had literally lost their spirit.'

Here was the decisive factor. On the evening of 1 September *Panzerarmee* had only enough petrol left for one day's operations – barely enough for a retreat, and far too little for aggressive mobile warfare. (Of the four remaining ships due to arrive with fuel the *Picci Fassio* was sunk on the 2nd, the *Bianchi* and *Padenna* on the 4th, when *Sportivo* alone reached Tobruk, bringing too little too late.) On the morning of the 2nd, therefore, Rommel gave orders for a withdrawal, setting out his reasons in a signal to OKW which listed all the points already noted – the unexpected delays in the minefields, the early disorganisation, the lack of fuel and the round-the-clock bombing. For the Afrika Korps it was a final stroke of bad luck that Montgomery refused to pursue.

Much ill-informed criticism has been made of this decision. Why did not Montgomery 'set the armour loose', as some at the time and many subsequently considered to be militarily correct? To any student of the techniques which Rommel and the Afrika Korps had evolved and refined it will be plain that, had this happened, DAK would have fallen back on the minefields and formed a protective hedgehog with its 88s, 50 mm *Pak*, the good Russian anti-tank guns now in service, and the murderous Mk. IV Specials of which a substantial number survived. 8th Army was denied the possibility of out-flanking by the Qattara Depression. Some sort of head-on conflict in the old style must have materialised. Of the three armoured brigades available 8 was totally ignorant of desert warfare, 23 consisted of the reinforced survivors from an almost total disaster, and only 22 had maturity – but it was battle-weary, and it is to be doubted whether it had grown out of all the bad old ways, though it had fought a most able defensive action on the 31st.

Montgomery was wise to avoid the likelihood of another Cauldron, and the Afrika Korps was unlucky, after what was an open defeat, to lose the opportunity for what must surely have been a certain revenge. By an odd chance the one opportunity offered for a riposte was grasped by the Italians, who during the night of 3 September took the weight of an attempt to close the minefield gaps before the Afrika Korps could complete its retirement. The attack was a poorly co-ordinated effort by 5 New Zealand Brigade, whose spirit and skill took them to and beyond their objective, and the raw 132 Brigade from 44 Division whose only achievement was its own confusion. This ill-judged effort – the past re-asserting itself – made no significant impact on *Panzerarmee*'s movements, and is brushed aside by Rommel in his *Papers*. Yet the casualties – 275 New Zealanders and 697 from 132 Brigade – represent almost exactly half 8th Army's total for the whole Alam Halfa battle.

By 6 September the Axis troops were comfortably established in and behind the most westerly of the three British minefields which had caused such embarrassment. If the hail of fire which the ordinary soldier in DAK had just experienced did not bring the truth home to him, certainly Rommel, his staff and his commanders were aware that they had merely been granted a breathing-space. And next time would be different.

9

Decision at Alamein

'Enemy situation unchanged.'
Evening report of *Panzerarmee* to OKH, 23 October 1942

The Afrika Korps was perhaps never at a greater disadvantage than when the desert darkness was violated, during the night of 23 October, by the famous cannonade which preceded the final battle of Alamein. Rommel's increasing fear of what he called 'position warfare' was principally due to his knowledge that in this mode of fighting – the war of solid and static defences, of prolonged and expensive artillery duels – the qualities of his mature DAK would have the least opportunity to flower. Fluid manoeuvre, effective speed of thought, tested tanks and superior crews, the finger-tip-feel which so many of his commanders now possessed had paid a whole series of dividends, but once the two sides settled down after Alam Halfa and began to establish a kind of Western Front between the sea and Qattara he felt about his most precious capital, the skill of the Afrika Korps in mobile operations, as did Milton about his eyes:

> '. . . and that one talent which is death to hide
> Lodg'd with me useless.'

In any case, the Field Marshal was not long with the *Panzerarmee*. He needed to be rested physically and psychologically. For a week or two, however, he continued to work energetically – and courageously, making it clear in his Alam Halfa after-battle report to OKW and *Comando Supremo* that 'the German troops of the Panzer Army Africa, who are bearing the brunt of the war in Africa against the finest troops of the British Empire, must be provided with an uninterrupted flow of the supplies essential for life and battle. . . . Failing this, the continued successful maintenance of the African theatre of war will be impossible. . . .'* But the Axis had allowed Malta a new lease of life, and with increasing intensity right up to 23 October the destruction of the shipping-lines continued. Fuel, ammunition, armour, artillery, food were all short to a dangerous degree, and as the old hands of DAK lined up at sick parade with their various desert ailments there seemed no prospect of further reinforcement by competent German soldiers. 22 Air Landing Division, pulled out from long service in Russia for transfer to Africa, was sent instead to Crete.

The classic situation for an army in such straits is withdrawal, but for the *Panzerarmee* this was both unthinkable and impracticable. Hitler, not to speak of Mussolini, would never have sanctioned retirement, and in any case (as was painfully obvious after the battle had been lost) the transport available was inadequate for an orderly extrication of the Italian infantry divisions. To stand and prepare for the worst was the only alternative. In this, at least, the Afrika Korps was fortunate, for until 1940, it will be recalled, Rommel had been an infantryman. He was not ignorant of siege tactics and fortress defences, the great continental tradition running back for centuries. Moreover, he was by nature interested in and inventive of mechanical devices (as Normandy in 1944 would illustrate). The arrangements which he put in hand for the protection of the Axis front before his departure to Germany were therefore both sensible and, within the limits of the material available, remarkably effective. There was not enough barbed wire to festoon the 40-odd miles of sand, ridge and depression, but with half a million mines, bulked at danger-points and interconnected by lateral fields, an explosive carpet was laid to a depth ranging between two to four miles. And within these main belts random mixtures of booby-traps and anti-personnel mines were used to create man-killing zones suitably nick-named 'the Devil's gardens'. Such defensive works, calling for ingenuity, discipline and intensive labour, suited the German temperament: the fathers of the Afrika Korps had been notable experts in Flanders. And so, by 23 October, 'the Devil's garden' might well have been applied to the whole of the sinister barrier which 8th Army must seek to penetrate.

A minefield of such depth and scope presents a formidable challenge to the attacker, particularly when, as at Alamein, both flanks are denied by impassable obstacles. The difficulty is to maintain impetus through a breach, since the process of clearing tracks through the field under fire is inevitably slow, and the problem of the assault troops is how to reach the other side before an alerted enemy has been able to gather his reserves and block the exit. At Tobruk the Afrika Korps had only faced a miniscule version of the conundrum

---

* When von Mellenthin returned to Germany on 9 September Rommel sent with him a personal message to the Chief of the General Staff which stated that if supplies did not arrive 'despite its bravery the *Panzerarmee* will sooner or later suffer the fate of the Halfaya garrison'.

set by the *Panzerarmee*'s defences at Alamein. The new spirit of confident professionalism which Montgomery was now injecting into 8th Army can be observed in every aspect of his planning, though his armchair critics (who do not refer to the duration of CRUSADER) complain that his victory took too long and therefore his plan was bad. But the truth is that any battle for a break-through at Alamein was bound to be long and hard. However tired and weak, the Afrika Korps behind an extensive Devil's garden was not to be easily brushed aside.

Since the inevitability of his attack was obvious, Montgomery sought to diminish the difficulty of a breakthrough by achieving surprise – surprise about the date, the time, and the place. A fully orchestrated deception pro-gramme, more elaborate than that for CRUSADER, aimed at persuading his enemy that the main effort would be made in the south – all the tricks being employed of dummy vehicles, mimic pipelines, spurious radio traffic. This had some effect, though perhaps less than has been trumpeted. There is no doubt that even before 23 October an attack was expected by *Panzerarmee* – the day on which a visiting staff officer from OKW announced that his masters saw no likelihood of a British offensive for the time being! But in truth, the scale of preparation and the precise plans for the largest assault so far mounted in North Africa were mainly disguised from the opposition.

Certainly the weight and ferocity of the opening barrage created surprise. The Afrika Korps had experienced concentrated fire from a few artillery regiments during the July battles, but the technical efficiency, the great extent and the lavish fire-plan of the Alamein bombardment were of a different order, menacing in their assurance and hinting at unlimited resources. Taking the best advice, during September and October Montgomery integrated his abundant artillery into a single, flexible weapon. This was new in Africa. For the first time, too, DAK was faced by an army meticulously trained. Its morale was also high, but so it had been on the eve of CRUSADER. The extra factor was Montgomery's searching insistence on specific unit training for individual tasks. Minefield clearance, for example, was intensively practised at far greater levels of efficiency. 8th Army was not yet a unified professional team to the same degree as the Afrika Korps, but it was moving fast on the right road. The clarity and confidence of Montgomery's orders and expositions, filtering down to the lowest rank, helped to bond 8th Army together while diminishing the vagueness which encourages inefficiency.

Nor was there anything vague about the plan of attack. Montgomery always intended to feint in the south – where a major breakthrough would have been difficult to exploit – and to crack the mined carapace of the *Panzer-armee* somewhat north of centre. At first Operation LIGHTFOOT envisaged a passage of the British armour right through the minefields into open country along the Rahman track by Tel el Aqaquir. But by 6 October Montgomery grasped that this formidable task was beyond his army's capacity. (His armoured commanders disliked it: the scarred minds of men like Morshead, Pienaar and Freyberg assumed that once again the armour would be laggard.) By a simple but vital adjustment, therefore, he decided that on reaching the far side of the minefields his tanks would stand fast, to hold off the predictable counter-attacks while his infantry divisions eliminated the Axis troops still within the Devil's garden. This was the blueprint on which the opening stages of Alamein were fought, and at times during the battle even this limited objective was made to seem unattainable by the astonishing resistance of the Afrika Korps.

But though the amplitude and intricacy of the Devil's garden to some extent made up for the fact that in every department of war – generalship, equipment, munitions, reserves and other resources – 8th Army was now a transformed opponent, Rommel was right to christen the coming conflict 'The battle without hope'. If some of Montgomery's commanders themselves began to lose hope during the dog-fight, he himself was wiser in never abandoning his belief that the enemy must ultimately crack. The Italian element in the *Panzerarmee* was large but lightweight. It was the Afrika Korps that mattered, and Montgomery, fed by his intelligence staff and by ULTRA information which, at this stage, was providing a full and detailed picture of the *Panzerarmee*'s order of battle, knew that the Germans were thin on the ground.

This was indeed the case. In the whole *Panzerarmee* there were not many more than 50,000 German troops – including 164 Light Division and Ramcke's parachutists. Moreover, though the minefield barrier was wide and deep, two factors compelled Rommel to dissipate his Germans in disconnected groups. The 54,000 Italians in the line must be expected to buckle and break under pressure. German units were therefore sandwiched among their allies to make instant counter-attacks at a point of penetration, and 'plug the gap'. Similar considerations caused Rommel to mix his mobile reserve, the two panzer divisions of DAK, with *Littorio* and *Ariete*. But it was the second factor – the perennial shortage of fuel – which drove him to divide the reserve into two, placing 15 Panzer and *Littorio* behind the northern sector of the front and 21 Panzer with *Ariete* in the south. For *amour propre* it was arranged that orders should be given to both the German and Italian armoured commanders – a curious scheme which worked in practice, since it was the DAK man on the spot who took the decisions. (Montgomery, as will be seen, also used this unworkmanlike method at the time of the 'left hook' at Mareth when he sent orders simultaneously to Freyberg and Horrocks.) The consequence of these second-class but unavoidable solutions was to make it far more difficult, once battle was joined, for the Afrika Korps to be used *en masse*. 'For their defence girdle (to abuse the metaphor of Brigadier Williams, Montgomery's senior Intelligence officer) the German command had fashioned a corset strengthened with German whalebone.'*

From north to south – from the sea to Qattara – the detailed layout was as follows: XXI Corps (164 Light, *Trento, Bologna,* plus two Ramcke battalions) flanked by X Corps (*Brescia, Pavia, Folgore,* plus two Ramcke battalions) with the inevitable Reconnaissance Unit 33 covering the right of the line. 15 Panzer and *Littorio* lay behind XXI Corps and 21 Panzer, with *Ariete,* behind X Corps. The only reserve in depth was represented by 90 Light and *Trieste,* held back along the coast at Daba and Fuka. 288 Special Force (which had been trained for operations in Persia, and usually worked with 90 Light – and which Heinz Werner Schmidt joined on his return from leave) was stationed at Matruh and never got drawn into the battle.† 77,000 Italian troops elsewhere in North Africa were a mere irrelevance.

If the tactical dispositions of the *Panzerarmee* left much to be desired, the comparative equipment states were even more ominous. Guns must matter most at Alamein, and 8th Army's total of field and medium weapons had now risen to 908: the Germans had rather over 200, plus 260–300 Italian pieces. The British anti-tank gun figure was 1,451 (of which – an index of the reinforcement since Gazala – no fewer than 849 were six-pounders). In August Rommel's original Flak Regiment 135 was strengthened by the arrival of Flak Regiment 102 and the HQ of 19 Flak Division, but even so, for the front line itself, there were only 86 88 mms available on 23 October: 68 of the good 76 mm and 290 of the 50 mm made up the total. Montgomery had around 1,000 tanks – including the recently arrived Shermans. Of the 500-odd tanks in *Panzerarmee* less than half were German: of these, divided fairly equally between the two panzer divisions, 88 were Mk. III Specials and 30 Mk. IV Specials. As 8th Army's muster was 195,000 men, against the combined Axis figures of 104,000, it will be seen that in purely quantitative terms the overall superiority of the British was approximately two to one.

But it is generalship that injects quality, and for the Afrika Korps it was certainly a tragedy that on the eve of its supreme battle the dynamic, ubiquitous, stimulating Rommel of the old days was not at its head. All the defensive arrangements so far outlined had either been put in hand by him, or prescribed, before he departed, but when at last he flew back to Germany for medical treatment, on 23 September, the 'Russians' took over from the 'Africans'. General Stumme, the new commander of the *Panzerarmee,* had directed an

---

* Barton Maughan, *op. cit.,* p. 655.

† Reinforcements for this unit during September comprised ex-Merchant Navy seamen and Germans who had served in the French Foreign Legion. Its role was presumably to deal with British raids from inland or from the sea – there had been several abortive attempts.

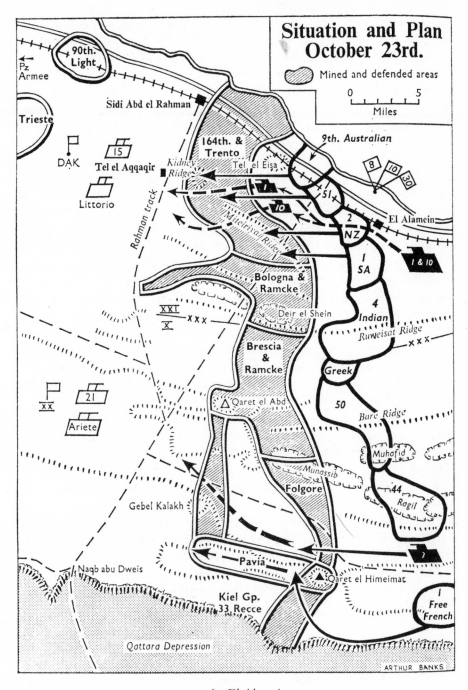

Situation and Plan
October 23rd.

Mined and defended areas

0   5
Miles

MAP 6   El Alamein

armoured corps in Russia and previously in Greece. Von Thoma, who was given the Afrika Korps, also came from the Russian front – so many months after his first negative reconnaissance of the African shores. Both were sound soldiers, practised in war, but for DAK the timing of their arrival was disconcerting. New men mean new ideas, new methods, new disciplines, new staffs: the old 'Africans' were bound to feel 'dicky on their perches', as Montgomery used to say.

Rommel was determined to profit by his absence, and to bring home to the Axis authorities the reality behind his pessimistic signals from the front. His talks *en route* with Cavallero and Mussolini elicited promises of men and supplies to build a road behind the front and improve the coastal railway: neither materialised. When he reached Hitler's headquarters, moreover, the atmosphere was not propitious, for on 24 September the *Führer* had dismissed the Chief of the General Staff, Halder, because of his pessimism about Stalingrad and the Caucasus. This was no time for defeatism. Surprisingly, Rommel was received amicably, with promises of *Nebelwerfers* (the multiple rocket-projectors), Tiger tanks and the special *Siebelfahren* ferries for work on the Mediterranean crossing. But all this was cosmetic: the Afrika Korps saw none of them. Rommel performed the necessary propaganda routine, with declarations that his army was poised for the conquest of Egypt, but when he withdrew to the Semmering, a mountain health resort near Vienna, that depression which alternated with euphoria in his nature must have been profound. It was a lonely vigil, nor was the occasional report he received from Africa therapeutic. And then, on the afternoon of the 24th, Keitel telephoned to say that a British offensive was in full spate, Stumme was missing, and Rommel must be prepared to return. Further calls, from Hitler himself, sent him on his way. 'I knew,' he wrote in his *Papers*, 'there were no more laurels to be earned in Africa.'

Montgomery's attack had opened at 2140 on the 23rd with the fire, on the main northerly front, of 456 guns whose tasks were co-ordinated under central control. This counter-battery programme on behalf of 30 Corps was paralleled in the south by 136 guns assisting 13 Corps, which was to make the diversionary assault. At 2200, zero hour for the advance of both Corps, all guns switched to that massive continuous bombardment which has entered history as 'The Alamein barrage'. The effect on the communications system of the *Panzerarmee* was shattering. At his headquarters near the coast Stumme could hear the thunder of the guns and observe the lightning of their flashes amid the darkness, but situation reports were meagre. By dawn the fog of war was still impenetrable, so Stumme set out on a personal reconnaissance.

He died almost immediately. Until next day, when his body was discovered, his fate was obscure, but finally it emerged that while examining the situation on the left of the line, where 9 Australian Division was attacking with customary dash, he and his staff officer had come under fire, his companion had been killed, and Stumme, holding on to his truck as it tried to get away, had collapsed under a heart attack. Until Rommel arrived during the evening of the 25th von Thoma took over the *Panzerarmee* command. There is no doubt that the Russians' ignorance of the army they commanded and of the character of their enemy combined with Stumme's death to induce a certain lethargy. During the first two days of the Alamein battle reactions on the Axis side were certainly less energetic or imaginative than would have been the case had Rommel been present.

And this was unfortunate, for during those two days 8th Army was struggling desperately to overcome the central problem – how to maintain momentum while driving an adequate breach through to the far side of an extensive minefield, and then place its armour in positions where it could act as a defensive shield without being savaged in counter-attacks. By the morning of the 24th it was clear to Montgomery that the 'break-in' phase, as he called it, had not, as he planned, been completed during the first night. On a front running, roughly, from Tel el Eisa down to the Miteirya Ridge the four infantry divisions of 30 Corps – 9 Australian, 51 Highland, 2 New Zealand and 1 South African – had attacked in line. With variations, the general picture was one of early successes followed by increasing delays. For all their previous training, ramifying minefields caused the clearance task forces great and unexpected problems. At dawn, therefore, the situation was confused. Some of the infantry were on their objectives, some were not. Sufficient gaps had been cleared for some but not all of the follow-up tanks to crawl forward, but the armoured shield behind which the enemy's troops in the minefields could be destroyed had yet to be established. Nor had things gone well in the south, where the diversionary attack by 13 Corps made little progress, though it served its hidden purpose of pinning down 21 Panzer.

15 Panzer and *Littorio*, intermingled on the left flank of the Axis line, had been separated into three groups, each Italo-German. North Group lay by the coast, around Sidi Abd el Rahman, where the north-south Rahman track cuts across the railway and the metalled road. On its right, Centre Group was positioned due east of the Rahman track, and South Group was effectively situated to cover any breakthrough beyond the Miteirya Ridge. It was Centre and South Groups who took the burden as, during the day and night of the 24th, 8th Army sought again to establish its armour indisputably on the enemy's side of the minefields. Heavy fighting with 1 Armoured Division during the afternoon, which held the British still short of their objective, cost Centre Group some 30 tanks. But it was during the night that the first real turning-point at Alamein occurred.

The British plan was for 10 Armoured Division to force its way, in the darkness, through and beyond the minefields on the New Zealand Division's front. *Luftwaffe* bombing, South Group's artillery and the usual intractability of the Devil's garden caused such confusion that the armoured brigadiers feared their tanks would be caught at dawn exposed on the open western slope of the Miteirya Ridge. They wanted to halt. The commander of the armoured 10 Corps, Lumsden, with Leese of 30 Corps, put the point to Montgomery at an uncomfortable meeting, about 3.30 a.m., when they were uncompromisingly instructed that the attack would continue. Any armoured commander without the will would be replaced. The issue was simple. Montgomery was not pre-pared to waste tanks fruitlessly, as his predecessors had so often done. But where a generous expenditure of tanks might bring a critical gain he was ready to spend, secure in the knowledge that while he must nurse his infantry his reserves of armour were copious. The message got through, and for the Afrika Korps it was a sinister development in that for the rest of the battle, perhaps for the rest of the campaign, there was no more of that divisive spirit, that questioning of orders from above, that sense of *apartheid* which in the past had so often prevented the British armour from behaving as though it were a part of the army.

Though the forward squadrons of 10 Armoured Division did in fact manage to debouch from the congested minefield gaps, experience proved that their commanders' fears were justified. In daylight the west side of Miteirya was lethal, so the armour dropped back to its reverse slope. 'The men of the 10th Armoured Division had proved Montgomery's belief that, with their own resources, they could fight their way through to an objective, but the enemy guns had shown that they could not stay there by daylight alone.'* The guns were, of course, those of DAK's habitual anti-tank screen whose line, formed not only from guns but also from dug-in tanks, had been set up even before the battle began, with splendid observation and fields of fire, along what was approximately the original objective of the British armour. But in spite of the immense difficulties experienced by the British as they struggled to deploy, the cost of keeping the Axis gun-line intact was punishing. By the 25th Mont-gomery had lost about 250 tanks (many recoverable), but 15 Panzer's loss of 75 out of a total of 112 boded ill. What would happen if a battle of manoeuvre followed a break-out? 21 Panzer's loss of a mere 15 reflected the failure in the south of 13 Corps's efforts which, after a second night attack, failed to carry 7 Armoured and 44 Infantry Divisions forward. Montgomery therefore closed down operations on his left flank.

Indeed, by the time Rommel arrived and started to weigh up the situation

---

* Barton Maughan, *op. cit.*, p. 685.

Montgomery had turned his attention to the seaward flank, where the Australians had been fiercely thrusting and probing. Here the 'crumbling' which was to follow the 'break-in' might begin, since over the centre of his front something near to chaos still reigned, as tanks, guns and supply vehicles clustered in the narrow minefields gaps, attracting fire not only on themselves but on infantry exhausted by nights of action and days of heat and dust. Without demur, therefore, Montgomery accepted Morshead's proposal that during the night of the 25th his Australians should drive northwards towards the sea, cutting out the enemy troops isolated by 8th Army's offensive and seizing the tactically valuable Point 29 which, though only 20 feet higher than the surrounding terrain, dominated the northern flank in the area west of Tel el Eisa.

The Australians had a stroke of luck. At dusk on the 25th a German group was surprised near their forward posts: prisoners included the regimental and one of the battalion commanders of 125 Regiment which, with an Italian admixture, had the special task of guarding the invaluable observation post represented by Point 29. They spoke too freely, and the battalion commander's map gave away not only his troops' positions but also the minefield layout. The Australians could now choose a safe line of approach. Consequently, when their attack developed at about midnight they were able, with a brilliant unorthodoxy, to send in a spearhead company mounted on carriers, four abreast, which hurled them straight on to the objective. There was vicious fighting that night, with the unaccustomed use of bayonets at close quarters. 173 prisoners were taken from 125 Regiment, another 67 from *Trento* and *Littorio*. But the main point was not the success of a neat local action: its true significance was its effect on Rommel's mind and on the subsequent use of his German troops.

He reached *Panzerarmee*'s command post on the evening of the 25th and after hearing reports from von Thoma and Westphal reached a conclusion from which he hardly budged during the rest of the battle – that Montgomery's aim was to break through not simply in the northern sector, but actually on the very right flank of 8th Army's line. The attack on Point 29 started a suspicion which was daily confirmed – for the underlying theme of Alamein, often overlooked by analysts, is the unremitting pressure exercised by 9 Australian Division and the frequent attempts made by Rommel to conform by shifting his weight to the north.

Because he was ultimately defeated, and because Montgomery made a sudden change of plan, students forget that Rommel's reading of his opponent's initial purpose was correct. On the 26th it was clear that 8th Army was making no important headway. Montgomery's coolly calculated decision, which caused such flutterings in Whitehall, to hold on his central front until he could withdraw the New Zealanders and 10 Armoured Division, thus forming a reserve with which a new offensive called SUPERCHARGE might be launched, was eminently sensible, and, in the event, successful. But in assessing Rommel's counter-moves, it must be remembered that Montgomery's first intention, as given by him to Freyberg at midday on the 28th, was for the New Zealanders to maintain the Australians' pressure by moving into their sector during the night of the 29th/30th and then, with the support of armour and other infantry brigades, *to advance along the coast*. Such was the pattern of thinking on both sides which now enmeshed the Afrika Korps.

Three moves by Rommel on the 26th illustrate the magnetism of the north. As the fall of Point 29 implied a further advance westward by his enemy, he tried to recover the ground lost in this sector by a counter-attack launched jointly by 15 Panzer, 164 Light and the Italian XX Corps. But the Axis army, and particularly its panzer core, were weakened by an inexorable logic. Fuel was short: re-supply was improbable (*Proserpina*, with 3,000 tons of fuel, and *Tergestea* with 1,000 were both sunk that day); the constant pattern-bombing and dense artillery concentrations involved wasteful evasive manoeuvre and consumed hundreds of gallons that could have been better used in offensive action. So this attack failed. At the same time Rommel started to edge 90 Light eastward along the coast to Sidi el Rahman, and by the late evening he had begun to shift 21 Panzer and a portion of *Ariete* northward under heavy attack from the night-bombers. Perhaps this was, historically, a moment of nadir for the Afrika Korps, for in spite of the signs that Rommel was seeking to concentrate his panzers, 8th Army's superiority of tanks in the central sector was such that Montgomery, unconcerned, left 7 Armoured Division quiescent in the south. When had a British commander in the desert last felt confidently able to leave a whole armoured division off-stage, knowing that DAK was gathering its strength?

Rommel's redeployment led next day to one of the most extraordinary episodes of the whole battle – extraordinary because he then thought he was mounting a major counter-attack while the British, pre-occupied with their own problems, were largely ignorant of its significance – except a portion of one battalion, 2 Rifle Brigade, which with its own 6-pounder anti-tank guns plus a few from the Royal Artillery, 19 in all, for the first time in the desert war crippled the Afrika Korps by the very skills in which it had for so long specialised.

Rommel's plan was to attack Point 29 again, this time with 90 Light (who failed). But also – south-west of the Australian sector, and like a cork in the orifice of the main northerly corridor which the British had been driving through the minefields – there stood the feature known from its conformation as Kidney Ridge to the 8th Army: the Germans (when not confusing it with

Point 29) called it Point 28. Here on the 27th, after much inexcusable confusion between armour and infantry about map-reading, 1 Armoured Division pushed forward in the early hours Colonel Turner's Rifle Brigade battalion to set up a position, called SNIPE, which with its dug-in anti-tank defences could form an advance pivot of manoeuvre as the Division sought to push its armour westwards during the day. But it was precisely in the region of SNIPE and Kidney Ridge that Rommel had decided to make his main effort on 27 October.

The result was that in an increasing tempo throughout the day the SNIPE defenders found themselves dealing with 15 Panzer, *Littorio* and, as they came in from the south, elements of 21 Panzer and *Ariete*. At least once they were engaged by their own 24 Armoured Brigade. When they retired at the end of the day, hauling their one remaining gun out of action, they had accounted for at least 37 tanks or self-propelled guns, as a searching committee of enquiry established soon afterwards. 1 Armoured Division had failed to advance, but the men at SNIPE had not only kept the pivot secure, they had disrupted the first combined operation by the Afrika Korps at Alamein. (If one jumps forward to Medenine, one sees that from now on there was little left for DAK to teach 8th Army about setting up an anti-tank screen – and the bulk deliveries of six-pounders had made it possible to apply the lesson effectively.) Colonel Teege's 8 Panzer Regiment of 15 Panzer was particularly hard hit. *

The arithmetic of Alamein was daily becoming more obvious. The *Panzer-armee*'s infantry was essential for holding on to the minefields or counter-attacking lost positions. But the panzers and 88s formed the only true line of resistance: if this snapped, Montgomery's armour must be expected to pour through the breach into open desert. Actions like that at SNIPE, sapping DAK's strength, could no longer be endured. The crux of the battle was approaching, for while neither Rommel nor his staff could believe that the *Panzerarmee* was capable, at best, of doing more than prevent a fatal breakthrough, it was equally evident that Montgomery, in view of his great resources, must make at least one more major effort. Rommel, as has been seen, identified the northern sector as the decisive area, and it was here, instinctively, that he continued to concentrate his trusted veterans from DAK and 90 Light. Many, he knew, were 'desert-happy', over-strained and physically weakened by 18 months of almost continuous service at the front. But they were the best he had. And so the *Panzerarmee*'s order of battle, which on 23 October had shown Germans and Italians intermingled along the whole length of the front, by the morning of the 29th indicated to the intelligence staff at 8th Army that all the

---

* Teege himself was soon to die, as was the redoubtable Colonel Baade, commanding the Division's 115 Infantry Regiment, whose name is to be found in so many earlier action reports.

German divisions had been filtered off to the north.

It was this discovery that caused Montgomery to make a change of plan. Having built up his reserve, he aimed to propel the New Zealand Division and its attached brigades westwards along the coast during the night of October 30/31. Savage and not entirely successful assaults by the Australians prepared the way. But the discovery that during the night of the 28th the whole of 90 Light had been committed on the Australian front led Montgomery to make the centre-line of SUPERCHARGE run somewhat further to the south: as his advisers had been arguing, this would avoid marching straight at the Germans, and ought to direct the attack on to Italian-held positions. Here was one of those small shifts of emphasis which can be decisive in a great battle. The amendment, which Montgomery made at 11 a.m. on the 29th, was not so perspicacious as his memoirs suggest, since the junction-point between 90 Light and its neighbour, *Trento*, was further to the south than had been assumed, so that when SUPERCHARGE was launched 8th Army's forward troops in fact overlapped much of the German line. Still, it was sufficient – and it certainly surprised a Rommel who, in his heart, had already accepted defeat.

The Field Marshal's feelings are made plain in his *Papers*. 'I spent the whole of that night [*the 28th/29th*] with a number of my officers and men on the coast road . . . from where we could see the flash of bursting shells in the darkness and hear the rolling thunder of the battle. . . . No one can conceive the extent of our anxiety during this period. That night I hardly slept and by 0300 hrs. was pacing up and down turning over in my mind the likely course of the battle, and the decisions I might have to take.' In his heart he knew what he must do. Replacement of fuel was minimal: 70 tons flown over the previous day hardly made up for the loss of the tanker *Prosperpina* outside Tobruk followed by the news that its replacement *Louisiana* had also been torpedoed. The Italian infantry would have to be sacrificed in what seemed an inevitable withdrawal, while as many tanks and guns as possible were salvaged. His mind turned that morning to a fall-back position somewhere between Fuka and the Qattara Depression. But first 'we were going to make one more attempt, by the tenacity and stubbornness of our defence, to persuade the enemy to call off his attack'.

The 'rolling thunder' to which Rommel and his staff listened during the night of the 28th was part of the almost continuous noise of battle which persisted in the north until SUPERCHARGE was launched, as the Australians endeavoured to cut through to the sea and 'kill Germans'. For the Afrika Korps the consequences were important, since Rommel (against the advice of subordinates, who wanted to start disengaging from this unprofitable sector), refused to stop attacking. Instead he committed 90 Light (as has been seen), and even part of 21 Panzer, with the result that when the real test came of his army's ability to discourage its opponent its dispositions were unbalanced, while tanks and 88s invaluable for the next phase had been squandered in the graveyards around Point 29.

For the real test was SUPERCHARGE, and the main burden, inescapably, fell on the Afrika Korps. Launched neither at the time nor in the place where Montgomery had first intended, it had a vital significance for both sides. The *Panzerarmee* could only roll with the punch, hoping that effective resistance might demoralise the enemy and, if not, that some sort of effective disengagement might be contrived. But Montgomery only had one option: to break through. The image of Alamein as a glorious victory has too often obscured the fact that before SUPERCHARGE there were many, from Churchill downwards (and including high officers in Egypt) who were pessimistic and critical. It obscures, too, the concern Montgomery was beginning to feel about the attrition of his infantry – particularly the good Commonwealth divisions whose gaps could not be filled. There were tanks in plenty: but how long could he supply the foot-soldiers for lethal assaults through fire-swept minefields against fixed defences? Neither Montgomery's personal position nor, perhaps, the morale and fighting efficiency of his army would have been the same if SUPERCHARGE had failed.

Nor was it an instant success. Freyberg demanded a postponement, partly on behalf of his exhausted infantry and partly because the problem of redeploying men, guns and tanks in the congested area of the minefields was enormous. The initial infantry attacks to prepare the way for SUPERCHARGE did not go in, therefore, until the night of 1 November, and it was not until about 0600 next morning that the hard point of the assault, 9 Armoured Brigade, started to feel its way into the open. It was too late. The early light allowed 15 Panzer and *Littorio* to react violently, and the supporting tanks from 1 Armoured Division, which were supposed to maintain the impulsion of the attack, were baulked and blocked in the smoke and dust of the minefield corridors. Though the number of 88s available was not large – perhaps no more than two dozen at the peak – the gun-line of *Pak* and panzer held, inflicting on 9 Armoured Brigade the crippling loss of 70 tanks and many of its best officers.

In a sense, therefore, the first explosion of SUPERCHARGE had failed – though Montgomery had been prepared to accept 100 per cent casualties in 9 Armoured Brigade for a success. The British had made an advance but not a breakthrough. During the morning, however, the true crisis-point emerged as von Thoma at Afrika Korps, at last convincing Rommel that the north was a secondary sector, called in 21 Panzer and organised a counter-attack with 21 Panzer striking from the north and 15 Panzer, plus elements of *Littorio* and *Trieste*, from the west. Not even Sidi Rezegh had a greater intensity than this swirling conflict along the Rahman Track by Tel el Aqaqir. Their own constant bombing and massive concentrations of artillery were new factors for the British – and this was the first of such actions in which they possessed, in the high-explosive shells from the Sherman's gun, a direct answer to the 88. Soon after midday Rommel and von Thoma accepted defeat – Rommel going so far as to summon up from the deep south the last units of *Ariete* and most of the artillery. It was *tout le monde à la bataille*, if anything more was to be done.

But there was nothing. 9 Armoured Brigade's self-sacrificial action, followed by the morning's fire-fight, had reduced DAK's strength to 35 tanks and its ammunition, by comparison with British abundance, was fading away. And so, signalling to Hitler that a breakthrough was inevitable next day, Rommel issued orders for withdrawal to the Fuka line which had been so much in his mind. (ULTRA picked up the signal.)

There was sporadic fighting at various points during the night, mainly due to local efforts by the British to advance their positions. But when he visited the coastal road during the morning of the 3rd Rommel was astonished and relieved to learn from von Thoma and Bayerlein that DAK was now under very little pressure. Relief, however, disappeared when he got back to *Panzerarmee* HQ in the early afternoon and was presented with Hitler's reply to his own signal, ordering him to stand fast. 'As to your troops, you can show them no other road than that to victory or death.'

Rommel's words about the reactions of himself and his staff are more convincing than what he says about his men. 'The order had a powerful effect on the troops. At the *Führer*'s command they were ready to sacrifice themselves to the last man. An overwhelming bitterness welled up in us when we saw the superlative spirit of the army, in which every man, from the highest to the lowest, knew that even the greatest effort could no longer change the course of the battle.' Nevertheless, the Afrika Korps and the best of the Italians did continue the hopeless fight. Though Rommel reversed his orders, it was not entirely possible to halt a retreat which, once started, developed an impetus of its own. In the south, particularly, the Italian X Corps was making for the west, its more or less defenceless infantry harassed by 8th Army's armoured cars.

By the morning of the 4th, however, a sort of line still existed nearer the coast – DAK and 90 Light, then the remains of the Italian armour, then *Trento*, Ramcke's parachutists, and X Corps. 90 Light fought doggedly from 0800 to mid-day, fending off swarms of tanks. During the afternoon 7 Armoured Division caught and encircled *Ariete*, which fought to extinction in a running battle which made all previous German observations about Italian pusillanimity out-of-date. And by now von Thoma himself was missing. As *Ariete*'s tin-can tanks were exploding, DAK's commander had insisted on taking part in a clash between his two panzer divisions and 1 Armoured Division on the old killing-ground about Tel el Aqaqir. Von Thoma's tank was hit, and he surrendered. Bayerlein was nearly lost with him, but managed to escape on foot and, in the evening, take over the DAK command.

There was nothing left with which to prevent 8th Army's masses of tanks, plentifully supplied with fuel and ammunition, from racing over the desert and cutting off the whole *Panzerarmee*. Rommel had assessed Montgomery already as a cautious general, but as yet he had no evidence to suggest that he would be as slow in pursuit as he had been sure in the battle of position. For DAK, for his whole command Rommel was justified, on the afternoon of the 4th, in seeing only one prospect. 'So now it had come, the thing we had done everything in our power to avoid – our front broken and the fully motorised enemy streaming into our rear. Superior orders could no longer count. We had to save what there was to be saved.' Bayerlein agreed – as had Kesselring during a morning visit. By the end of the afternoon the whole army had received orders to retreat. It mattered little, now, that both Hitler and Mussolini endorsed them next morning.

No Laurels in Africa?

The Italians suffered the greater purgatory.

Names steeped in history passed out of existence alongside others newer but no less glorious. The infantry of *Pavia* had had a hundred years or more of life, though they really dated back to the French-named regiment of Savoy; *Brescia* had originally been composed of volunteers of 1848; *Bologna* of men recruited in Venetia and Romagna in 1859. Nothing was left of them. Nor of the youthful *Ariete* and *Littorio*. Nor of the new-born *Folgore*, reduced finally to the most painful of all sacrifices. . . . It was like an ant-hill being overwhelmed by a flood. *

In a copybook retreat the weakest fall back first, covered by the strong. After Alamein this was impossible. Sheer military necessity required that priority over fuel, over food and over ammunition should be given to the Afrika Korps and the other German units within the *Panzerarmee*, and only thereafter to the Italians. If Rommel was to keep 'an army in being' such a course was inevitable even if it meant, in practice, the abandonment of an ally.† In fact the disposition of troops on the ground was decisive. Concentrated mainly in the south, far from the coastal road and short of vehicles, the Italian divisions had to be left to fend for themselves – to thirst, short rations, capture. It is not surprising that a cynical rumour spread among them: the quick change of

---

* Caccia-Dominioni, *op. cit.*, p. 242.

† In his *Papers* Rommel maintained that he intended if *possible* to stand on the Fuka line 'until the infantry withdrawal was complete', but this was an unrealistic concept from the start.

orders, 'Retreat', 'Stand Fast', 'Retreat', was the Germans' trick to allow their own troops a greater opportunity to escape.

This, at least, was not the case: and the need for Rommel to preserve the Afrika Korps as a nucleus of Axis power at the eastern end of the Mediterranean was ominously confirmed during the morning of the 8th, when Westphal reported to the Field Marshal that an Anglo-American force had landed in North-West Africa. What Montgomery had naturally anticipated when he launched LIGHTFOOT was now a reality. Until the end of the campaign the fortunes of DAK would be conditioned by the consequences of TORCH. And Rommel's judgement was unqualified. 'This,' he wrote, 'spelt the end of the army in Africa.'

Whatever the Italians may have invented about the escape plans of the Germans, however, the truth is that 'the end of the army' should have been consummated as an immediate result of defeat at Alamein. During the aftermath of Montgomery's victory TORCH was an irrelevance, since its fruits were already waiting to be plucked. Until the Afrika Korps reached the next good defensive position, or disengaged sufficiently far to the west, it was powerless to prevent on its own what no other formation in the *Panzerarmee* can even be imagined preventing – an encirclement, that is to say, by the full strength of the 8th Army's mobile divisions. For DAK it was an uncovenanted and wholly unexpected mercy that this did not occur: that lack of foresight, inadequate planning by exhausted staff and the appalling confusion of the battle area caused the British to fumble what should have been their final blow. 'Some of the pursuing formations were delayed by real difficulties, some by imaginary ones, some by their own lack of impetus. None evinced the initiative or drive needed to snatch the prize.'*

Yet the remains of the German contingent amounted to a mere handful. Even by 10 November, when its scattered units had been more or less reassembled, the two panzer divisions of DAK contained only 2,200 men, with 11 tanks. 90 Light was down to 1,000 and 164 Light, which had been pulverised during the fighting in the Australian sector, mustered a mere 800. Ramcke's parachute brigade had 700 survivors. And in the whole German group there were precisely 25 anti-tank guns, of which the Afrika Korps possessed 10. Yet 8th Army still had tanks by the hundreds (of the 500 lost during the battle about 300 were recovered and repaired), while in all other respects its quantitative superiority had actually increased. After every excuse and explanation has been taken into account it still seems, in retrospect, an extraordinary error on Montgomery's part to have allowed the Afrika Korps, his principal opponent, to slip away.

---

* Barton Maughan, *op. cit.*, p. 741.

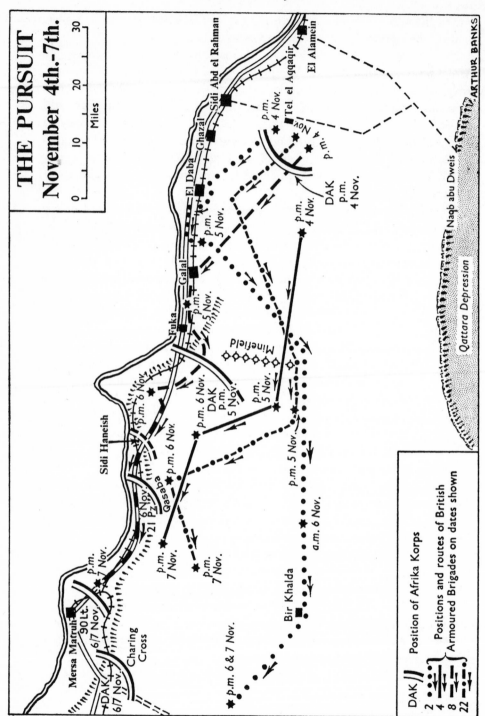

THE PURSUIT
November 4th.-7th.

Miles
0   10   20   30

El Alamein
Tel el Aqqaqir
Sidi Abd el Rahman
Ghazal
El Daba
Galal
Fuka
Sidi Haneish
Qasaba
Mersa Matruh
Charing Cross

Minefield
Bir Khalda

Qattara Depression
Naqb abu Dweis

p.m. 4 Nov.
DAK p.m. 4 Nov.
p.m. 5 Nov.
p.m. 5 Nov.
DAK p.m. 5 Nov.
p.m. 5 Nov.
p.m. 5 Nov.
p.m. 5 Nov.
p.m. 6 Nov.
DAK p.m. 6 Nov.
p.m. 6 Nov.
6 Nov.
21 Pz
p.m. 7 Nov.
p.m. 7 Nov.
p.m. 7 Nov.
p.m. 7 Nov.
90 Lt.
6/7 Nov.
DAK 6/7 Nov.
a.m. 6 Nov.
p.m. 6 & 7 Nov.

DAK ‖   Position of Afrika Korps

2 ••••
4 ↓↓↓   Positions and routes of British
8 - - -   Armoured Brigades on dates shown
22 —

ARTHUR BANKS

MAP 7   Pursuit across the desert

By the 11th DAK was clear of the Halfaya bottleneck and the pressure relaxed. It was between the 4th and 11th that 8th Army had its main opportunity, for at a number of points from Alamein to the escarpment it should have been possible to outflank Rommel's disorganised troops, constantly battered as they were from the air, and by striking north to cut the coastal road. But analysis reveals that in spite of some 270 tanks of three armoured divisions (1, 7 and 10), as well as the mobile New Zealand Division, the British failure to do so was essentially self-generated. There were some brisk actions: but hook after hook to the coast was abortive, either because it was not first driven far enough to the west, or because tanks ran out of fuel, or because the units for an out-flanking force could not be married together in time. The rains which fell on the 6th and 7th were a contributing factor, but it has long been accepted that they alone do not account for Montgomery's anticlimax. It was due, far more, to a decline in organisation and a temporary relaxation of will.

Already, however, the political parameter was re-emerging. Rommel intended to hold the approaches to Halfaya and Sollum only so long as might be necessary to let his army pass westwards through the defiles. By the 8th the inevitable argument had started: through Cavallero Mussolini insisted that a rearguard must stick it out as long as possible. A new gambit was used by the Duce on the 10th, when he declared that if Halfaya could not be held there must be a 'systematic' retreat back to El Agheila, where a final stand must be made. Rommel's view was that 'the vital thing now was to get every German and Italian soldier and as much material as possible away to the west to enable us either to make a stand somewhere farther back, *or to ship them back to Europe*'. At the very beginning of the retreat, therefore, one observes a basic difference about strategy which would continue virtually to the end. And how fortunate for the Afrika Korps that its commander resisted the political pressure which might have forced it into a fight-to-the-death among the old hunting grounds of Sollum, Capuzzo, Sidi Omar – with a few dozen tanks and guns, a few thousand weary men and no hope!

Among those now filtering to safety across the escarpment were some who felt as harshly towards Rommel and the Afrika Korps as did the Italians. These were Ramcke's survivors. After the success of SUPERCHARGE they were isolated beside their Italian allies in the south, with little transport, and they felt – arrogant as always – a deep sense of grievance against Rommel's command. Their kin had deserted them. Nevertheless, after setting out on the long tramp westwards they managed to ambush some British vehicles on which, after a lively skirmish with the Household Cavalry, they finally reported back to Rommel on the morning of the 7th. This fine achievement by General Ramcke and his men did not diminish their sense of outrage, so they were now put on lorries and sent to the rear for a rest. There is no doubt that these *Luftwaffe* troops thought themselves to be as good as, if not better than the DAK – a reminder that the Afrika Korps, indisputably an *élite*, nevertheless had its jealous rivals.

But jealousy was an emotion which, from now on, would infiltrate the Afrika Korps itself, as the bush telegraph with increasing magnifications of the truth brought rumours of special treatment being accorded to their fellows in Tunisia. *Nebelwerfers*, Tiger tanks, enormous *Giganten* transport gliders, the latest 88s, frequent convoys, effective air cover . . . all that was lacking in the east seemed to be going to the west. But Hitler had ordered Rommel and his army to forget Tunisia, and concentrate on their own affairs. In so doing they might at least keep another front in being.

Once the escarpment was reached, and the bombed columns struggled back through Tobruk's minefields and the gaps in the old Gazala line, there was no question of even establishing such a front until the Mersa Brega/El Agheila position on the Gulf of Sirte could be re-occupied. Indeed, the fear was that the British might get there first. Recollections of O'Connor's cut-off at Beda Fomm, and their own memories of successful outflankings and encirclings on the Cyrenaican plateau in the springs of 1941 and 1942, made Rommel and many an Afrika Korps veteran assume that before Benghazi could be evacuated and the whole army passed westwards through Agedabia Montgomery would have sent his forward tanks and mobile troops in strength by, say, Msus and Antelat. An armoured brigade of Shermans at Agedabia, early enough, was all that was required for a decisive interception.

In practice Montgomery took counsel of his fears. The record and reputation of the Afrika Korps – in spite of its present weakness, which was evident to him – were still powerful deterrents. He had no intention of being caught off balance, like his predecessors, by an unexpected counter-attack from El Agheila, and he was convinced that he would have to carry the position itself by one of his set-piece assaults. His advance through the Jebel and across its neck were therefore cautious, light forces only being used to probe in the south and threaten DAK's withdrawal. In consequence, while 8th Army returned to Benghazi on the 20th, the remains of the *Panzerarmee* were able to complete their occupation of the Mersa Brega/El Agheila defences during the night of the 23rd/24th.

The British skirmishers were hampered by rain, but rain is an impartial enemy of the just and unjust: the Afrika Korps was also slowed down. More to the point was the system introduced by DAK at an early stage in the retreat, of denying abandoned ground by every variant of mine and booby-trap. The new Chief Engineer who had arrived on the 8th, General Buelowius, was considered by Rommel to be one of the best in the German Army. Certainly the impact of this denial programme was considerable, not only on 8th Army's advance guards but also on the supply services on which Montgomery depended for his logistic build-up. Forward airfields, in particular, had to be slowly and meticulously searched before they could be made operational. 'The first airfield found to be systematically prepared was Derna; Benina, Barce and Berka were even worse, having been furnished with a great variety of infernal devices.'*

As for the El Agheila position, to have arrived there was one thing, to stay there another. Nobody but a *Führer* or a Duce would have dreamed that a stand could be made against a determined and properly planned assault. Rommel, certainly, was not convinced – but then Rommel had seen from the first, and seen rightly, that after Alamein the only correct military solution was for the *Panzerarmee* to make as fast as possible for Tunisia. In particular, he looked back avidly even beyond the Mareth Line and its French-built, solid defences to the Gabes Gap, where on the Wadi Akarit he could block the sole and narrow passage between the sea and the Qattara Depression of Tunisia, that vast range of trackless salt marsh called the Chott-el-Fedjadj. But so sensible a withdrawal was politically impossible. The Afrika Korps had therefore to prepare for at least a token gesture at El Agheila.

During a heated discussion with Kesselring and Cavallero on 24 November Rommel nevertheless argued his case, and extracted a conditional agreement from the latter that in the event of attack by a superior force he might withdraw to Buerat at the western end of the Gulf of Sirte. Still dissatisfied, on the 28th he flew to see Hitler at 'The Wolf's Lair', his command post near Rastenburg in East Prussia. The *Führer* was icy. He had been right, he declared, to order 'No retreat' in Russia during the first desperate winter: there would be no retreat in Africa now. Supplies would be made available and Goering would return to Italy with Rommel to ensure their delivery.

Rommel had already given his minimum requirements to Kesselring and Cavallero on the 24th – demands so modest that they vividly reflected the attenuated state of the Afrika Korps. 50 Mk. IV Specials: 50 75 mm anti-tank guns: 78 field guns: 4,000 tons of petrol and 4,000 tons of ammunition make a modest shopping-list for an army commander in Rommel's circumstances. The figures reveal, perhaps, a realistic pessimism about the possibility of deliveries, for by sea and air his enemy maintained an iron grip on the Mediterranean seaways, while his own supply services found it hard to move more than about 50 tons of fuel per day from the only remaining port, Tripoli, to the army at the front. In any case Hitler's promises (like his previous ones) were not fulfilled: Russia and North West Africa were his present concerns. And

---

* Playfair, Vol. IV, p. 98.

Goering's abrasive presence failed to oil the wheels in Italy. 'Flying back to Africa,' Rommel recalled, 'I realised that we were now completely thrown back on our resources and that to keep the army from being destroyed as the result of some crazy order or other would need all our skill.'

The several weeks which Montgomery allowed for his preparations gave his opponents ample time to prepare for an attack which was foreseen and which Rommel had no intention of allowing to provoke a battle. By 15 December an outflanking force of New Zealanders, with a few tanks, had travelled wide to the south over the bad inland going and now, having turned north, was just short of the coastal road. 'Someone at Division,' wrote Kippenberger, then commanding 5 New Zealand Brigade, 'told me that Afrika Korps was "in the bag": the rest had gone, but we had Afrika Korps, 15 and 21 Panzer Divisions, and 90th Light, the élite of the German Army.'* The wish had fathered the thought, for Rommel was on the *qui vive*, the move of the New Zealanders was spotted by the *Luftwaffe*, and orders for a withdrawal were given in sufficient time for every element of the *Panzerarmee* to escape once again with minimal loss. All accounts draw attention to the intensive mining and booby-trapping, which held up the advance of 51 Highland Division against the main position on the coast, while Heinz Werner Schmidt, still serving with the Special Group 288, has recorded how generously he and his Group laced the inland tracks with explosives. To force a way between the New Zealanders and the sea the panzer troops had to fight a kind of naval action, covering the softer vehicles like destroyers defending a convoy from the flank.

By the 17th everyone had travelled far down the Gulf of Sirte, beyond Nofilia, where a screen was set up to protect the road against attacks from the south. The Afrika Korps guarded Nofilia itself: then came two Reconnaissance Battalions, then Panzer Grenadier Regiment *Afrika*, and finally 90 Light. To the west, at Sirte, lay the Italian Young Fascist Division and a combat group from the relics of *Ariete*. This was well, for on the 17th the New Zealanders, driving ahead at speed, launched an attack straight from their transport on 15 Panzer's positions. But their accompanying tanks were too few, and the attack failed to penetrate defences whose professional layout pleased the professional eye of Brigadier Kippenberger. And he noted with admiration the customary combination-of-all-arms which the Afrika Korps used as instinctively in defence as in attack. The skills persisted as fuel and equipment dwindled.

All the way to Tripoli this was the prevailing pattern. The hunting pack gathered its strength, and pounced: the lean wolf snarled, and retreated.

---

* Sir Howard Kippenberger, *Infantry Brigadier*, p. 250.

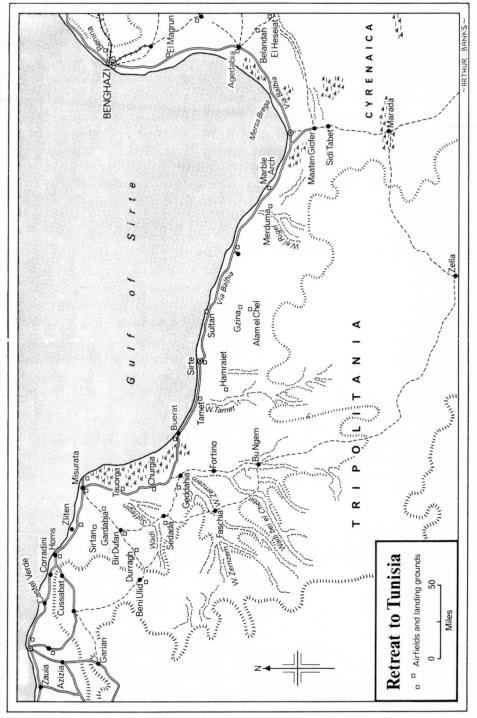

Retreat to Tunisia

□ Airfields and landing grounds

0   50

Miles

MAP 8   Withdrawal into Tunisia

Though the Afrika Korps was steadily closing up on its Tripoli base, while 8th Army had travelled 1,200 miles from Cairo, two images of Christmas Day 1942 illustrate their comparative well-being. Group 288 that day was lying just to the west of Sirte. It actually watched 8th Army's patrols entering the village during the afternoon and start the inevitable clearing of the air-strip.

> What a strange night to celebrate! We vamped up a Christmas-tree out of a wooden pole in which we had bored holes to carry camel-thorn branches. We decorated the tree with silver paper and we improvised candles of a sort. As Christmas fare each of my men received three cigarettes – we had been hoarding them for some time. The contents of a light mail-bag of letters from home were handed out. The letters were the best of Christmas presents.*

By contrast the New Zealanders, comfortable at Nofilia, were feasted on turkey and roast pork, *fresh* vegetables, plum pudding and two bottles of beer per man.

Morale was nevertheless astonishingly high in the Afrika Korps. And the old sense of personal leadership was still there. On Christmas Eve Rommel wrote to his wife: 'I'm going off very early this morning into the country and will be celebrating this evening among the men. They're in top spirits, thank God, and it takes great strength not to let them see how heavily the situation is pressing on us.' There was nothing here of the atmosphere during another desperate retreat, as described by Rifleman Harris when he recalled General Craufurd on the road to Corunna: 'If he stopped his horse, and halted to deliver one of his stern reprimands, you would see half a dozen lean, unshaven, shoeless and savage riflemen standing for the moment leaning upon their weapons, and scowling up in his face as he scolded. . . .'

Yet the first month of 1943 was a watershed in the history of the Afrika Korps. By the end of January its character had been irreversibly altered, and the change occurred as a result of what Rommel called the heavy pressure of the situation. Between the rearguard operations at Nofilia in mid-December and the evacuation of Tripoli in mid-January Rommel was in a persistent state of angry dialogue with the Italian High Command, whose emotional demands for the defence of Tripoli and its approaches seemed merely childish to the Field Marshal. Though he thought Montgomery was amazingly slow to act, he nevertheless realised that the 8th Army's patient build-up of troops and supplies was not a peacetime exercise. When the enemy struck, the Afrika Korps and still more the immobile Italians and other units would be in danger

---

* Schmidt, *op. cit.*, p. 152. The *Panzerarmee* staff, it is true, supped delicately on – gazelles!

of being outflanked and surrounded. (The hapless position of von Paulus at Stalingrad was ever-present in Rommel's mind.) Moreover, the campaigns in the east and the west were now fusing. Throughout the retreat a main objective had always been to get the Afrika Korps through the Gabes Gap as soon as possible. But about 10 January a new danger seemed imminent. The Anglo-American army in Tunisia looked as thought it might cut the Gabes escape route.

And so, as the arguments between Rommel, Bastico, Cavallero and Mussolini flashed to and fro the Italian dislike and suspicion (and, no doubt, envy) of their *Panzerarmee*'s commander at last expressed themselves in action. On the 22nd Rommel received 'a severe rebuke from Rome'. On the 26th, the day he had actually moved his headquarters across the Tunisian frontier, he was informed by *Comando Supremo* (to whom he was technically subordinate) that on grounds of poor health he must surrender his command, on a date of his own choosing, once his army had withdrawn as far west as the Mareth Line. (A fortnight previously, at Cavallero's request, he had detached 21 Panzer and sent it off to Southern Tunisia to protect this sensitive zone.*)

Thus though Rommel, as it soon turned out, was not yet entirely *hors de combat*, and though 15 and 21 Panzer each had much fighting before them, it may fairly be said that after January the magic was dissipated. Never again would the complete Afrika Korps of two panzer divisions, associated with a 90 Light which by its prowess had become a blood-brother, fight its own battle as an entity under the man who had formed, shaped, trained and inspired this unique war-machine. And the test is very simple. In the battles still to come, like Kasserine or Medenine, even though Rommel and at least some of his veterans were to some degree involved, 'old Africa hands' at the time and military critics subsequently have pointed to a wide discrepancy between the quality of performance and that of earlier days. Something had been fractured.

But if the delaying actions before Tripoli during this climactic month were fought by an Afrika Korps already doomed, there was no shame in their conclusion. The British entry into the port on 23 January, which some thought should have happened two years previously, was militarily unavoidable. The force that finally moved in on Tripoli consisted of 51 Highland Division, as usual inching its painful way amid the minefields of the coastal road, and a mobile group striking from the southern hinterland via Beni Ulid, Tarhuna and Castel Benito. This comprised 7 Armoured Division (with well over 150 tanks) and the New Zealand Division. There was thus heavy pressure down all the routes leading to Tripoli. In 21 Panzer's absence, 15 Panzer and 90 Light

---

* 21 Panzer was actually dispatched to Sfax on 14 January without its guns or tanks, which were handed over to 15 Panzer. Re-equipment was easier in the west.

– with the remains of 164 Light and the parachutists – fought stubborn delaying actions of great import, since there were 30,000 Italian troops to be
extricated, while the harbour and warehouses of Tripoli had to be cleared and
demolished. (No less than 93 per cent of the stores had to be shifted by road.)
But even courage and craters (109 were blown on the route between Buerat
and Homs) could only defer and not prevent. By the end of January the Royal
Navy was starting to discharge cargoes at Tripoli, and 'on the 15th of February,
1943', Rommel recorded with relief, 'the rearguard of the 15th Panzer Division
finally withdrew into the forefield of the Mareth Line and the great retreat
from Alamein to Tunisia was over'.

It was only a qualified relief. The pre-war French defences constituting the
Mareth Line, along the potential tank-trap of the Wadi Zigzaou which runs
inland from the coast about 20 miles east of Gabes, had grave limitations. Both
Hitler and *Comando Supremo* were anxious for the usual prolonged stand, but
Rommel knew that it was badly sited and overlooked by hills to occupy which
would drain his diminishing army. Moreover, as events would prove, it could
be outflanked by a determined enemy, and he accepted that, far from being
able to block such a move, he would scarcely have the capacity to delay it.

Nevertheless the two Axis armies now in Tunisia, von Arnim's in the west
and Rommel's in the east, at least had the advantage of operating on interior
lines. The detachment of 21 Panzer was an immediate example, and von Arnim
soon put it to use. From the map of Tunisia it is obvious that the broken
mountain-chain running roughly southwards from Bou Arada to Gafsa, and
usually known as the Eastern Dorsal, was the stop-line on which the Anglo-
Americans could be prevented from breaking into the coastal lowlands.
Alternatively it might provide sally-posts for counter-assaults on the enemy.
In any event, to command the five passes, Karachoum, Kairouan, Fondouk,
Faid and Maknassy was of paramount importance. During the latter part of
January, therefore, von Arnim set about this essential task, using his 10 Panzer
Division in the north. At Faid 21 Panzer, now rested and re-equipped, shattered
a weak Franco-American combination, while at Maknassy the Americans
virtually eliminated themselves by panic and inefficiency. The whole of the
Eastern Dorsal became Axis property.

When a division had been drained of its strength on the Western Front, at
Ypres or on the Somme, it would be sent to a 'cushy sector' to recover. 21
Panzer must have felt like this at Faid. And still more so when, on 14 February,
von Arnim took Eisenhower and his advisers by surprise. Convinced that the
next big attack was coming further north, at Fondouk, they and their virgin
troops were in no posture to accept a vicious converging thrust through the
southern passes by 10 and 21 Panzer Divisions. In a three-day operation the
American 2 Corps lost two tank, two infantry and two artillery battalions: its

commander, Fredendall, was discredited. The quality of the captured equipment, its lavish scale, the succulence and abundance of American rations were a revelation to the men from the desert, who emerged virtually unscathed.

And now Rommel was on the way. Though the Italian General Messe had arrived from Russia at the end of January – an excellent, experienced, if stolid commander – to take over the *Panzerarmee*, its leader had no intention of vacating his post until his troops were reasonably secure. In typical Rommel fashion he saw that if he could shift his veterans to the west, deal the Americans a crushing blow, and then rapidly move east again to hit 8th Army on the nose before its main body and great supply dumps had been lifted forward, he might at least ensure a provisional security for his men, giving the *Panzerarmee* and Arnim's formations the opportunity to knit together into a powerful bridgehead garrison. By 15 February, therefore, he was already in Gafsa and pressing forward, bringing with him an Afrika Korps Group (commanded until the 17th by Liebenstein, who was then wounded and was succeeded by Buelowius): it contained armour from 15 Panzer, Panzer Grenadier Regiment *Afrika*, and *Centauro* as a make-weight.

The arguments between Rommel, Kesselring, von Arnim and Rome about what should follow are complicated and may be summarised by saying that Rommel, the man with the surgical mind, wanted to cut right through the soft enemy defences as far as Tebessa; thus, at a stroke, seizing the main Anglo-American administrative centre and supply-depot in the south, and opening up the whole of central Tunisia. More restrictive views prevailed. Nevertheless, on the 19th a double-pronged attack was launched which might well have led to an Allied disaster. No military student will forget the word Kasserine.

21 Panzer's first operation in Tunisia had been to assist in clearing the passes of the Eastern Dorsal. But further inland, at no great distance, ran a further and parallel range generally known as the Western Dorsal. It was this, the last barrier covering Tebessa, Le Kef, and other critical Allied centres, that Rommel now proposed to breach. As a result of the High Command arguments he had recovered control of 21 Panzer and won the loan by von Arnim of 10 Panzer – though von Arnim, mentally fixated on operations further north, never released the whole of the division and, in particular, withheld the battalion of Tiger tanks which he had promised. The pattern of the two Dorsals on the map discloses that if Rommel was not to make for Tebessa direct, via Thelepte (which *Comando Supremo* had rejected), there remained the options of thrusting through the pass at Kasserine or, further to the east, driving up the road from Sbeitla (now in German hands) through the Allied positions at Sbiba and so on to Le Kef.

A wise gambler, Rommel kept his options open. He sent 21 Panzer up to Sbiba (under its latest commander, Hildebrandt), and held 10 Panzer at

Sbeitla until he could estimate whether the Sbiba attack was more promising than the one he launched at Kasserine with the Afrika Korps Group under Buelowius. <u>Everything went wrong.</u> 21 Panzer stuck at Sbiba, checked by minefields and an unyielding defence by a Guards brigade and American units. Though Rommel therefore switched 10 Panzer to Kasserine, he found to his chagrin that <u>his DAK veterans were less skilled in mountain warfare than the Americans, who were quick to apply the North West Frontier technique of seizing the commanding heights.</u> Even when the pass was cleared, and 10 Panzer rolled uncomfortably up the sloping valley towards Thala on the crest, the British 26 Armoured Brigade with decrepit Crusaders gallantly held it in check. During the crisis night of 20/21 February a complete regiment of American medium and field artillery arrived, going straight into action after a 800-mile forced march from Oran. In retrospect it seems that if 10 Panzer had possessed the fire and dynamism of the Afrika Korps in its great days Rommel would have obtained a victory. The Allied defences were truly a 'thin red line', and there should have been a breakthrough at Thala – with incalculable consequences. <u>In practice DAK was down to a day's supply of fuel and ammunition,</u> the attack had lost impetus, and to the astonished relief of his opponents (but with Kesselring's agreement), Rommel called a halt and began the return journey which, he hoped, might enable him to savage 8th Army's forward troops before their concentration was complete.

Though 21 Panzer and the core of 15 Panzer were employed at Kasserine, and <u>though Rommel was in command, the battle was not a true Afrika Korps operation.</u> Rommel himself was uneasy – no longer sure of his position, hostile to an unfriendly von Arnim, and carrying out what he believed to be an unsatisfactory plan. Co-ordination had been the key-note in the desert battles, but this time the Sbiba and Kasserine actions were like separate, private battles. And a menacing fact emerged. Though both Rommel and his men were awe-struck by the quality and quantity of the captured American equipment, and though the fighting capacity of the American troops was at times pathetic, a larger truth could be discerned. It did not escape Rommel that <u>though the Americans had fought like children in their first engagements, their ability to learn and mature at speed was astonishing.</u> Already in the hill-fights at Kasserine some were acting coolly and competently, while the technical skill of their artillery impressed a Field Marshal who had experienced Alamein.*

---

* Exultant panzer crews munching American chocolate may have forgotten – but it can hardly have escaped Rommel, and should certainly not be overlooked by the military student – that the 8th Army they had come to respect and admire had once also earned their contempt for the puerile quality of its tactics. In the first assault on Tobruk DAK itself had revealed its ignorance of important skills. <u>All the armies in Africa had to learn the hard way.</u>

And Alamein, oddly enough, is often recalled by the next of DAK's battles. Just as Montgomery preceded his triumph there with a quick, effective defensive action at Alam Halfa, so his even more rapid <u>defensive victory at Medenine</u> <u>on 6 March</u> anticipated his success later in the month at the Mareth Line. But there is a more important analogy: in each case <u>the ULTRA intercepts provided</u> him with vital advance information about his <u>enemy's intentions and even the</u> <u>date of the attack.</u>

In the case of Medenine such knowledge was critical. During February Montgomery had been gradually propelling his army forward with the ultimate object of cracking the Mareth Line, and by the end of the month, partly in answer to pleas that he should aid his allies in Tunisia by creating a diversion, 51 Highland and 7 Armoured Divisions had arrived at Medenine. Now forewarned, his staffs rushed forward the New Zealand Division, 201 Guards Brigade and 8 Armoured Brigade. By 6 March all were dug in and ready, with 460 anti-tank guns, 350 field and medium guns, and 300 tanks. Ammunition was abundant and 70,000 mines had been sown. A feature of the most perfect defensive position 8th Army ever created was the fact that the infantry took second place. For the first time on a large scale all the anti-tank guns were scientifically sited, in enfilade if necessary, for the prime purpose of killing tanks. The attack was awaited with total confidence.

Rommel, who after Kasserine had been put in command of all the Axis forces in Africa, felt something more akin to despair. <u>His latest view, which</u> Hitler rejected, was that his old *Panzerarmee* (now under Messe and rechristened 'Italian First Army', or AOK 1) should withdraw immediately right back to the mountainous heart of Tunisia where the great *massif* comes down to the sea at Enfidaville. And so, as the panzer divisions reported back from Kasserine, the plan for attacking 8th Army at Medenine went ahead under Messe's direction – with Rommel virtually washing his hands of it.

The main assault, by DAK, came out of the hills to the west of Medenine, roughly from a start-line between the Hallouf Pass and the Medenine–Metameur–Toujane road. Further north, down the main Medenine–Mareth road, came Column Bari – the latter under Graf von Sponeck and consisting of his 90 Light Division and *Spezia*. DAK, whose new commander Cramer had only taken over on the previous day, contained 10, 15 and 21 Panzer Divisions as well as a mixture of German and Italian battle groups. All were short of fuel and ammunition.

Many detailed and extensive accounts exist of the catastrophe that followed. German contempt for the Americans' ineptitude at Kasserine could well have been turned on themselves. Seasoned warriors among the Highlanders, the New Zealanders and the armoured brigades could scarcely believe their eyes as they watched the panzer grenadiers and the following panzers deploy in

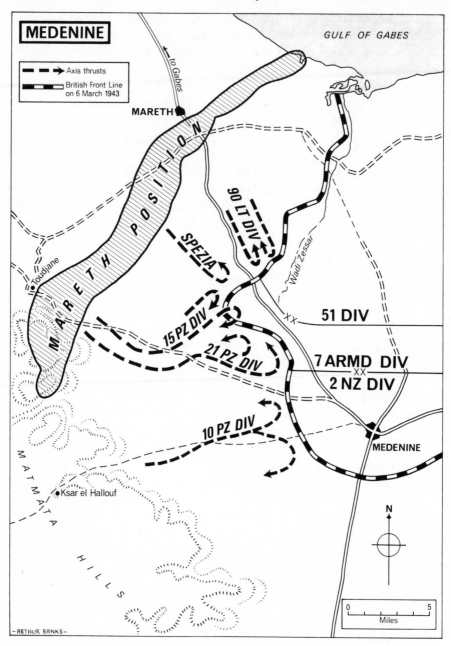

MAP 9   The assault at Medenine

ways which ran counter to every lesson of the desert war. For the anti-tank gunners it was like shooting on a range. There seemed to be no heart or impulsion in the attack, and though it was renewed, almost as a ritual, during the afternoon Rommel called it off by nightfall – the last battle, for him, in Africa, since he returned to Europe on the 9th after handing over to von Arnim. The figures are eloquent – around 50 panzers eliminated without meaningful damage to the enemy or the gain of a yard of ground. There is no aspect of Medenine that identifies it as an Afrika Korps battle – except that the Afrika Korps participated.

The stage for the next act was set in the course of the usual high-level exchanges. Von Arnim wanted a brief – and got it on the 17th in an order from *Comando Supremo* that the Mareth and Akarit Lines were to be defended to the last. But Messe also wanted to know where he stood. He must hold at Mareth, von Arnim told him, and if pressed could fall back on Akarit – but only with von Arnim's permission. In the meantime 10 and 21 Panzer Divisions were withdrawn again to the west, where Eisenhower's forces offered the greater threat. 15 Panzer still remained available for counter-attack at Mareth. In other words the fragmentation of the old DAK, inevitable once Tunisia was entered, remorselessly continued.

Montgomery's first intention was to break through the main defences of the Mareth Line, where the natural tank-trap of the Wadi Zigzaou, covered by block-houses and other fire-points, formed a taxing obstacle. The garrison was mainly Italian – the Young Fascists, *Trieste, Spezia,* and *Pistoia.* But seven battalions from 90 Light were centrally placed, and five miles behind the line lay 15 Panzer whose 30-odd tanks, though few, were to play a crucial part. As a long-stop-reserve 21 Panzer was near Gabes, and 10 Panzer near Sousse, comprising, jointly, 110 tanks. 164 Light (its able commander von Liebenstein restored to it) provided a flank force on the right in the hills beyond *Pistoia's* positions. About 450 field and medium guns stiffened the defences whose approaches, as usual, were thick with mines.

The main attack, which began just before midnight on the 20th, was made by 50 Division supported by 50 RTR. There was a heavy accompanying barrage, and confidence was high. (The author recalls the Durham Light Infantry moving through his gun position, on their way to the assault, as if they were going to a picnic. Later their baffled survivors were being rallied at the same spot.) But trust was misplaced, for after two nights' deadly work less than 50 aged Valentines had been edged over the difficult crossing into 50 Division's bridgehead – and no anti-tank guns. The defenders were now fully alert. Shortly after midday on the 22nd 15 Panzer counter-attacked with a vicious ferocity. After Medenine they had scores to settle. 30 British tanks were soon destroyed, leaving the infantry who still survived on the far side of

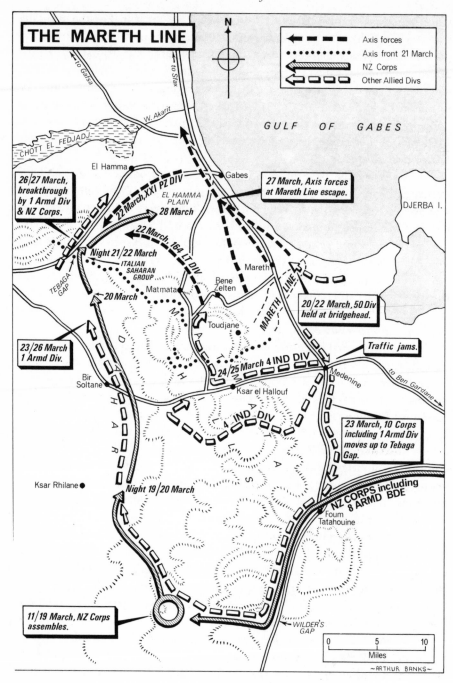

MAP 10   The Mareth Line

the crossing unprotected. Though fighting and fresh planning continued, 15 Panzer had in fact brought the first phase of the Mareth battle to a dead stop. Montgomery accepted the truth at 2 a.m. on the night of the 22nd/23rd.

But there was a second phase. For many weeks the feasibility had been examined of sending a strong mobile force in an enormous sweep through the hill country south of Mareth. It would then turn north till it reached the Tebaga Gap, pass through this bottleneck and sweep via El Hamma down to Gabes and the sea, thus taking in the rear the garrison and defences of Mareth. The full and fascinating story belongs elsewhere. By the 22nd, however, a New Zealand Corps under Freyberg (comprising 2 New Zealand Division and 8 Armoured Brigade) had overcome all obstacles and was approaching Tebaga. Montgomery decided to convert this outflanking march into his main thrust, and on the evening of the 23rd 1 Armoured Division set off from Medenine to reinforce Freyberg's Corps.

Montgomery also sent off Lieut-General Brian Horrocks, to exercise 'dual control' with Freyberg. What he failed to provide was time. Between them Messe, Bayerlein, his Chief of Staff, and von Liebenstein, who acted with constructive energy, were able to use the space between the fight on the Wadi Zigzaou and the ultimate assault at Tebaga to cobble a defence together. On the afternoon of the 25th a classic *Blitz* began, with the Desert Air Force in squadron relays bombing and shooting the New Zealanders on to their objectives, followed by 1 Armoured Division which, under the moon, drove through the night for El Hamma. 21 Panzer and 15 Panzer had taken the strain, but the disintegration was such that if von Liebenstein, in the early hours of the 24th, had not scraped together two 88s, four 50 mm and four field guns, to form a rudimentary anti-tank screen, 1 Armoured Division might well have breakfasted in Gabes. 'Though a platitude, it is a practical truth that in battle a gift of time is precious to anyone who is capable of using it. The enemy showed themselves to be thus capable, met the changing situation, and got themselves out of great danger.'*

That the most imaginative and, indeed, the most daring of all 8th Army's enterprises was robbed of the complete success it deserved had been due in large measure to the Afrika Korps, even though the panzer divisions had once again been employed independently as trouble-shooters. But an escape-route had been preserved. There was a deep irony in the fact that by the end of the month in which Rommel left Africa for ever his cherished DAK, together with the rest of Messe's 'First Italian Army', was able to fall back unimpeded (except from the air) and establish itself on the safe side of the Wadi Akarit – the haven for which Rommel had yearned ever since his defeat at Alamein.

---

* *The Mediterranean and the Middle East*, Vol. IV, p. 354.

The Field Marshal's departure was inevitable. The mood of desperation that had prevailed since the previous October was now acute: he believed that 'for the Army Group to remain longer in Africa was now plain suicide'. (Indeed, he made some ineffectual efforts to draft back to Europe the best of his officers before the predictable débâcle.) He was sick at heart and physically in poor condition. Hitler missed nothing: he is recorded as having observed at one of his *Führer* conferences 'there you have the opposite ends of the scale. Rommel has become the greatest pessimist and Kesselring the complete optimist.' And so, on 9 March, he departed from Tunisia for ever, to be succeeded by von Arnim, and made his way to Rome where, in a friendly session with Mussolini, he failed to convince the Duce that the military advantages of withdrawal from Tunisia outweighed the political inconvenience. Then he flew to Hitler's headquarters in East Prussia, determined to plead the cause of his 'Africans'. All he got was a cool reception, a rejection of his request to be allowed to return to the front, and the Iron Cross (Oakleaves with Swords and Diamonds – the highest order). He trailed away on sick leave.

The Afrika Korps soldiered on. Rommel, like Montgomery, when he left 8th Army in Italy to prepare for D Day in Normandy, had in a sense become irrelevant. Each commander had performed his task to perfection, by training and welding his army to the point at which it could function efficiently without his presence. The Afrika Korps, moreover, was already so well accustomed to being broken up into independent sub-units that Rommel's passing, whatever regrets it may have caused, made no essential difference to its performance in action. Its spirit and its skill persisted to the end. There is a revealing contrast here with the impact on the 14th Army in Burma of the news that, after its victorious return to Rangoon, an attempt was being made by the Allied Land Forces commander, Sir Oliver Leese, to displace Slim from its head. The Army seethed: divisional commanders and headquarters staffs proffered their resignations – as did at least one highly placed airman. That was a teacup storm that soon settled, but the reaction is significant. The Afrika Korps admired and respected Rommel: it would follow him anywhere. (8th Army's feelings about Montgomery are roughly comparable.) But 14th Army worshipped Slim.

But what had seemed to Rommel a desirable haven unfortunately proved to be no more than a temporary resting-place. On 29 March Messe reported that all his units were in position and prepared for defence, but the trouble was that there were few positions to defend. All *Comando Supremo*'s energies had been directed to the Mareth Line and it was only now, at the last minute, that the Wadi was improved as an anti-tank ditch and extended further inland. Wiring was light, and minefields exiguous. But Montgomery, generous as ever in his gifts of time to his opponent, did not attack until the night of 5 April, when the topographical strength of the Akarit Line had been developed into at least the semblance of a defensible front.

From the sea to the salt marshes of the Chott is no more than 18 miles. Four miles of the Akarit Wadi, then the high ridge of Jebel Roumana, then a 5,000 yard gap flanked by Fatnassa, 'a towering, horrible-looking labyrinth of pinnacles, chimneys, gullies and escarpments', then broken hill-country across to Jebel Haidoudi and the marshes. Messe placed the Young Fascists and two battalions of 90 Light along the Wadi, *Trieste* around Roumana, then *Spezia* and *Pistoia* between Fatnassa and Haidoudi, where von Liebenstein and 164 Light lurked in the wings. The main body of 15 Panzer, and 200 Panzer Grenadier Regiment from 90 Light, formed a reserve in depth north of Roumana. Artillery was scarce, but of the 63 88s of 19 Flak Division 28 were deployed in an anti-tank role. The practice was habitual, but it would shortly have a decisive effect.

Montgomery intended a conventional thrust between Roumana and Fatnassa, but Tuker of 4 Indian Division persuaded the C-in-C to authorise a silent night-attack on the latter, the key feature, by his mountain-wise infantry. Though 50 and 51 Divisions had a hard time on the approaches to Roumana, the surprised Italians on Fatnassa soon succumbed, and early in the morning of the 6th all seemed set for the armour of Horrocks' 10 Corps to cross the anti-tank ditch spanning the gap between Fatnassa and Roumana before cascading westwards. Unaccountably – and the word is used with emphasis – the armour, with the New Zealand Division at its head – was set in motion too slowly and too late. Not more than two or three 88s, firing in enfilade along the ditch, were then sufficient to halt the leading tanks and prevent the forward movement of a whole Corps.

During the afternoon more and more reserves from 15 Panzer and 90 Light were sucked into the battle, but there was a prevalent feeling of disenchantment. By seven in the evening 90 Light was recording in its War Diary:

> The enemy has captured all the commanding features of the Akarit Line and thus brought about its collapse. All the troops have been thrown into the Italian Divisions' sectors and there are no more reserves. But the Army cannot make up its mind to retreat. By tomorrow this will be impossible.

Actually von Arnim, after the almost mandatory arguments with Messe, Bayerlein and Cramer, issued orders the same evening for a limited withdrawal. By the morrow the whole of AOK 1 was *en route* for the rear, and 8th Army had missed another opportunity for achieving a decisive result. Messe's comment on Akarit has already been quoted – *non é stata una bella battaglia*: this was not a good battle – but a strictly technical assessment suggests that Montgomery, considering all his advantages, might well have made a similar comment. Certainly it was not an action for which either 15 Panzer or 90 Light needed to offer any apologies.

The end of the road now lay ahead – Enfidaville, where some 25 miles south of the Cap Bon peninsula the switchback mass of mountains and valleys that constitutes the bulk of Tunisia falls down to within gun-shot of the sea, and between the coast and the mountains' rim a narrow plainland forms a passage northward from Enfidaville to Hammamet. In the high ground that looms over the little town and the surrounding flats, giving perfect observation, Messe by mid-April redisposed his army – 90 Light occupying, as it would do to the last, the corner of the hills between town and sea.

This is a moment when to continue to refer to the Afrika Korps ceases to be meaningful. Once 'Fortress Tunisia' was occupied transference of units from south to north, to meet sudden emergencies within the contracting perimeter, became unavoidable and were indeed declared by von Arnim to be a matter of policy. As 8th Army closed up on Enfidaville Montgomery strove ruthlessly, until restrained by Alexander, to steal a march to Tunis, and many New Zealanders, Indians and British troops died to no purpose under the fire of DAK and its Italian allies. From enviably strong positions in the nooks and crannies of the Jebels, they repulsed, sometimes bloodily, every attack until Alexander decided to switch 8th Army divisions to the Medjez-el-Bab/Tunis front, and Montgomery was left as the sitting tenant of ground that had suddenly lost its significance.

15 Panzer also departed, on what proved to be its death-ride. At the beginning of May all the armour and much of the artillery in Messe's army was transferred northward – a move as natural as Alexander's shift of the 8th Army divisions. And thus it was that when the final all-out drive on Tunis occurred on 6 May, the oldest of the Afrika Korps' formations was at its heart. The report of Army Group Africa tells its own story:

> Between the Medjerda and the Medjez-St Cyprien road the enemy has achieved his decisive breakthrough to Tunis. This sector was heroically defended by 15th Panzer Division . . . but these troops could not survive an assault mounted by numerically far superior infantry and armoured formations with massive artillery support, and accompanied by air attacks of an intensity not hitherto experienced. The bulk of 15th Panzer Division must be deemed to have been destroyed.

Though Tunis was entered on the 7th it took some days to complete the surrender of about 150,000 Germans whom Hitler had ordered to hold out to the last man and the last round. Twice, on the 10th and 11th, Freyberg asked von Sponeck to capitulate with his old opponents of 90 Light. How many memories must have been in Freyberg's mind! But von Sponeck merely ignored the suggestion. It was not until midday on the 13th that Messe (who had been promoted Marshal of Italy on the previous day) made a general surrender of all the German and Italian troops under his command. It happened that the author's observation post was on the low ground between the sea and the positions occupied by 90 Light. He saw the white flags go up: first in small clusters, turning into larger groups as platoons merged with companies. White everywhere, as if butterflies were dancing over the hills. It had been a long haul from Alamein, and exhilaration predominated. But there was a sense of compassion, too: this had been a good enemy. And Rommel had been wrong when, in the previous October, he despaired about the possibility of winning further distinction. The last phase in the life of the Afrika Korps had been entirely worthy of its astonishing *début*. When all was over its famous sign, the palm tree, could have been fittingly surrounded by a wreath of laurels.

Bibliography

Apart from the relevant volumes in the British Official History I found the following volumes in the Commonwealth series particularly helpful. In the Australian series, Barton Maughan's *Tobruk and El Alamein*; in the New Zealand series, *Battle for Egypt: the summer of 1942*, by J.L. Scoullar; in the South African series *The Sidi Rezegh Battles, 1941*, by J.A.I. Agar-Hamilton and L.C.F. Turner. Other books consulted include:

Barnett, Corelli, *The Desert Generals*, Kimber
Bender, R.J. and Law, R.D., *Uniforms, Organisation and History of the Afrika Korps*, R.J. Bender Publishing Company
Bergot, Erwan, *The Afrika Korps*, Wingate
Blumenson, Martin, *Kasserine Pass*, Houghton Mifflin

Caccia-Dominioni, Paolo, *Alamein 1933–1962*, Allen and Unwin
Carell, Paul, *The Foxes of the Desert*, Hutton
Carver, Michael, *Tobruk* and *El Alamein*, Batsford
Churchill, Winston, *The Second World War*, Cassell
Ciano, Count, *Diary 1939–1943*, Heinemann
Clarke, Dudley, *The Eleventh at War*, Michael Joseph
Clifton, George, *The Happy Hunted*, Cassell
Connell, John, *Auchinleck*, Cassell, and *Wavell*, Collins

De Guingand, Sir Francis, *Operation Victory*, Hodder and Stoughton
Douglas, Keith, *Alamein to Zem Zem* and *Collected Poems*, Faber
Douglas-Home, Charles, *Rommel*, Weidenfeld and Nicolson

Hood, Stuart, *Pebbles from my Skull*, Hutchinson
Horrocks, Sir Brian, *A Full Life*, Collins

Jackson, W.G.F., *Alexander of Tunis* and *The North African Campaign 1940–1943*, Batsford
Joly, Cyril, *Take These Men*, Constable

Kennedy-Shaw, W.B., *Long Range Desert Group*, Collins
Kesselring, Field-Marshal, *Memoirs*, Kimber
Kippenberger, Sir Howard, *Infantry Brigadier*, Oxford University Press

Lewin, Ronald, *Rommel as Military Commander* and *Montgomery as Military Commander*, Batsford. *Man of Armour: the biography of Lieutenant-General Vyvyan Pope*, Leo Cooper
Liddell Hart, Sir Basil, *The Tanks*, Vol. II, Cassell

Macintyre, Donald, *The Battle for the Mediterranean*, Batsford
Macksey, Kenneth, *Afrika Korps*, Ballantine
Mellenthin, Maj.-Gen. von, *Panzer Battles, 1939–1945*, Cassell
Montgomery, Field Marshal the Viscount, *Memoirs*, Collins
Moorehead, Alan, *Mediterranean Front, A Year of Battle* and *The End in Africa*, Hamish Hamilton

Nicolson, Nigel, *Alex*, Weidenfeld and Nicolson

Peniakoff, Vladimir, (Popski), *Private Army*, Cape
Phillips, C.E. Lucas, *Alamein*, Heinemann

Rommel, Field-Marshal Erwin, *The Rommel Papers*, (ed. Liddell Hart), Collins

Schmidt, Heinz Werner, *With Rommel in the Desert*, Harrap
Strawson, John, *The Battle for North Africa*, Batsford

Tuker, Sir Francis, *Approach to Battle*, Cassell

Verney, G.L., *The Desert Rats*, Hutchinson

Wilmot, Chester, *Tobruk 1941*, Angus and Robertson

Young, Desmond, *Rommel*, Collins

Index

For convenience of readers military and air formations and units are under national headings e.g. British Indian Army under Indian Army, British. Places beginning with the Arabic 'El' are in order of the second word. German names are indexed by the name after 'von'. Only book-titles not appearing in the Bibliography have been indexed.

Abbreviations used: n – footnote; Bib. – *see also* Bibliography